TO
PREACH
OR
NOT TO
PREACH?

David C. Norrington

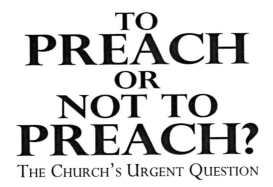

TO
PREACH
OR
NOT TO
PREACH?
THE CHURCH'S URGENT QUESTION

A New Introduction by Jon Zens of Searching Together
and "Norrington Replies to the Critics"

TO PREACH OR NOT TO PREACH

by David C Norrington

Library of Congress Control Number: 2012956371

Publisher's Cataloging-in-Publication data

Norrington, David C.

   To preach or not to preach : the church's urgent question / David C. Norrington ; a new introduction by Jon Zens.

   p. cm.

   ISBN 978-1-938480-01-0

1. Pastoral theology. 2. Clergy --Office --History. 3. Preaching. 4. Integrity --Religious aspects --Christianity. I. Zens, Jon. II. Title.

BV4211.2 .N6 2013

253 --dc23   2012956371

This volume is printed on acid free paper and meets ANSI Z39.48 standards.

Cover design and layout by: Rafael Polendo

Formerly published by Paternoster Press, Carlisle, Cumbria UK

Omaha, NE

TABLE OF CONTENTS

PUBLISHERS NOTE:

In our effort to restore this special book to the body of Christ we've stayed true to Norrington's original work with only a few exceptions. Several typos were fixed and British spelling was changed to American spelling. A few stylistic changes were also made but they do not affect the message or readability. We've changed the chapter sections a bit to orient the material a little better and simplify the table of contents. In the process, there were no reductions to Norrington's work at all.

One thing that could not be fixed: on page 33 (page 12 in the original) you will notice footnote numbers jump from 94 to 96. However, in the endnotes, on page 41 (page 19 *in the original*) there is a 95. We do not know where the actual placement of the footnote was to have appeared in the chapter content.

This version features more white space and narrower columns so you do not have to spread the pages to read the edges closest to the spine. As noted on the cover this volume also contains an expansive section [Appendix III—Norrington Responds to Critics]. Another adaptation of this work is available in eBook format. Look for it online with the ISBN: 978-1-938480-02-7

The republishing process was lengthy and ardous to say the very least. And while we have streamlined, fixed and added content, no doubt there are little things that might have missed our notice. For this we apologize. If you find errors, please contact me and we'll update the interior copy as seems necessary.

Sincerely,

Timothy L. Price
Ekklesia Press
tim@ekklesiapress.com

ACKNOWLEDGEMENTS

This work is offered to the reader with mixed feelings. I am, of course, pleased that something which has been in my thoughts for many years is finished at last. And yet, to part with it is another matter. I have been adding, deleting, revising judgments and amending footnotes right up to the last moment and would be happy to continue doing that indefinitely. But an end has to be made (thanks to gentle pressure from the publisher) and the book must now go into the world and perform its task.

This study has not been written by one in the mainstream of scholarly activity but is, rather, the work of a private student. Even so, many hands have helped and I should particularly like to mention the following: the staff at the libraries of Blackpool and the Fylde College, Poulton-Ie-Fylde, Lancaster University, Cambridge University and Tyndale House, Cambridge; Robert J. Banks, George Ellison, the late Donald Guthrie, John G. Pouncy, Stephen V. Rees, Harold H. Rowdon, Klaas Runia and Derek J. Tidball who read earlier drafts and provided extensive suggestions most of which have been incorporated into the text; Kaye Keir who worked with me and has helped me to say what I mean and to say it more clearly than would otherwise have been the case; Mandy Reeves who transformed a handwritten manuscript into a word processed document; Peter Cousins, of the Paternoster Press, who helped to transform that into a book; Monika Dobson, Jeanette Linington and Joyce Stainton who, for many years, have supplied me with books; Kevin Cosgrove, Stephen Pipe and Simon Woods who gave me books and encouragement; and my mother who provided material assistance and put up with a house always overflowing with books and papers. To all these I extend my gratitude.

—David C. Norrington
Poulton-le-Fylde
12 December 1995

INTRODUCTION
by
Jon Zens

This book was first recommended to me by Graham Wood several years after it was published in the UK. After reading it, I concluded that it remains a worthy and valuable contribution to inspire the renewal of Christ's life in His body.

To Preach is structured around four main points that encourage us to re-think the whole concept of "church." First, David shows that there was a lot of "preaching" going on in the early days since Pentecost, but he also reveals that the New Testament contains no evidence to support the ritual of a regular weekly sermon. "Preaching" was directed to those outside of Christ.

For example, the noun "preacher" is applied to Noah, and it is clear that his message fell on the ears of those who would experience water-judgment. It was not until the 3rd century that the sermon became a fixed tradition in the meeting, and dominated over the expression of Christ through His body.

Second, he unfolds how such a distorted focus on one individual and the "sermon" resulted in the virtual elimination of the one-another ministries that are prominent in the New Testament.

Third, he points out that there was actually no professional clergy in the earliest churches, and that the growth of the Lord in His body was a natural process of Christ living out His life in His people, mutual caring for one another, and expressing Christ together as depicted in the New Testament.

IX

Lastly, David illustrates just how ineffective the monologue sermon is as a means to promote the expression of Christ through His body.

After its publication in 1996, its reading audience was mainly based in the UK. As could be expected, this book evoked some strong reaction. David said to me in a February, 2006, email: "You may know that *To Preach* has been widely criticized. I have, at long last, responded. My response was intended for the Evangelical Quarterly (which has published some of my earlier material), but the editor thought it too late and thought a 'dignified silence' more in my interest." Unfortunately, David died in October, 2007, but his replies to the critics were published in Searching Together (2009). They have been included in this re-issue of *To Preach*.

One drawback of "the centrality of preaching" that is often overlooked is the reliance on the expert mentality. John Robbins manifested this mind-set when he wrote:

> Martin Luther understood the dependence of the practical men [plumbers, carpenters, doctors] on the scholars. In his essay on the "Duty of Sending Children to School," he wrote: "...Without scholars [preachers] it would not be long till businessmen in their perplexity would be ready to dig a learned man out of the ground ten yards deep with their fingers; for the merchant will not long remain a merchant, if preaching and the administration of justice cease. I know full well that we theologians and jurists must remain, or else all other vocations will inevitably go to the ground with us; where theologians perish, there perishes also the Word of God, and nothing but heathen and devils are left.... But what the merchant will gain when peace vanishes, I shall let his ledger tell him; and the use of all his property when preaching ceases, let his conscience show him" ("A Christian University," *The Trinity Review*, #155, January, 1998).

To Preach or Not To Preach? is a wonderful corrective to the unhealthy and unbiblical reliance we have come to have on the sermon in the gatherings of the believers. The Lord will use this book to foster the expression of Christ through all the parts of His body, not just one or a few!

ORIGINAL INTRODUCTION
by
David C. Norrington

The sermon has been under attack from many quarters and for many years but still functions as a major form of biblical instruction and the centerpiece of many Christian gatherings. The sermon has survived, not because criticisms have been examined and refuted, but because they have been ignored or misunderstood or have emanated from sources hostile to Christianity. The continued popularity of the sermon may even represent a desire by some to secure at least one fixed point in a world of rapid social change, just as others may seek that security in an antique translation of the Bible.

The purpose of the present essay is to show that the sermon delivered to Christians had only a small part to play in the life of the primitive church and that much contemporary practice not only lacks a biblical foundation but is injurious to the life of the Christian community. The scarcity of such sermons in the New Testament has been noticed but usually only as a curiosity without particular significance. Consequently, the discovery has prompted little research. There are at least two reasons for this. First, the power of tradition— this is great and seldom recognized, for it is no easy task to step out- side one's own culture and pass an informed, biblical judgment upon it. To some extent this has shielded the sermon from discussion.

Second, the atomistic nature of research in particular biblical research: small areas are examined in microscopic detail, presumably in the belief that if every tree is so treated then the nature of the whole wood will become clear.

Perhaps it should be so but all too often this is not the case, particularly as issues of significance to the professional theological community are seldom directly related to church life or studied in a way conducive to hearing a word from God. This approach is currently under scrutiny.

In order to understand any given issue in detail, an analysis of the larger system will usually be necessary because issues cannot be detached cleanly from the systems in which they arise.[2] The problem of the sermon, for example, ultimately raises educational, sociological, organizational and structural issues and forces us to ask questions concerning the nature and aims of the church.[3] In order, therefore, to understand this problem it has been tackled in the present essay from as many angles and using as many disciplines as practicable, given the limitations of the writer. As this is God's world, all truth is God's truth so that it is appropriate to bring truths to bear from a variety of disciplines in the elucidation of any biblical issue. Moreover, the biblical issues raised here have been examined in the light of present day concerns. These can frequently open our eyes to further biblical truths which otherwise might be missed.

Taken by itself, the failure of the sermon would not necessarily be significant. If activities like domestic religion, the serious reading of the Bible and other Christian literature and Christian group life were flourishing, then the failure of the sermon might be a trivial matter. But since these activities are not as fruitful in contemporary western society as they might be, the sermon is expected, in many churches, to make up for all these deficiencies. Sadly, it fails to do so.

ENDNOTES

1. C. West Churchman, *The Systems Approach and its Enemies*, 1979, pp. 12f; W. Wink, *The Bible in Human Transformation*, 1973, pp. 1-18; L. Morris, *I Believe in Revelation*, 1976, pp. 92-108; E. Linnemann, *Historical Criticism of the Bible: Methodology or Ideology?*, 1990; idem, *Is There a Synoptic Problem? Rethinking the Literary Dependence of the First Three Gospels*, 1992; D.C. Steinmetz, 'The Superiority of Pre-Critical Exegesis, *Theology Today*, 37, 1980, 27-38
2. C. West Churchman, *Systems Approach*, pp. 4-7
3. On the rewards and dangers which result from applying sociology to biblical material see D.J. Tidball, *An Introduction to the Sociology of the New Testament*, 1983, pp. 11-22; R.J. Banks, 'Setting "The Quest for the Historical Jesus" in a Broader Framework', *GP*, 1981, II, 70-74; S.C. Barton, 'Social Scientific Approaches to Paul', *DPL*, pp. 892-900

Abbreviations

ABD - D.N. Freedman (ed), *The Anchor Bible Dictionary, 6 vols., 1992*

ABR - *Australian Biblical Review*

AJT - *Asia Journal Theology*

A-NF - Ante-Nicene Fathers, 1864ff

ANRW - H. Temporini and W. Haase (eds), *Aufstieg und Niedergang der romischen Welt, 1972ff*

AV - Authorized Version

BA - *Biblical Archaeologist*

BAFCS - Winter et al (eds), *The Book Acts in its 1st century Setting, 6 vols., 1993ff*

BAGD - Bauer, W.F. Arndt, F.W. Gingrich and F.W. Danker, *A Greek English Lexicon of the New Testament,* ²1979

BJRL - *Bulletin of the John Rylands Library*

Burton, *Syntax* - E. de W. Burton, *Syntax of the Moods and Tenses in New Testament Greek,* ³1898

CBQ - *Catholic Biblical Quarterly*

CH - *Church History*

CHB - P.R. Ackroyd et al (eds), *The Cambridge History of the Bible, 3 vols., 1963-1970*

Class Phil - *Classical Philology*

col - column

Compendia Compendia rerum Iudaicarum ad Novum Testamentum, 1974ff

DCA - *W. Smith and S. Cheetham (eds), A Dictionary of Christian Antiquities,* 2 vols., 1908

DCG - J. Hastings (ed), *Dictionary of Christ and the Gospels,* 2 vols., 1906-1908

DJG - J.B. Green, S. McKnight and LH. Marshall *(eds), Dictionary of Jesus and the Gospels,* 1992

DPL - G.F. Hawthorne, R.P. Martin and D.G. Reid (eds), *Dictionary of Paul and his Letters,* 1993

DSCHT - N.M. de S. Cameron et al (eds), *Dictionary of Scottish Church History and Theology,* 1993

EB - English Bible

EBC - The Expositor's Bible Commentary

EDNT - H. Balz and G. Schneider (eds), *Exegetical Dictionary of the New Testament,* 3 vols., 1990-1993

EEC - A. Di Berardino (ed), *Encyclopedia of the Early Church,* 2 vols., 1992

EGT - Expositor's Greek Testament

Enc Jud - C. Roth et al (eds), *Encyclopaedia Judaica*, 16 vols., 1971

Ep - Epistle

EQ - Evangelical Quarterly

ERE - J. Hastings (ed), *Encyclopaedia of Religion and Ethics*, 13 vols., 1908-1926

ET - English Translation

Exp T - Expository Times

GP - R.T. France, D. Wenham et al (eds), *Gospel Perspectives,* 6 vols., 1980-1986

HJP - E. Schürer, *The History of the Jewish People in the Age of Jesus Christ (175BC-AD135)*, 4 vols., 1973-1987

HTR - Harvard Theological Review

HUCA - Hebrew Union College Annual

IDB - G.A. Buttrick (ed), *The Interpreter's Dictionary of the Bible,* 4 vols., 1962

IDBS - K. Crim (ed), *The Interpreter's Dictionary of the Bible Supplementary Volume,* 1976

IRM - International Review of Missions

ISBE - G.W. Bromiley (ed), *The International Standard Bible Encyclopedia,* 4 vols., 1979-1988

JBL - Journal of Biblical Literature

JCE - Journal of Christian Education

JEH - Journal of Ecclesiastical History

JETS Journal of the Evangelical Theological Society

JJS - Journal of Jewish Studies

JPT - Journal of Psychology and Theology

JQR - Jewish Quarterly Review

JScSR - Journal for the Scientific Study of Religion

JTS - Journal of Theological Studies

LN - J.P. Louw and E.A. Nida, *Greek-English Lexicon of the New Testament based on Semantic Domains,* 2 vols., 1988

LSJ - H.G. Liddell, R. Scott and H.S. Jones, *A Greek English Lexicon, with supplement, 1968*

m - Mishnah

MM - J .H. Moulton and G. Milligan, *The Vocabulary of the Greek Testament Illustrated from the Papyri and Other Non-Literary Sources, 1930*

Moulton, *Grammar* - J .H. Moulton, *A Grammar of New Testament Greek,* vol. 3, *Syntax by N. Turner,* 1963

nd - no date
NEB - New English Bible
NIDNTT - C. Brown (ed), *The New International Dictionary of New Testament Theology*, 3 vols., 1975-1978
NovT - Novum Testamentum
NRSV - New Revised Standard Version
NT - New Testament
NTS - New Testament Studies
OT - Old Testament
PBSR - Papers of the British School at Rome
PIC - R.J. Banks, *Paul's Idea of Community: The Early House Churches in their Historical Setting*, 1980
P&P - Past and Present
repr - reprinted
Robertson, *Grammar -* A.T. Robertson, *A Grammar of the Greek New Testament in the Light of Historical Research,* [4]1934
RSR - Religious Studies Review
RTR - Reformed Theological Review
RV - Revised Version
SJT - Scottish Journal of Theology
ST - Searching Together Magazine
TDNT - G.W. Bromiley (ed), *Theological Dictionary of the New Testament*, 10 vols., 1964-1976
TDOT - G.J. Botterweck and H. Ringgren (eds), *Theological Dictionary of the Old Testament*, 1974ff
TS - Theological Studies
TynB - Tyndale Bulletin
VE - Vox Evangelica
Vol - volume
WTJ - Westminster Theological Journal
WUNT - Wissenschaftliche Untersuchungen zum Neuen Testament
ZNTW - Zeitschrift für die neutestamentliche Wissenschaft

Editions are indicated by small superior figures before the date of publication. Standard abbreviations have been used for biblical and other ancient literature.

'But the Emperor has nothing at all on!' said a little child. 'Listen to the voice of innocence!' exclaimed his father; and what the child had said was whispered from one to another.

'But he has nothing at all on!' at last cried out all the people. The Emperor was vexed, for he knew that the people were right; but he thought, 'The procession must go on now!' And the lords of the bedchamber took greater pains than ever to appear holding up a train, although, in reality, there was no train to hold.

Hans Christian Andersen (1805-1875)

Truth is always a surprise.
Lord Kenneth Clark (1903-1983)

A new scientific truth does not triumph
by convincing its opponents
and making them see the light,
but rather because its opponents eventually die,
and a new generation grows up that is
familiar with it.
Max Planck (1858-1947)

1 Speeches in the Bible and Early Church

In this chapter, biblical and early church data will be examined in order to assess the extent to which the modem form of the sermon was used. For the purposes of this discussion, the sermon will be defined as follows: a speech, essentially concerned with biblical, ethical and related material, designed to increase understanding and promote godly living among the listening congregation, delivered by one in good standing with the local Christian community and addressed primarily to the faithful in the context of their own gatherings. J.I. Packer maintains that, in Christian preaching, the message is brought by God himself through the words of the spokesperson.[1] Two objections may be brought against this view: (*i*) sermons need not necessarily be from God as Packer himself later notes,[2] (*ii*) the sermon is not the only form of discourse, which may be inspired by God. Consequently, I have not included Packer's point in the above definition.

Today such sermons occur almost every time Christians gather together on Sundays. In fact, the sermon occurs at most major meetings where the local church as a whole is gathered. In the present essay, the term 'regular sermon' will be used to indicate this kind of frequent and regular occurrence. At this point I shall not be offering any criticism of the sermon as defined here but rather seeking evidence for the use of the regular sermon in the Bible and early Christian writings.

(Abstract definitions can create as much darkness as light and so the reader who places little faith in them may ignore the above definition and, instead, utilize other sources of information.[3] The contextual analyses which follow should provide sufficient material to make the matter plain.)

SERMONS IN OLD TESTAMENT AND JEWISH LITERATURE

Throughout the biblical period, information was largely communicated orally rather than by the written word. The skillful speaker was highly regarded in Israel and speeches were common (Exod. 4:10-16; 1 Sam. 16:18). They included political speeches, farewell addresses, speeches directed to various spiritual purposes, monologues and dialogues (Deut. 32f; Josh. 23-24; 1 Sam. 12; 1 Kings 2:1-9; 1 Macc. 2:49-68).[4]

Speeches were common in the prophetic period and the prophets were the principal public speakers engaged in teaching, particularly during the latter part of the Old Testament period; their efforts were supplemented by those of rulers, priests and others.[5] Occasionally addresses were given by groups (2 Chron. 28:12f—perhaps one speaking on behalf of the group?) but more usually by individuals.

The audiences were diverse and included individuals (frequently leaders), groups (perhaps prophets)[6] and the nation itself. Few recorded speeches seem to have been aimed at the lowest strata of society but the poor might have heard the prophets and others when they spoke in public places. In many cases, however, precise identification of the audience is difficult if not impossible.

Given that sacred and secular, and religion and politics are not sharply differentiated in Hebrew and Jewish thought, it is frequently difficult to label material as 'political' and to be sure that it is altogether without religious significance although a broad distinction between political and religious speeches can be made, as is done by Otto Eissfeldt.[7] Furthermore, Old Testament sermons are difficult to define and opinions vary on an appropriate definition.[8] For my purposes, it will not be necessary to define the term here because speeches and related material of all kinds will be examined and, where necessary, dealt with in context.

Difficulties are compounded by the fact that we are dealing with literary texts and it is not easy to know whether they represent verbatim reports, summaries of speeches or summaries of general discussions. This makes it difficult to assess the length of speeches. It may be that most of the 8th century prophets could not hold the attention of their hearers for long and delivered short prophetic units

(Amos may be an exception here) and that this did not change until the time of Ezekiel and the post-exilic prophets.

Many speeches occurred in response to specific events. For example, many of the speeches of Moses and Joshua were delivered to audiences where a good number appear to have stood in need of the same exhortation, encouragement, reproof or information—or where all were required to make a decision and act upon it (Deut. 1:1, 5:1, 27:1,9; Josh. 23:1-24:15). This is also true of some of the later prophetic speeches but, as J. Lindblom reminds us, the majority of the prophetic discourses 'were caused by the apostasy and the sins of the people in general. Thus the prophets appear as ordinary but inspired preachers of repentance and heralds of doom or bliss.'[9] Lindblom further maintains that most of the utterances in the prophetic books were delivered as public speeches or sermons.[10] Eissfeldt is less confident on this point, especially with respect to the older prophetic material such as Amos, Hosea, Isaiah and Micah.[11]

Such speeches utilized a variety of forms, including parables, poetry, proverbs, songs and the relating of visions. The occasions upon which speeches were given were similarly diverse. It would not have been difficult to gather together an audience in most of the towns and villages of Palestine[12] and the prophets were thus able to speak in the streets (Jer. 11:6) and the gates of the cities (Jer. 17:19). Some speeches were delivered or read aloud at religious sites (Jer. 36:6-23; Amos 7:10-17; and perhaps Hos. 4: 1ff)[13] but there is no evidence to suggest that speeches were ever a regular part of the Israelite cult either at the Temple or other shrines.[14] Ezekiel addressed people on a regular basis when they came to hear him give a word from the Lord. This happened occasionally and perhaps regularly in Ezekiel's own house (Ezek. 8:1, 14:1, 20:1, 33:31-33).[15] In common with the work of the majority of the prophets, Ezekiel's task centered on proclaiming a message to those who stood in opposition to God (although the elders mentioned in Ezekiel 8:1 may have been godly).[16] As W. Eichrodt puts it, referring to the typical listener 'The interest now being awakened marks, rather, a revival of the old creature of the twilight which wants to have a share in the divine salvation without going so far as to be converted.'[17] Furthermore, the precise form of address or instruction used by Ezekiel is not given. There is a prophecy in Deuteronomy

18:15-22 to the effect that God would raise up prophets throughout the course of Israel's history. The form in which they would instruct is neither stated nor implied. This silence is not surprising given the wide range of means used by the prophets in achieving their ends.[18]

In addition to speeches, public readings occur in the Old Testament. Moses read to the people (Exod. 24:7) and he required the public reading of parts of the law every seven years during the Feast of Tabernacles (Deut. 31:10-12) but there is no evidence available on the extent to which this ruling was implemented. Public readings are mentioned later on but there is little in the contexts to suggest that such readings were widespread Josh. 8:34f; 2 Kings 22:10,23:2; Neh. 8:1-8, 9:3; Jer. 51:61-63). Some may have been punctuated by explanatory comments and contemporary applications.[19]

Prophets were not the only teachers in Israel. Much teaching was done by priests and Levites, perhaps supplemented by that of village leaders.[20] The priests had teaching duties from at least the 8th century BC but were frequently rebuked by the prophets for their rejection of God, ignorance of his ways and, by implication, their failure to instruct others Jer. 2:8; Hos. 4:4-10; Mic. 3:11; Zeph. 3:4).[21] The competent performance of these duties required a good knowledge of the law and included giving instruction on cultic and ritual matters (Lev. 10:9-11, 14:33-57) and passing judgment on specific legal questions (Hag. 2:11).[22] Priestly instruction might be given at the sanctuaries. Similarly, the Levites were involved in teaching the law (2 Chron. 17:7-9, 35:3; Neh. 8:7f).[23] Both priests and Levites delivered speeches but there is little to suggest that speeches were a major factor in the teaching of either group.[24]

Parental instruction, particularly that of the father, was considered important but speeches hardly appear in the family circle. Let us now summarize the Old Testament material and the extent to which it reflects the use of regular Sermons. First, the regularity and frequency of Old Testament speeches of any kind is difficult to determine, as is the precise form in which speeches were delivered. Length cannot be determined either. Second, as audience participation was common, many speeches may have been interrupted, unlike modern Sermon s which seldom provoke interruption, at least in an English setting (Isa. 5:3f; Amos 3:3-8).[25] Third, many of the prophets were not in good standing with those whom they addressed (*cf.* Matt. 23:29-35; Luke 6:23, 26, 11:47f). In these circumstances, there could have been little agreement on the authority or interpretation of the biblical material under discussion. Fourth the Old Testament offers little indication of a sermon-based ministry aimed at building up already mature Jewish groups although this may simply be the result of the difficulty of accurately identifying such groups from the text.

Speeches also occur in Jewish writings of the Hellenistic and Roman periods but there is nothing comparable with regular sermons. For example, the Qumran writings reveal great concern for Torah study and appear to contain sermonic material but the precise techniques used in the delivery of the latter seem beyond recovery.[26] In conclusion, the Old Testament and related writings provide no clear parallel to modem regular sermons.

SERMONS IN THE NEW TESTAMENT PERIOD

It will not be necessary to identify material in early Christian texts as sermonic merely by considerations of form and content which, in any event, are difficult to define.[27] My concern here is to identify occasions when addresses were delivered. In a given case, there may be some uncertainty as to what constitutes an address, but straightforward indications in the text will generally be sufficient for identification purposes and the net will be cast widely in the hope that most of the relevant material will be examined.

SERMONS IN THE SYNAGOGUE

The sermon appeared on a more regular basis as part of the activities of the synagogue on the Sabbath. The earliest evidence for synagogue sermons comes from the: New Testament where both Jesus and Paul frequently taught in synagogues. Unfortunately, there is little contemporary Jewish evidence to fill out the picture. Later Jewish writings (mainly post-200AD) provide a more comprehensive account but it is difficult to assess how far these writings reflect 1st century practice.[28]

Bearing this point in mind, if we combine New Testament and later Jewish material, the following tentative picture emerges. The delivery of the sermon was not restricted to an ordained class and any competent person such as a priest or lay teacher might speak.[29]

In some synagogues, anyone who wished to address the brethren might do so but others were more restrictive and only a priest or an elder might speak (Mark 6:1-5; Luke 4:15-27; Acts 13: 15, 17:2; Philo, *Hypothetica* 7:12f).[30] The sermon, however, was not an integral part of the proceedings and if no competent person were present it was omitted.

The form was different from modern sermons and involved interruptions and perhaps a good deal of discussion, generally after the sermon, but possibly in answer to questions posed by the speaker during the sermon.[31] Occasionally, the architecture and seating arrangements may have encouraged such interaction.[32] Occasionally points raised by the speaker provoked immediate opposition—mild or militant (Matt. 13:54-57; Luke 4:28f, 13:14; Acts 18:6).[33] Questioners might be Jews or interested Gentiles for pagans often had access to synagogue services, perhaps by invitation. Consequently, the sermon may have had apologetic overtones.[34] J. Heinemann assumes sermons would usually be based on the Torah readings but that on special Sabbaths sermons might be based on the prophetic readings. This is possible but in this respect, as in those already mentioned, the absence of biblical laws relating to synagogues meant that practice varied.[35] There is no clear evidence that the Jews had a fixed lectionary as early as the 1st century AD.[36]

Sermons were common not only in synagogue but in the theological schools as well.[37] Eventually, the Jews carne to hold the sermon in the same reverence as we find later among the Reformers.[38]

SERMONS IN THE MINISTRY OF JESUS

The ministry of Jesus took place in a community, which was accustomed to preaching, possessed some rhetorical sophistication and had some skill in scriptural discussion.[39] In his early ministry, Jesus made extensive use of the synagogue and, in particular, the sermon as a platform for announcing the arrival of the kingdom of God. The reference to his attending the synagogue at Nazareth according to his usual custom (Luke 4:16) probably concerns his use of the synagogue for teaching.[40] From the beginning, Jesus' visits to synagogue seem to have had missionary overtones. Unlike John the

Baptist, Jesus was willing to utilize the existing religious and social forms of the nation as were the prophets before him—a significant point as Jesus often cut across social conventions where these did not serve his purposes[41] and instructed his disciples to act similarly (Luke 10:4, 25-37; 14:7-24).[42]

Jesus may well have been sought out as an able preacher, but the freedom of the synagogue was not his to enjoy for long—opposition quickly made an effective ministry there difficult. It is difficult to ascertain how far gospel material is arranged in chronological order but the main events follow a chronological arrangement and this may also be the case for Jesus' missionary tactics but it would be difficult to establish this beyond doubt.[43] For example, the last occasions recorded in the synoptic gospels when Jesus taught in a synagogue occur at Mark 6:1-6 and Luke 13:10 although we may deduce a later occasion just prior to Jesus' invitation to dine with a leader of the Pharisees (Luke 14:1) as it was customary to invite the visiting speaker for a meal after the meeting (cf. Luke 11:37). Jesus may have made a formal break with the synagogue as a result of opposition but he may have continued to speak there throughout his ministry (cf. John 18:20).[44] Jesus' use of the Temple as a place for teaching appears to have been more occasional (Luke 19:47; 21:37f; John 7:14, 28; 8:2, 20; 10:22-39).

Jesus often taught in the open air—a common procedure in Judaism, particularly among the prophets. The instruction of disciples in the open, air was undertaken by later rabbis in Palestine and Babylonia and may have been customary in the 1st century.[45] Jesus seems to have commenced his public ministry with open air preaching (Mark 1:14) although the first large audience appears after hostility from the synagogue (Mark 3:7). The advantages were numerous: the setting as a whole was under Jesus' authority and meetings could be conducted as he wished without the disadvantage of criticism from above; all those in attendance chose to be there; unlike the synagogues and small towns there was more than sufficient room for all, including those from larger cities; although the larger cities such as Sepphoris and Tiberias seem to have been avoided by Jesus, many from such places came out to see him as his activities and whereabouts were widely publicized (Matt. 4:25, 8:34; Luke 6:17; John 6:23; Mark 1:45,

5:14);[46] city dwellers who worked in the fields might have seen Jesus more easily than if he had gone to their cities—those already present in the fields might have included both sexes, all ages, masters and servants especially during the harvest when whole families might live in temporary accommodation (Ruth 2:1-5; 2 Kings 4:18); the weather in the region generally favored open air work for much of the year but when it did not, Jesus undertook other activities (John 10:23); finally the disciples would be less likely to encounter the barbed questions of the religious leaders which could hardly have been answered by novices (*cf.* Matt. 9:11) and which might have endangered their faith. In the light of these advantages, there can be little doubt that Jesus used the open air for its positive benefits rather than just as a negative response to the antagonism of the synagogue. But there was at least one disadvantage. Jesus' teaching inevitably attracted large numbers of the merely curious. The combination of teaching and miracles could result in an unhealthy interest and spurious discipleship. Jesus' response was to withdraw, send the crowds away or to emphasize more challenging aspects of his teaching. Mass hysteria and the abuse of group dynamics were thus carefully checked (Mark 1:36-38, 6:45; John 6:60-71).[47]

Jesus' use of speeches here is significant for he was not merely utilizing conventions imposed upon him. Crowds were occasionally with Jesus for more than one day (Mark 8:2) and the starting point in their instruction seems to have been the sermon. The 'Sermon on the Mount' may be a fairly typical specimen of Jesus' early sermons but may be no more than a summary.[48] It appears to have been addressed to disciples, primarily, with the crowd as a secondary audience.[49] The disciples, however, are not clearly defined.[50] As written, the sermon is short but may have been punctuated by interruptions and numerous periods of silence, particularly after the more dramatic sayings.[51] Doubtless, Jesus preached at greater length—for the ancients, especially in the East, had great stamina when it came to listening to lengthy speeches.[52] Utilizing the natural theatres of Palestine would have enabled him to address large audiences without either raising his voice much or being physically far from the most distant listener, particularly as the air was clear and extraneous noises were few.[53] Thus a measure of informality could be achieved which might encourage discussion.

Speeches were useful to introduce Jesus' message (Matt. 5:1, 7:28) or to provide instructions when all stood in the same need of information (Matt. 10 and perhaps Luke 24:27),[54] but for detailed instruction to those who were maturing in their understanding and likely to become leaders, one-way communication was inadequate. Recent studies indicate that lectures are often useful for simply transmitting data but that discussion and participation are better for critically examining ideas, stimulating thought and changing attitudes.[55] Not surprisingly, Jesus spent time in the private instruction fan inner core of disciples.[56] This is clearest in the gospel accounts of the latter part of his ministry although such instruction may have begun earlier.[57] This apparent shift from crowd instruction to private training should not be seen as merely a negative response to the facile nature of his popularity with the masses nor just as an attempt to avoid Herod Antipas who was threatening his life, although this need not be entirely excluded (Matt. 11:7-24; Mark 6:1-6; John 2:23-25, 6:25-66). [58] The change appears to be a positive recognition of the need for a trained nucleus to carry on Jesus' work beyond his earthly ministry.

The Twelve were not the only ones to receive more detailed instruction than that given to the crowds. There was a wider sphere of disciples who attached themselves to Jesus at various times. The mission of the 70 or 72 (Luke 10:1) may give some idea of the size of this group at one particular time.[59] There is a tradition, recorded in the Fourth Gospel, that Jesus addressed a more learned audience in Jerusalem, particularly in the synagogues or the Temple.[60] Here he was able to tackle the religious leaders on their own ground and using their own methods. I am assuming here that the Fourth Gospel is, contrary to much contemporary opinion, historically reliable.[61]

How did Jesus conduct his teaching? The disciples were instructed to be as 'wise as serpents' (Matt. 10:16), capable of using in full measure the gifts they had received (Matt. 25:14-30; Luke 19:12-27). Jesus presented himself as a pattern and he used a wide variety of teaching methods. These included enigmatic sayings, Jewish history, visual aides, familiar ideas, projects, figures of speech, irony, poetry, logic, problem-solving, humor, looks, gestures and movement, silence, repetition, questions, discussion, rest and relaxation, together with frequent avoidance of dogmatic answers and precise definitions, withholding of material until it was requested, emphasis on how to think rather than what to think and sparing use of correction. This approach will have stretched his listeners, particularly the Twelve, to the full. They were not just given a barrage of right answers in order to become orthodox talking-machines[62]—although nothing would have been easier, particularly as such an approach was congenial to the Jewish mind (*m Aboth* 2:8 but, *cf.* 5:15). Rather, their intellectual and spiritual powers were developed, which facilitated real maturity of thought and action. In this respect, the teaching style of Jesus anticipates much of the best in modern teaching methods and his training of leaders has much in common with contemporary management training practices.[63]

Speeches played only a small part in the later instruction of the Twelve (perhaps Matt. 18).[64] They were given something approximating to a farewell address at the Last Supper but that included questions put by both Jesus and his hearers (Luke 22:15-37; John 13:31-16:33).

SERMONS IN THE PRIMITIVE CHURCH

In the primitive church speeches continued to be used, particularly in mission—as on the day of Pentecost by Peter (Acts 2:14-36) and subsequently in synagogue addresses by Paul and perhaps Stephen (Acts 6:8-11). Not all speeches were missionary in intent for they occurred also at times of crisis and farewell (Acts 15:13-21,32, 20:7-12,17-35). Jewish homiletic forms seem to have been followed frequently and, as before, there might have been questions from the speaker or the floor (Acts 26:24-29).[65] With the establishment of Christian communities outside the synagogue system, sermons seem to play little part; they may have been used with nascent Christian groups to present basic material but detail is lacking. In particular, sermons, as defined above, are scarce.[66] There are, however, several examples of what might appear to be sermons and it will be necessary to examine each case.

PASSAGES THAT SUGGEST USE OF SERMONS

About thirty different words are used in the Greek New Testament for proclaiming the word of God but in the Authorized or King James Version (AV) they are usually rendered 'preach.'[67] This is important because, in England, the AV has been the most influential of all Bible translations and continues to be influential, particularly in this area, in spite of the appearance of later versions, which are superior in their rendering of terms for communication. Even so, some continue to overwork the term 'preach.' G. Friedrich notes that this deficiency in translation 'is a sign, not merely of poverty of vocabulary, but of the loss of something which was a living reality in primitive Christianity.'[68] The loss is emphasized by the fact that whenever the word 'preach' occurs in our versions, the tacit assumption is often made that the activity under consideration is similar to that undertaken by Christian clergy in their pulpits. This assumption often results in a serious misunderstanding of the text.

Many who write about preaching preface their remarks with lengthy analyses of the more significant Greek words. This is usually a futile exercise because the essential problems this: no word used for verbal communication in the New Testament can give much of a clue concerning context, length, place of delivery, regularity or audience; and, as A.C. Thiselton reminds us, 'It is a mistake to insist on a greater degree of precision than that suggested by the text.'[69] Many of the Greek words used for verbal communication suggest a particular form of communication and this aspect of the words most relevant to the present study will be examined below but often the precise interpretation will depend upon the context.[70] It is absurd to quote a New Testament statement that someone 'preached,' as though this clearly proved a regular Western-style preaching ministry. The point is reinforced by G.B. Caird who warns that:

> It is precisely when theologians have claimed biblical authority for their own beliefs and practices that they have been particularly exposed to the universal temptation...of jumping to the conclusion that the biblical writer is referring to what they would be referring to were they speaking the words themselves.[71]

Our examination of individual passages begins with the speeches in Acts. There are many views on the precise nature of these speeches—

whether they are verbatim accounts, summaries of actual speeches, or creations by Luke. Our present concern however is with the presence or absence of sermons and, more particularly, regular sermons in the text of the New Testament. The precise nature of the text is a separate question from the presence or absence of sermons in the passages under consideration and so current discussion about the nature of the speeches need not detain us unless a particular verse proves crucial for our purpose.

- *Acts 6:2-4 Choosing the Seven*
  This is hardly a sermon after the definition given above but rather a one-off piece of church business.

- *Acts 15:32 The Council of Jerusalem*
  On this occasion, all the listeners stood in need of the same encouragement, exhortation and explanation of recent events. A common need such as we see here is the basic requirement of the use of a sermon is to be appropriate. Prophetic gifts were probably used and there may have been questions during or between the addresses.[72] The plurality of speakers serves to emphasize the singularity of the event. It was not one of a series.

- *Acts 20:7-12 A Sermon at Troas*
  Up to the interruption caused by the fall of Eutychus, this may have been a formal discourse. The use of *dialegomai* and *logos* could suggest this[73] but these terms need imply nothing more formal than a conversation.[74] The second part of the evening centered on familiar conversation—*homilesas*, 'talked with them' (Acts 20:11).[75] Also, this was a farewell address (Acts 20:11-13)76 and, as R.C.H. Lenski notes, the whole gathering was 'a special service in every way' and thus attempting to deduce normal procedures from such an isolated instance, is unjustified.[77]

Manfred Hauke suggests that Paul's conversational style here, and elsewhere, is consistent with what is known of roughly contemporary Jewish practice and, hence, what we might expect from one trained at Gamaliel's rabbinical school. He concludes that '...we cannot project our present-day conception of the Sunday sermon back on the preaching of the word in the communities of Saint Paul.'[78]

- *Acts 20:17-38 Paul's Address to the Ephesian Elders*
  This is a farewell address which follows a common Old Testament pattern.

- *Romans 1: 15 Paul Wishes to Preach in Rome*
  All of the 42 occurrences of *euangelizomai*, from the beginning of Acts onwards, refer to proclaiming good news. The recipients are usually unbelievers except at 1 Thessalonians 3:6 and Revelation 10:7 (and possibly Gal. 1:8,9; Acts 5:42, 15:35; 1 Pet. 4:6) and the present verse, where the recipients of good news may be believers. It is not clear at Romans 1:15 whether Paul intended to preach the gospel (for outsiders might well be present) or to undertake some other aspects of his ministry.[79] More significantly for our purposes, there is nothing in the text to suggest that Paul planned a series of addresses or that his speech would fit into an already existing pattern of sermons at Rome.

- *1 Corinthians 1:21*
  A widely quoted comment of Paul on 'the foolishness of preaching' (AV) is misleading. *Kerugmatos* in this verse is commonly interpreted in, two ways:

  1. It may refer primarily or exclusively to the content of the preaching with little or no reference to form.[80] In this case we can infer nothing as to the form of delivery.

  2. It may refer to both content and form as intimately connected but with the emphasis on form.[81] The reference is then to Paul's failure to utilize classical rhetoric in his presentation of the gospel. But in this case there is still nothing to indicate that regular sermons for specifically Christian consumption were in mind in this verse. Rather, the context of this passage indicates that non-Christians

were the intended audience for this preaching and there is no necessary connection with Christian gatherings.

- Corinthian Christians
They seem to have believed that eloquence and wisdom were intimately connected and that rhetorical eloquence was divinely inspired. Other churches may have felt similarly. It may be that Apollos used rhetorical devices in presenting the gospel and building up the Christian community at Corinth (1 Cor. 3:6), that this was greatly appreciated by one section of the church and that this contributed to the divisions at Corinth.[82] Be this as it may, there is no evidence for regular sermons in the Corinthian church of this period.

- *1 Corinthians 9: 16*
Paul reminds the Corinthians that he is called to preach the gospel—to non-Christians, means not stated.

- *1 Corinthians 11: 26*
The proclamation of the Lord's death at the Lord's Supper is not necessarily the same as preaching a sermon. The use of *katangello* is not decisive as the precise meaning must be judged from the context.[83] The proclamation might be achieved through the meal itself rather than with words but, even if it refers in whole or in part to a verbal declaration, there is insufficient detail in the text to give a clear idea of what is happening.[84] There is certainly no indication of length or that verbal proclamation was the dominate feature of the gathering.

- *Colossians 1:28*
We are concerned with technique but for the most part this verse is not. Paul commits himself to no particular means here. C.A. Evans comments, 'What the writer is describing here is not a philosophy of parish preaching but a philosophy of Apostolic ministry.'[85]

- *1 Timothy 4:13 Instructions to Timothy*
Te paraklesei—exhortation. This might refer to some kind of address, as was requested of Paul at the synagogue in Pis-

idian Antioch (Acts 13:15) or prophecy (1 Cor. 14:3) or a request.[86] Here the reference is probably to expounding the scriptures, possibly to counteract the false teaching already mentioned (1 Tim. 4:1-5).[87] The precise form of the communication is unknown but since there was a major point to be made and all stood in need of the same information, a sermon would be entirely appropriate.

Te didaskalia—the teaching. Since there is no hint as to the form, which this teaching might take we have no warrant for assuming that sermons are in mind.

- *1 Timothy 5:17 Preaching and Teaching*
  There are several possible meanings of *en logo* although it is usually rendered 'in word' or 'in speech' (1 Cor. 4:20; 2 Cor 6:7; Col. 3:17; 1 Thes. 1:5, 4:15; 1 Tim. 4:12). In the present verse it is usually rendered 'preaching' but the context makes no particular interpretative demands.

- *2 Timothy 2:2*
  C.K. Barrett's comment on this verse is worth quoting:[88]

'The things you have heard from me through many witnesses commit to trustworthy men, who will be able to teach others too' (2 Tim. 2:2). But what of the Pauline fellowship, where everyone had a psalm, a teaching, a revelation, a tongue, an interpretation (1 Cor. 14:26)? of the Pauline church, in which every member had its function or ministry, like the organs and limbs of a body (1 Cor. 12:4-27)? This, it seems, has disappeared.

Careful reading of the verse shows however that 2 Timothy 2:2 states an *end*—the instruction of followers who will then teach others. The text says nothing of the *means* to that end. Barrett has inferred means where none is mentioned or implied and, therefore, his reasoning is invalid.[89] The reasoning might be invalid but the conclusion true. However, as we shall see, mutual ministries continued to operate into the sub-apostolic period and there is nothing in the Pastorals to indicate their abandonment. Moreover, there is nothing in 2 Timothy 2:2 to indicate a ministry of sermons.[90]

- *2 Timothy 4:2 'Preach the Word'*
  The use of *kerusso* here is rather surprising as it is used primarily for the proclamation of Jesus and the gospel to unbelievers outside Christian gatherings. But here (as in 2 Cor. 11:4) it seems to refer primarily to addressing the faithful although the possibility of the occasional presence of unbelievers cannot be ruled out and may even have been in mind when the epistle was penned. 'Preach' is not a good translation of *kerussein*[91] but at least it does suggest that something is to be taught. The form and duration of the teaching, both as regards Paul's intentions and Timothy's performance, are beyond recovery. The reference may be to a sermon, or even a series of sermons, but it need not be. The reason for Timothy's action is given in the text. The danger of which Paul had warned the Ephesian elders had materialized and Timothy was asked to take action against it (Acts 20:29f; 2 Tim. 2:14-18, 3:1-14, 4:1-5, 14f). The sermon, if such it was, was an aid in the battle but there is nothing here to suggest that it was already a regular feature of church life or that it should ever become such, although it might be repeated if needed to counter other errors in the future.[92]

The imperatives are usually rendered 'preach...reprove, rebuke, exhort...' In my opinion, the natural interpretation of this instruction is that reproving, rebuking and exhorting should be done as and when necessary rather than at fixed or regular times, irrespective of other considerations. The precise significance of 'in season and out of season' is not clear[93] and in any case there is no reason to restrict its application to *keruxon ton logon*. Hence, the context provides no evidence for regular sermons.

- *Possible Homiletic Material*
  Several writers contend that some of the epistles, notably Ephesians, Hebrews, James, 1 Peter and Jude, contain

homiletic material, perhaps reworked sermons in some form or another. This may be so but precise details seem beyond recovery and can, therefore, hardly enter our discussion.[94]

- *Public Reading*
  There were occasional public readings in Christian gatherings. The material read might include the Old Testament and the letters of Paul (Col. 4:16; 1 Thes. 5:27; 1 Tim. 4:13). Precise detail is lacking but this activity is not strictly comparable with preaching sermons.

The speeches mentioned in this section cover those to non-Christians, specific problems in the life of the church, farewell addresses and greetings to previously unknown brethren. There is nothing here to indicate regular sermons in the context of Christian gatherings although this does not amount to a proof that they were not delivered.

THE SERMON: NEW TESTAMENT TO EARLY FATHERS

THE SUB-APOSTOLIC LITERATURE

When we move into the sub-apostolic period, the picture is broadly similar. Ignatius of Antioch (early 2nd century) recommended Polycarp to prepare a homily (*homilia*)—perhaps more than one—to combat a specific problem relating to false teachers (Ign *Poly* 5:1).[96] The form is unknown but, at this time, it might have been as informal as a conversation.[97] According to Irenaeus (as reported by Eusebius), Polycarp delivered discourses (*dialexeis*). These may have been sermons or even conversations (Eus *HE* 5:20:6).[98] If sermons are in mind here, their frequency cannot be determined from the word or its context. Another possible reference to a sermon (Ign *Phil* 7:1) appears to refer to an alleged prophecy rather than a sermon.[99] The *Second Epistle of Clement*, itself a sermon (*2 Clem.* 19:1), makes reference to what may be sermonic presentations (*2 Clem.* 17:3). Detail is lacking but the congregation does seem passive and perhaps unresponsive.[100] M. Staniforth finds it tempting to see the sermon in the latter part of the *Epistle to Diognetus* (11:6)[101] but the reference is obscure and this section of the epistle is probably late although not easy to date.[102] In the *Didache* (40-150AD?)[103] there is no justification for translating *tou lalountos soi*, 'the one who speaks,' by 'the one who preaches' (*Did.* 4:1) as is done by J.B. Lightfoot, J.R. Harmer and M.W. Holmes.[104] The reference here is to *speaking* the word of God. No further detail is given and the context provides no clear guide to a more precise translation.

Aside from these few examples, the sermon does not appear and there is nothing to suggest it was a regular part of Christian gatherings. This is not surprising as mutual ministries (which will be discussed below) were still in evidence although the precise part they played in Christian gatherings of this period is difficult to ascertain (*1 Clem.* 2:6, 37:5, 38:1; *2 Clem.* 17:2; *Did.* 4:2f,8, 15:3; *Ep Barn* 19:12, 21:4; *Poly Phil* 10:2).[105] References to preaching generally concerned unbelievers but set-piece evangelistic speeches were not common after the 3rd century. Missionaries like Paul, who travelled the Empire taking the gospel hither and thither, were not numerous even in the 1st century and by the second 'and third centuries they were scarce.[106]

The evidence from the New Testament and sub-apostolic literature that we have so far examined suggests that the sermon appeared only as an occasional item—an extra, delivered to deal with a specific problem needing attention or on a special occasion. There is no clear evidence for regular sermons.

THE EPISTLES OF PLINY (ABOUT 112AD)

The description of early Christian meetings given in the epistles of Pliny (10:96:5-8) makes no mention of sermons but this is not significant as the account is very brief and provides only a summary of activities.

THE EARLY FATHERS

The writings of Justin Martyr (mid-2nd century) contain a reference to what may be the sermon delivered to the faithful on a regular basis (Justin **1** *Apo1* 67) but the use of *dia logou* and *proklesin* does not necessarily demand a sermon after the modern fashion as defined above, particularly as these terms do not generally refer to addresses in Justin's writings.[107] Justin appears to have travelled widely and may have possessed an extensive knowledge of contemporary ecclesiastical practices.[108] It is, nonetheless, difficult to know whether Justin's reference to 'the sermon' (whatever we are to understand by it) indicates common practice or not.[109]

According to C.W. Dugmore, we have a 'sermon' in the *Acts of John* 106f and although this source is of limited historical value, its mention of the sermon might at least reflect the procedures of the time (latter part of the 2nd century). On closer inspection, the 'sermon' proves to be yet another farewell address and not necessarily part of a series.[110]

By the time of Clement of Alexandria, Tertullian and Origen— late second to mid-3rd century—sermons seem entrenched—even in Montanist circles (Tert *De Anima* 9)—although apparently not without opposition from those who had to endure them. Origen regularly preached for an hour or more, usually in a simple, Attic style with imperatives and rhetorical questions but his congregations often grew restive, talked throughout, left before the sermon started or attended irregularly.[111] The audiences probably did not appreciate the subject matter or speaker. Clement of Alexandria lamented that the sermon had so little effect on some Christians.[112] But opposition was futile and eventually the sermon became standard practice, possibly however as late as the 4th century.[113]

W.O.E. Oesterley says of Justin's reference to the sermon that 'it is doubtless in the light of these definite statements that the vague allusions to the subject in earlier Christian writings must be read.' Oesterley's view is widely held but the evidence, as we shall see, points elsewhere.[114]

Finally, it is worth noting that even when sermons were delivered they were not yet the passive occasions so frequently experienced in churches today. Just like the sermons in synagogue, Christian sermons were often punctuated by interruptions such as applause, foot stamping, restlessness, suggestions to the preacher, discussion among a group in the audience, joining in the reciting of biblical passages, tears, laughter and dialogue between preacher and congregation. On occasion there might even be violence as in the theatre.[115] As Alexandre Olivar points out, there was considerable frankness and openness between audience and preacher and this seems to have applied even when non-Christians were present.[116]

ENDNOTES

1. 'Authority in Preaching' in M. Eden and D.F. Wells (eds), *The Gospel in the Modern World*, 1991, p. 199
2. 'Authority in Preaching,' p. 200
3. Some of the issues involved in defining are discussed in S.L Hayakawa, *Language in Thought and Action*, [4]1978, pp. 49-58, 157-160; E.A. Nida and J.P. Louw, *Lexical Semantics of the Greek New Testament*, 1992, pp. 3f, 18f, 25f, 37f
4. O. Eissfeldt, *The Old Testament: An Introduction*, 1965, pp. 12-15
5. O. Eissfeldt, *Old Testament*, p. 16; A. Bentzen, *Introduction to the Old Testament*, [2]1952, 1, 207f
6. Mic 3:6: J.L. Mays, *Micah*, 1976, pp. 83f
7. *Old Testament*, pp. 12-17.
8. R. Mason, *Preaching the Tradition: Homily and Hermeneutics after the Exile*, 1990, pp. 142, 257f
9. J. Lindblom, *Prophecy in Ancient Israel*, Oxford, Blackwell Publishers, 1963, p. 153
10. *Prophecy*, p. 153; similarly W.H. Schmidt, *Introduction to the Old Testament*, 1984, p. 173
11. *Old Testament*, p. 16
12. For the swift gathering of a crowd in New Testament times see K.E. Bailey, *Poet and Peasant: A Literary-Cultural Approach to the Parables in Luke*, 1976, pp. 181f
13. D.A. Hubbard, *Hosea*, 1989, p. 100
14. H.H. Rowley, *Worship in Ancient Israel*, 1967, p. 224; E. Jacob, *Theology of the Old Testament*, 1958, p. 270 n1; R. Mason, *Preaching the Tradition*, p. 259
15. W. Eichrodt, *Theology of the Old Testament*, 1967, II, 250f; *cf.* 2 Kings 6:32
16. W.H. Brownlee, *Ezekiel 1-19*, 1986, pp. 122, 128; *cf.* W. Eichrodt, *Ezekiel*, 1970, pp. 121, 179
17. W. Eichrodt, *Ezekiel*, London, SCM Press Ltd., 1970, p. 466
18. 1 Kings 11:29-31, 18:20-46, 19:19-21; 2 Kings 13:14-19; Isa. 7:3, 8:1-4, 20:1-6; Jer. 13:1-11,16:1-9, 18:1-12, 19:1-13, 27:1-28:17, 32:6-15, 43:8-13, 51:59-64; Ezek. 2:8-3:3, 3:26 (24:27), 4:1-17, 5:1-4, 6:11-14, 12:1-20, 21:6-17, 24:15-24, 37:15-17; Hosea 1:2-9; Mic. 1:8; Zech. 6:9-15: W.D. Stacey, *Prophetic Drama in the Old Testament*, 1990, pp. 75-214
19. F.D. Kidner, *Ezra and Nehemiah*, 1979, p. 110
20. A.J. Saldarini, *Pharisees, Scribes and Sadducees in Palestinian Society*, 1989, pp. 52, 274
21. The priests continued with their teaching duties into the New Testament period (E.P. Sanders, *Judaism: Practice and Belief 63BCE-66CE*, 1992, pp. 170-182)
22. S. Wagner, *TDOT*, VI, 343f; H.H. Rowley, *Worship*, pp. 101f; R. de Vaux, *Ancient Israel: Its Life and Institutions*, [2]1965, pp. 353-355
23. H.G.M. Williamson, *1 and 2 Chronicles*, 1982, pp. 282f, 405; idem, *Ezra, Nehemiah*, 1985, pp. 289-291
24. Priestly speeches: 2 Chron. 26:17f, 31:10; Ezra 8:28f, 10:10f; Neh. 8:9f and perhaps 2 Chron. 24:20-22. Levitical speeches: 2 Chron. 20:14-17; Neh. 8:9-11
25. J.N. Oswalt, *The Book of Isaiah: Chapters 1-39*, 1986; p. 154; D.A Hubbard, *Joel and Amos,* 1989, pp. 148f
26. L. Wills, 'The Form of the Sermon in Hellenistic Judaism and Early Christianity', *HTR,* 77, 1984, 293-296; O. Eissfeldt, *Old Testament,* p. 17; J.I.H. McDonald,

Kerygma and Didache, 1980, pp. 46, 164 n65; B.T. Viviano, *Study as Worship: Aboth and the New Testament,* 1978, pp. 143-152

27. J.W. Bowker, 'Speeches in Acts: A Study in Proem and Yelammedenu Form', *NTS,* 14, 1967, 96f; K.P. Donfried, *The Setting of Second Clement in Early Christianity,* 1974, pp. 25f

28. W.R. Stegner, 'The Ancient Jewish Synagogue Homily' in D.E. Aune (ed), *Greco-Roman Literature and the New Testament: Selected Forms and Genres,* 1988, p. 51; W.A Meeks, *The First Urban Christians,* 1983, p. 146; *HJP,* II, 449; P.S. Alexander, 'Rabbinic Judaism and the New Testament', *ZNTW,* 74, 1983, 244f

29. S. Safrai, 'The Synagogue', *Compendia* I:2, 915, 932; *HJP,* II, 336, 453; H.B. Rowley, *Worship,* p. 236; E.P. Sanders, *Jewish Law from Jesus to the Mishnah,* 1990, p. 79; idem, *Judaism,* pp. 177, 201

30. E.P. Sanders, *Judaism,* pp. 199, 201f

31. J. Heinemann, 'Preaching', *Enc Jud,* XIII, col 995f; A. Edersheim, *The Life and Times of Jesus the Messiah,* ³1887, I, 445, 448f

32. E.P. Sanders, *The Historical Figure of Jesus,* 1993, pp. 100f; idem, *Judaism,* p. 200

33. A. Marmorstein, 'The Background of the Haggadah', *HUCA,* 6, 1929, 204

34. R.C. Worley, *Preaching and Teaching in the Earliest Church,* 1967, p. 60; L.M. White, *Building God's House in the Roman World,* 1990, p. 92

35. J. Heinemann, 'Preaching', *Enc Jud,* XIII, col 995; E.P. Sanders, *Jewish Law,* pp. 78f

36. L. Morris, 'The Gospels and the Jewish Lectionaries', *GP,* III, 134-139; P.F. Bradshaw, *The Search for the Origins of Christian Worship,* 1992, pp. 21f, 31f

37. S. Safrai, 'Education and the Study of the Torah', *Compendia* I:2, p. 967

38. J. Heinemann, *Enc Jud,* XIII, col 994; I.H. Levinthal, 'The Uniqueness of the Classic Jewish Sermon', *Conservative Judaism,* 27, 1973, 77-80

39. J.J. Murphy, *Rhetoric in the Middle Ages: A History of rhetorical Theory from Saint Augustine to the Renaissance,* 1974, pp. 272f, 275

40. I.H. Marshall, *The Gospel of Luke,* 1978, p. 181; R.J. Banks, *Jesus and the Law in the Synoptic Tradition,* 1975, p. 91; J. Nolland, *Luke 1-9:20,* 1989, p. 195; *cf.* D.G. Peterson, *Engaging with God: A Biblical Theology of Worship,* 1992, p. 131

41. For example, women traveling with him (Mark 15:40f; Luke 8:1-3), his teaching style (Mark 1:22), his use of the Sabbath (Mark 3:1-5), his willingness to eat with outcasts and reinterpretation of eating restrictions (Mark 7:1-23; Lk 5:29f). Other examples are given in K.E. Bailey, *Through Peasant Eyes,* 1980, pp. 14f, 27, 28f

42. I.H. Marshall, *Luke,* p. 418; E.F.F. Bishop, *Jesus of Palestine: The Local Background to the Gospel Documents,* 1955, p. 170; K.E. Bailey, *Through Peasant Eyes,* p. 48; R.L. Rohrbaugh, D.E. Oakman and J.H. Neyrey in J.H. Neyrey (ed), *The Social World if Luke—Acts: Models for Interpretation,* 1991, pp. 140-147, 175, 385

43. See the discussion of gospel chronology in R.H. Stein, *The Synoptic Problem: An Introduction,* 1988, pp. 34-37, 43f, 155f, 218; E. Linnemann, *Is There a Synoptic Problem?,* 1992, pp. 165-170

44. V. Taylor, *The Gospel According to St Mark,* ²1966, p. 298; S. Freyne, *Galilee, Jesus and the Gospels,* 1988, p. 250; W.D. Davies and D.C. Allison, Jr., *A Critical and Exegetical Commentary on, the Gospel According to Saint Matthew,* 1991, II, 455; I. Abrahams, *Studies in Pharisaism and the Gospels,* First Series, 1917, pp.

12f

45. A. Büchler, 'Learning and Teaching in the Open Air in Palestine', *JQR*, 4,1913-14, 485-491; S. Krauss, 'Outdoor Teaching in Talmudic Times', *JJS*, 1, 1948,82-84.

46. G.E.M. de Ste Croix, *The Class Struggle in the Ancient Greek World*, 1981, pp. 427-430

47. D.J. Tidball, *An Introduction to the Sociology of the New Testament*, 1983, p. 45

48. Many modem writers from John Calvin onwards maintain that the 'Sermon on the Mount' (and other speeches of Jesus) does not represent an interrelated whole, delivered as a sermon by Jesus, but is rather a collection of elements taught by him on various occasions and arranged by the author of Matthew's gospel or even in part written by him (J. Calvin, *Commentary on a Harmony of the Evangelists*, 1845, I, 258f; W.D. Davies, *The Setting of the Sermon on the Mount*, 1964, p. 5; R.T. France, *Matthew: Evangelist and Teacher*, 1989, pp. 160-163; R.A. Guelich, *The Sermon on the Mount*, 1982, pp. 33-36). Objections to the unity of the 'Sermon on the Mount' are answered by D.A Carson, *Matthew*, EBC, 1984, VIII, 122-126. Reasons for assuming the unity of all the lengthier speeches in Matthew's gospel are given in C Blomberg, *The Historical Reliability of the Gospels*, 1987, pp. 138-146 and, from a slightly different perspective, G.A. Kennedy, *New Testament Interpretation Through Rhetorical Criticism*, 1984, pp. 39-72

49. M.J. Wilkins, *The Concept of Disciple in Matthew's Gospel*, 1988, pp. 149f; *cf.* G.A. Kennedy, *NT Interpretation*, pp. 40f

50. On the identity of the disciples see D.A Carson, *Matthew*, 128; R.T. France, *The Gospel According to Matthew*, 1985, p. 107; W.D. Davies and D.C Allison, *A Critical and Exegetical Commentary on the Gospel According to Saint Matthew*, 1988, 1, 425; R.B. Gundry, *Matthew: A Commentary on His Literary and Theological Art*, 1982, p. 66

51. G. Highet, *The Art of Teaching*, 1972, pp. 169-172, *cf.* J.A Grassi, *The Teacher in the Primitive Church and the Teacher Today*, 1973, pp. 46, 108

52. See Appendix I

53. B. Cobbey Crisler, 'The Acoustics and Crowd Capacity of Natural Theaters in Palestine', *BA*, 39:4, 1976, 128-141; E.F.F. Bishop, *Apostles of Palestine: The Local Background to the New Testament Church*, 1958, p. 70

54. The unity of Matthew 10 is discussed in D.A. Carson, *Matthew*, 240-243. In Luke 24:27 we may have an uninterrupted discourse. There are textual variants here but the use of *dienneneuo* (whether we read an aorist or an imperfect) does not necessarily point to an uninterrupted address (LN, I, 405; BAGD, p. 194a; LSJ, p. 425b; I.H. Marshall, *Luke*, p. 897; AC Thiselton, NIDNTT, I, 581f)

55. J. Rogers, *Adults Learning*, [3]1989, pp. 119f; D. Legge in M.D. Stephens and G.W. Roderick (eds), *Teaching Techniques in Adult Education*, 1971, pp. 56-60, 66; S.S. Boocock, 'Toward a Sociology of Leaming: A Selective Review of Existing Research', *Sociology of Education*, 39:1, 1966, 12; D.A. Bligh, *What's the Use of Lectures?*, 1978, pp. 4-26, 156-159; R.M. Beard and J. Hartley, *Teaching and Learning in Higher Education*, [4]1984, pp. 185-194.

56. Small group instruction was characteristic of the sages of Israel and of Greek education at the higher levels (B. Witherington III, *Jesus the Sage: The Pilgrimage of Wisdom*, 1994, pp. 175-179; FAG. Beck, *Greek Education: 450-350BC*, 1964, p. 309)

57. Mark 4:11, 34: V. Taylor, *The Gospel According to St Mark*, [2]1966, pp. 147f. Privacy

was hardly known in the towns of Palestine. Consequently, when Jesus wished to be alone (or even alone with a small group), it was often advisable to escape to the countryside or wilderness (J. Wilkinson, *Jerusalem as Jesus Knew It*, 1978, p. 29)

58. H.W. Hoehner, *Herod Antipas*, 1972, pp. 200-202; *cf.* V. Taylor, *Mark*, pp. 635f

59. There is a textual problem here relating to the number 70 (72). See the discussion in I.H. Marshall, *Luke*, pp. 414f; B.M. Metzger, *A Textual Commentary on the Greek New Testament*, [2]1975, pp. 150f. The historicity of this mission has been challenged by many including J.A Fitzmyer, *The Gospel According to Luke*, 1985, II, 843; C.F. Evans, *Saint Luke*, 1990, pp. 442, 446. The challenge has been answered by A. Plummer, *A Critical and Exegetical Commentary on the Gospel According to S. Luke*, [5]1922, pp. 269-271; N. Geldenhuys, *Commentary on the Gospel of Luke*, 1950, pp. 302f; I.H. Marshall, *Luke*, pp.412f

60. D. Guthrie, *New Testament Introduction*, [4]1990, pp. 306-309; G.E. Ladd, *A Theology of the New Testament*, [2]1994, pp., 256f

61. See the discussion in D.A. Carson, *The Gospel According to John*, 1991, pp. 40-68

62. This expression is taken and adapted from Thomas Carlyle, 'Latter Day Pamphlets', No. 1, *The Present Time* (Edinburgh edition), 1911, p. 38

63. C.A. Wilson, *Jesus the Teacher*, 1974; J. Holt, *Teach Your Own*, 1981, p. 52; idem, *Learning all the Time*, 1991, pp. 127-162;]. McLeish, W. Matheson and J. Park, *The Psychology of the Learning Group*, 1973, pp. 88-90; A. Rogers, *Teaching Adults*, 1986, p. 74; J. Garnett, *The Work Challenge: Leaders at Work*, [5]1988.

64. On the unity of this passage see D.A. Carson, Matthew, 396

65. J. W. Bowker, 'Speeches in Acts: A Study in Proem and Yelammedenu Form', *NTS*, 14, 1967, 96-111

66. The point has been noticed: A.B. MacDonald, *Christian Worship in the Primitive Church*, 1934, pp. 86f; A. Richardson (ed), *A Theological Word Book of the Bible*, 1950, pp. 171f; E. Schweizer, 'Worship in the New Testament', *Reformed and Presbyterian World*, 24, 1957, 205; G. Reid, *The Gagging of God*, 1969, pp. 98f; C.A. Evans, ' "Preacher" and "Preaching": Some Lexical Observations', *JETS*, 24:4, 1981, 315-322; J. Zens, 'What is a "Minister"?', *ST*, 11:3, 1982, 19f; S.K. Stowers, 'Social Status, Public Speaking and Private Teaching: The Circumstances of Paul's Preaching Activity', *Nov T*, 26, 1984, 70; K. Craig, 'Is the "Sermon" Concept Biblical?' , ST, 1986, 15:1-2, 22-29; D. Birkey, *The House Church*, 1988, pp. 121f

67. This is also true, to some extent, of the English versions, which preceded the AV, particularly the Tyndale Bible, the Great Bible, the Geneva Bible and the Bishops' Bible. The Wyclif and Rheims versions exhibit greater freedom in rendering terms for verbal communication

68. G. Friedrich, *TDNT*, III, Eerdmans (Wm. B) Publishing Co., USA, 703

69. A.C. Thiselton, 'Semantics and New Testament Interpretation' in I.H. Marshall (ed), *New Testament Interpretation: Essays on Principles and Methods*, Carlisle, Paternoster Press, 1977, p. 94

70. On the importance of context as a guide to the meaning of words see K.L. McKay, 'Syntax in Exegesis', *Tyn B*, 23, 1972, 56; S.I. Hayakawa, *Language in Thought and Action*, [4]1978, pp. 54-58; J.P. Louw, *Semantics of New Testament Greek*, 1982; E.A. Nida and].P. Louw, *Lexical Semantics of the Greek New Testament*, 1992, pp. 11-13, 18-20, 37f; J.M. Frame, *The Doctrine of the Knowledge of God*, 1987, pp. 169f, 183-185, 194-196

71. G.B. Caird, *The Language and Imagery of the Bible*, London, Duckworth (Gerald)

& Co. Ltd., 1980, p. 80, *cf.* p. 10

72.   F.F. Bruce, *The Book of the Acts,* ²1988, p. 300

73.   E. Haenchen, *The Acts of the Apostles,* 1971, p. 584; J.A. Alexander, *A Commentary on the Acts of the Apostles,* 1857 repr 1980, II, 228f; G. Schrenk, *TDNT,* II, 94f; LN, 1:33:26 (p.392)

74.   F.F. Bruce, The Acts of the Apostles, ³1990, p. 425; LSJ, pp. 400, 1058f, (VI); LN, 1:33:446 (p. 439); G. Abbott-Smith, *A Manual Greek Lexicon of the New Testament,* 31937, p. 108; *cf.* BAGD, p. 185b

75.   J. A. Alexander, *Acts,* II, 233; R.J. Knowling, *The Acts of the Apostles,* EGT, 1901, II, 426; BAGD, p. 565b, *cf.* Luke's usage at Luke 24:14f; Acts 24:26 and similarly Justin *Dial Trypho* 28:2: K.N. Giles, 'Teachers and Teaching in the Church', Part 2: *JCE* Papers 71, July 1981, 57

76.   D.F. Watson, 'Paul's Speech to the Ephesian Elders (Acts 20:17-38): Epideictic Rhetoric of Farewell' in idem (ed), *Persuasive Artistry: Studies in New Testament Rhetoric in Honor of George A. Kennedy,* 1991, pp. 184f

77.   R.C.H. Lenski, *The Interpretation of the Acts of the Apostles,* Augsburg Fortress, USA, 1961, p. 825

78.   M. Hauke, *Women in the Priesthood?,* Ignatius Press, USA, 1988, p. 363

79.   C.A. Evans, '"Preacher" and "Preaching": Some Lexical Observations', *JETS,* 24:4, 1981, 317; J.D.G. Dunn, *Romans 1-8,* 1988, pp. 33f; N. Turner, *Grammatical Insights into the New Testament,* 1965, p. 92

80.   R.H. Mounce, *The Essential Nature of New Testament Preaching,* 1960, pp. 53-55; J.I.H. McDonald, *Kerygma and Didache,* 1980, pp. 1f; G.D. Fee, *The First Epistle to the Corinthians,* 1987, p. 73; G.K. Barrett, *The First Epistle to the Corinthians,* ²1971, p. 54; LN, 1:33:258 (p. 417)

81.   A.D. Litfin, *St Paul's Theology of Proclamation: 1 Corinthians 1-4 and Greco-Roman Rhetoric,* 1994, pp. 155, 160-173, 188-190, 198-209

82.   This view is argued in B. Witherington III, *Conflict and Community in Corinth: A Socio-Rhetorical Commentary on 1 and 2 Corinthians,* 1995, pp. 82-87, 100, 124f, 130

83.   LN, I: 33: 204 (p411); *cf.* BAGD, p. 409

84.   BAGD, p. 409a; G.D. Fee, *The First Epistle to the Corinthians,* 1987, p. 557; G.K. Barrett, *The First Epistle to the Corinthians,* ²1971, p. 270; I.H. Marshall, *Last Supper and Lord's Supper,* 1980, p. 113

85.   C.A. Evans, '"Preacher" and "Preaching": Some Lexical Observations', *JETS,* 24:4, 1981, 318

86.   BAGD, p. 618a; LSJ, p. 1313; LN, 1:25:150, 33:168 (pp. 306, 408);]. Thomas, *EDNT,* III, 24-27

87.   G.D. Fee, *1 and 2 Timothy, Titus,* 1984, p. 69

88.   G.K. Barrett, *Church, Ministry and Sacraments in the New Testament,* Carlisle, Paternoster Press, 1985, p. 92. The problems involved in reconciling the treatments of church order and ministry in the Pastoral Epistles with Paul's treatment elsewhere are examined in D. Guthrie, *The Pastoral Epistles,* ²1990; pp. 31-39; J.N.D. Kelly, *The Pastoral Epistles,* 1963, pp. 13-16; E.E. Ellis, *Pauline Theology: Ministry and Society,* 1989, pp. 102-107; R. St. J. Parry, *The Pastoral Epistles,* 1920, pplix-1xxx; R.Y.K. Fung, 'Charismatic Versus Organized Ministry?', *EQ,* 52,1980, pp. 206-210

89.   Confusing means with ends in connection with Paul's mission is commonplace

among theologians. Further examples may be found in A.J. Malherbe, *Paul and the Thessalonians*, 1987, p. 8; W.A. Meeks, *The First Urban Christians*, 1983, p. 26

90. See further Th Zahn, *Introduction to the New Testament*, 1909 repr 1977, II, 97

91. G. Friedrich, *TDNT*, III, 703. In 2 Timothy 4:2 'Proclaim the word (or message)' is a more accurate translation and relatively free from false associations and is so rendered in NRSV; HJ. Schonfield, The Authentic New Testament; idem, The Original New Testament; NEB; Revised EB; W. Barclay, The New Testament: A New Translation; C.K. Williams, The New Testament: A New Translation in Plain English; EJ. Goodspeed, The Student's New Testament; New Jerusalem Bible; D .H. Stem, Jewish New Testament

92. Views on the purpose of the aorist imperatives are legion and include adding authority and solemnity, indicating the vivid nature of the address, emphasizing the necessity for prompt action, indicating an action to be ended at a definite time and a stylistic variation (B.M. Fanning, *Verbal Aspect in New Testament Greek*, 1990, pp. 370-379). But given that the aorist tense is essentially undetermined or undefined or presents the action as complete or as a whole without regard to internal make-up (Burton, *Syntax*, 35; Robertson, *Grammar*, p. 824; F. Stagg, 'The Abused Aorist', *JBL*, 91, 1972, 221-231; Carson, *Exegetical Fallacies*, 1984, pp. 69-75; S.E. Porter, *Idioms of the Greek New Testament*, 1992, p. 35; B.M. Fanning, *Verbal Aspect*, pp. 86-98), the use of the aorist imperative—'preach the word'—tells us litde of the timing or arrangement of the event (Burton, *Syntax*, 184, 98). In order to imply repeated action by the verbal form alone, the present imperative might have been more appropriate (J.H. Bernard, *The Pastoral Epistles*, 1899, p. 140; C.F.D. Moule, *An Idiom—Book of New Testament Greek*, ²1959, 20; Moulton, *Grammar*, III, 74f; M. Zerwick, *Biblical Greek Illustrated by Examples*, 1963, 243 (p. 79). As is so often the case, in order to comprehend the matter further, we must pass from the grammar to the context.

93. See the discussion in A.J. Malherbe, "In Season and Out of Season": 2 Timothy 4:2', *JBL*, 103, 1984, 235-243; G.D. Fee, *1 and 2 Timothy, Titus*, 1984, pp. 233f

94. A.T. Lincoln, *Ephesians*, 1990, pp. xxxixf; W.L. Lane, *Hebrews 1-8*, 1991, pplxx-lxxv; idem, *Hebrews 9-13*, 1991, pp. 567-569; P.H. Davids, *The Epistle of James*, 1982, pp. 12f, 23; W.W. Wessel, *ISBE*, II, 962; J.N.D. Kelly, *The Epistles of Peter and of Jude*, 1976, pp. 15-20; J.R. Michaels, *1 Peter*, 1988, pp. xxxviiif, 73; P .H. Davids, *The First Epistle of Peter*, 1990, pp. llf; R.J. Bauckham, *Jude, 2 Peter*, 1983, p. 3

95. [Publisher Note: No actual note in text] In this section I have relied on C.A. Evans, "Preacher" and "Preaching": Some Lexical Observations', *JETS*, 24:4, 1981, 315-322

96. J.B. Lightfoot, *The Apostolic Fathers: S. Ignatius, S. Polycarp*, 1885, II, section 1, 346f; B. Reicke, 'A Synopsis of Early Christian Preaching' in A. Fridrichsen et al, *The Root of the Vine: Essays in Biblical Theology*, 1953, p. 150

97. LSJ, p. 1222a; MM, p. 448

98. LSJ, p. 401a; G.W.H. Lampe, *A Patristic Greek Lexicon*, 1961-1968, p. 356a

99. W.R. Schoedel, *Ignatius of Antioch*, 1985, p. 205

100. For the date of *2 Clem* see Appendix I

101. M. Staniforth and A. Louth, *Early Christian Writings: The Apostolic Fathers*, ²1987, p. 149 n 11

102. F.L. Cross favors around 200AD, *The Early Christian Fathers*, 1960, p. 28. L.W.

Barnard tentatively favors around 140AD, *Studies in the Apostolic Fathers and Their Background,* 1966, p.173

103. On the dating of the *Didache* see J. Draper, 'The Jesus Tradition in the Didache', *GP,* V, 269-271; C.N. Jefford, *The Sayings of Jesus in the Teaching of the Twelve Apostles,* 1989, pp. 4-18

104. J.B. Lightfoot, J.R. Harmer and M.W. Holmes, *The Apostolic Fathers,* InterVarsity Press, USA, ²1989, p. 151

105. B.E. Bowe, *A Church in Crisis: Ecclesiology and Paraenesis in Clement of Rome,* 1988, pp. 110f

106. C.A. Evans, 'Preacher', pp. 318-320; R. MacMullen, *Christianizing the Roman Empire AD100-400,* 1984, pp. 33f, 111; W.P. Bowers, *Studies in Paul's Understanding of His Mission,* PhD Thesis (Cambridge University), 1976, pp. 184f; E.G. Hinson, *The Evangelization of the Roman Empire,* 1981, pp. 38f, 216

107. For New Testament usage of *dia logou* see Acts 15:27,32; 2 Thess 2:2,15; 1 Tim 4:5. Logos is used in Justin 1 *Apol* with a wide range of meanings (A.W.F. Blunt, *The Apologies of Justin Martyr,* 1911, p. 150). *Dia logou* also occurs at 1 *Apol* 13, 55, 64, 66; 2 *Apol* 10. Addresses are not referred to in these cases with the unlikely exception of 1:55. *Proklesin* also occurs at 1 *Apol* 3 where it does not refer to a sermon. See also the discussion of Justin's use of *homilein* (*Dial Trypho,* 28:2, 85:6) in K.N. Giles, 'Teachers and Teaching in the Church', Part 2: *JCE* Papers 71, July 1981, 57

108. G.T. Purves, *The Testimony of Justin Martyr to Early Christianity,* 1888, p. 45; L.W. Barnard, *Justin Martyr: His Life and Thought,* 1967, pp. 133, 150

109. See the brief discussion in P.F. Bradshaw, *The Search for the Origins of Christian Worship,* 1992, pp.139f

110. C.W. Dugmore, *The Influence of the Synagogue Upon the Divine Office,* 1944, p. 26; *Acts of John* 111-115 culminating in the death of John

111. G.A. Kennedy, *Classical Rhetoric and its Christian and Secular Tradition from Ancient to Modern Times,* 1980, pp. 139f

112. 112 B.J. Kidd, *A History of the Church to AD461,* 1922, I, 405; C. Bigg, *The Christian Platonists of Alexandria,* ²1913, pp. 165-168; J.W. Trigg, *Origen,* 1985, pp. 177f, 196; J.T. Lienhard, 'Origen as Homilist' in D.G. Hunter (ed), *Preaching in the Patristic Age,* 1989, pp. 43f; Clem Alex *Paid* III .xi (A-NF, II, 290). A general estimate of the effects of preaching is given in A. Olivar, *Predicación Cristiana Antigua,* 1991, pp. 946-949

113. C.A. Evans, 'Preacher', pp. 320f; E. Hatch, *The Influence of Greek Ideas and Usages Upon the Christian Church,* 1897, p. 109

114. W.O.E. Oesterley, *The Jewish Background of the Christian Liturgy,* Oxford University Press, 1925, p. 118

115. F. van der Meer, *Augustine the Bishop,* 1961, pp. 427-429; B.J. Kidd, *History of the Church,* II, 392, 418; A. Olivar, *Predicación,* pp. 780-809, 850

116. *Predicación,* pp. 772f, 797

Origins of the Sermon

JEWISH ORIGINS FOR THE SERMON

It is widely assumed that the Christian sermon was developed by the first generation of Christians from the addresses given in the synagogue. As we have already seen, there is no suggestion of such borrowing in the New Testament but it might be possible to establish dependence on Jewish forms during the succeeding period. Although there was then mutual hostility between church and synagogue, especially from about 85AD, the intellectual and cultural break between the two was not complete[1] and the church did borrow Jewish practices,[2] just as in other periods of mutual hostility, the church borrowed from Islam and Judaism borrowed from Hellenism, often without even realizing it.[3] Even so, there is no direct evidence of such borrowing in this period. The early fathers are of small assistance here as they seldom discussed the synagogue.

Since the way in which rhetoric was used by many rabbis from Hillel onwards appears to have been influenced by Greco-Roman practice[4] it is possible that any borrowing from Judaism in this area might ultimately have been indirect borrowing from paganism, although as Birger Gerhardsson suggests:

> ...it is possible for similar institutions to grow up in one and the same cultural area, relatively independent of one another. We ought therefore to avoid too superficial talk about borrowing and influences.[5]

Bible readings in the synagogue, when in Hebrew, were subsequently translated, perhaps with additional comments, into Aramaic, Greek or some other living language. The synagogue sermon may have had its roots in this practice but the point cannot be established firmly and the ultimate origin of the synagogue sermon remains in doubt.[6] Consequently, if the Christian sermon is derived from the synagogue sermon, then its ultimate origin remains in dispute.

A PAGAN ORIGIN FOR THE SERMON

RHETORIC

Throughout the classical period the theory and practice of rhetoric did not change greatly and what follows is a brief outline of its main features in the Greco-Roman world.[7]

Rhetoric was particularly the province of the rich and powerful and was the most prestigious of all forms of learning. Furthermore, eloquence had become the principal aim of education; acquiring the art of speaking was perceived as the route not only to culture but also to thinking and acting correctly, since wisdom and eloquence (and social status) were believed to be intimately connected.[8] Acquiring rhetorical competence was a lengthy process and a hallmark of a higher education. It required the mastery of an elaborate technique dominated by the traditions of the past and centered on invention and arrangement of material, style, purity of language, memory, delivery, voice modulation and posture. The principal medium of rhetorical expression was the public speech or lecture and capable exponents of the rhetorical arts looked forward to a distinguished career, fame, wealth, power over others and the admiration of the populace.[9]

The Greeks were intoxicated by rhetoric and the Romans later fell under a similar spell. Roman rhetoric was an adaptation of the Greek form with perhaps less emphasis on persuasion and more on style and artistic effect.[10]

Rhetorical displays ranked with theatrical performances as great spectacles of entertainment—even if the audience could not understand the language of the speaker—for a fine rhetorical display was regarded as a true work of art (Philostratus *Vit Soph* 491, 589).[11] These performances could excite the same kind of enthusiasm as that generated by popular entertainers in our own day.

Not only was rhetoric popular, it had real merits. It offered a clear-cut framework within which practitioners could express themselves coherently and fluently. As these techniques were widely appreciated, rhetoric offered a common standard throughout the Greco-Roman world which all could appreciate, irrespective of education.[12] It demanded some thought, logical ingenuity and psychological observation.[13] Rhetoric also exercised a liberalizing influence. Rhetoricians were prone to argue for and against, with often the same rhetorician arguing both sides of a disputed case in quick succession. This demonstrated that there were two sides to each issue and that even the worst examples were entitled to a hearing.[14] Lastly, as G.A. Kennedy points out:

> In political debate there was in the best periods of ancient history a willingness to entertain the opinions of others when expounded with rhetorical effectiveness. At the very least rhetoric imparted vigor to ancient intellectual life; it has long been noted that oratory flourished most in the democracies and least under tyranny.[15]

For many, the virtues of rhetoric were self-evident and no alternative foundation for education was seriously considered.[16]

The problems with rhetoric surfaced early on and became increasingly severe with the passage of time. Indeed, when rhetorical studies dominated the timetable the disadvantages were formidable. First, style and form took precedence over substance to the extent that, for many listeners, content was immaterial.[17] Second, rhetoric was not primarily a method of instruction, encouraging a disinterested analysis of data, but rather a technique of persuasion more akin to seduction than ratiocination. As its emotional content was often high and its subject matter distorted, audiences were frequently swayed by specious argument. The rhetorician himself was likely to be swayed by his own speech even more than his audience.[18] Third, as the influence of rhetorical traditions gained in strength, rhetoric gradually discouraged independent thinking and intellectual curiosity, and in their place emphasized conventional content.[19] Fourth, in spite of a concern for honesty in rhetorical theory, rhetoric failed to encourage a love of truth. For many rhetoricians, since content was secondary to

victory in argument, truth was almost irrelevant.[20] Fifth, the rhetorician like any stage performer, was concerned, at least in part, to display his genius and to receive the acclaim of the audience.[21] Such a
method inevitably fostered egotism and arrogance (Philostratus *Vit
Soph* 616). This was particularly the case in the unreal atmosphere
of the schools where declaimers had difficulty at times in preserving
their own mental balance.[22] The judgment of Sir William Tarn that
rhetoric 'debased everything it touched' is perhaps not too severe,
particularly of rhetoric during the latter days of the empire, the period
the sermon came to prominence within the church.[23]

THE INFLUENCE OF RHETORIC IN THE CHURCH

A hundred years ago, Edwin Hatch argued that the extensive use of
the sermon arose under the influence of Greek rhetoric brought into
the church by those Christians who had been trained in rhetoric, and
perhaps even taught rhetoric themselves—before or after conversion—
and who subsequently achieved influence in the church. Many of
the church's fathers—Tertullian, Cyprian, Arnobius, Lactantius and
Augustine among them—had been professional rhetoricians before
becoming Christians.[24] Moreover, as rhetoric was the mainstay of
the educational system, the Christian community had little choice
but to recognize it and respond to it in one way or another.[25] But the
Christian use of speeches and rhetorical forms did not arise from
copying the activities of pagan religion. There were no 'sermons' in
Greco-Roman religion as, for the most part, it knew little dogma and so
required little use of formal teaching. The church, on the other hand,
valued dogma and used formal teaching methods. It was here that
rhetoric made its impact. The Christian rhetorician would expound the
sacred text of Scripture, just as the sophist would supply an exegesis of
the near-sacred text of Homer, although the Christian aimed to teach
the congregation, including the simple, and to change lives, rather
than to concentrate on the rhetorical arts.[26] Simplicity of style was
achieved on occasion as in the homilies of the 4th century[27] but, more
often than not, although the content was more or less Christian the
style was Greek. Often indeed the content was mixed, for pagan ideas
were corrupting Christian thought even by 100AD, as can be seen
from the writings of Clement of Rome; the influence of techniques cur-

rent in the schools is clearly visible in Augustine's biblical exegesis.[28] As the majority of great Christian leaders had received a better training in rhetoric than philosophy,[29] the finer points of philosophical debate frequently eluded them, with the result that pagan philosophical/ theological[30] ideas were unwittingly incorporated into the corpus of Christian doctrine even by those who, like Tertullian, claimed to despise pagan philosophy.[31] This tendency should not be confused with the deliberate use of pagan philosophy by Christians as a weapon against their opponents. The problem of inadvertently utilizing non-Christian ideas and thought forms in the explication of Christian faith is a perennial one.

It may be objected that Greek rhetoric entered the church at least as early as the apostle Paul and that later developments stem from his contribution. Paul's precise knowledge and use of rhetoric are still disputed, but his epistles reveal a considerable understanding of the rhetorical conventions taught in the schools.[32] Whatever the case may have been, rhetoric did not dominate Paul's presentation of the gospel in substance or form, and he rejected the cultural values associated with rhetoric (1 Cor. 1:10 - 2:5; 1 Thes. 2:1-12).[33] Moreover, although Paul relied on public speaking to a great extent in introducing the gospel to others, there is no reason to suppose that he was limited to this one method. As well as the home, the workshop and other locations may have been used for missionary activity among small groups or with individuals, using a variety of means. But it should be noted that there was often no sharp distinction between the home and the workplace.[34] Later, we shall see that Paul did not advocate the use of public speaking as a means to Christian growth. The church's use of rhetoric does not have its origin in the work of Paul.

When men such as Origen, John Chrysostom and Augustine made extensive use of the sermon, this was seen not as a distortion of New Testament methods but as a revival of the noble art of preaching as practiced by Paul. Many since have viewed preaching as as reawakening of spiritual power. But the use of Greco-Roman rhetoric depended for success entirely upon the skills and self-confidence of the individual rhetorician (to whom went the acclaim);[35] it involved forms designed to entertain and display genius rather than instruct or develop talents in others; it had little interest in the spiritual welfare of the hearers,[36] and it seldom required action on their part.[37] Such a method was not designed to foster Christian virtues or intellectual maturity, and there is little evidence to suggest that it can do so.[38] It seems that even the sermons of Augustine, delivered to his congregation at Hippo, failed to develop critical skills or independent judgment and were of questionable value in the development of spirituality.[39] Furthermore, as we shall see, the use of the sermon even without rhetorical coloring distorted New Testament practice considerably. The belief that methods in Christianity are unimportant, eloquently summed up in the assertion of Adolf Harnack that 'a living faith needs no special methods',[40] may sound deeply spiritual but is a distortion of the teaching of both testaments and certainly of the work of Paul, who was concerned with method as well as content— as we may see, for example, in his discussion of rhetoric, his practice of evangelism arid his attitude to money and gifts.[41]

From a Christian standpoint, the pagan origins of rhetoric do not pose a problem. There is nothing intrinsically wrong with the church embracing ideas from the surrounding culture. The Old Testament supplies several cases where the results of pagan influences were beneficial such as the appointment of judges to assist Moses (Exod. 18:13-26), the (possible) use of ancient Near Eastern concepts of wisdom and the design of the Tabernacle.[42] More frequently, however, syncretism and acculturation were harmful both to Israel and the church. This was because they led to the absorption of ideas and practices inimical to biblical faith and frequently to subsequent contempt for that faith.[43] So it was with rhetoric, with its insatiable demand for speeches as the medium for its artistic expression and its unavoidable confrontation with the more personal methods of the New Testament.

OTHER FACTORS CONCERNING THE RISE OF SERMONS

The dominance of the sermon was not achieved merely through the entrance of Greek rhetoric into the church. Several developments during the first four centuries helped to lay the foundation of most of our present ecclesiastical practices, and without these developments the sermon could not have secured such a prominent position. To these we now turn.

DECLINE OF THE CHARISMATIC MINISTRIES

Some of the charismatic ministries—in particular gifts of healing, working of miracles, tongues and interpretation—seem to have more or less ceased possibly during the lifetime of the generation after the apostles or as late as the 3rd century, and for reasons that are not entirely clear.[44] This opened the way to an increased emphasis on the importance of the more settled ministries of the church.

CHANGES IN FORMS OF TEACHING - DECLINE OF TEACHERS

Teaching techniques changed. The mutual ministries (of which more later), so characteristic of the earliest period of the church and requiring subtle and informed teachers, gradually faded. The prophets no longer played a significant role in instructing the church.[45] Serious study of the teaching methods used by Jesus and Paul declined.[46] In addition to neglecting New Testament methods, allegorical and typological methods of interpretation (sometimes borrowed from Judaism or paganism) were widely applied to the Old Testament, the verses of which were often interpreted without reference to context and with little historical awareness. The result was a distorted understanding of its message.[47] Inevitably, this further distorted the church's understanding of the New Testament. As it bears on the present issue, the real significance of a failure to comprehend the Old Testament is that the latter has often acted as a bulwark for the church against the infiltration of pagan ideas; without it the church easily falls prey to the spirit of the age.[48]

The educational void created by the neglect of biblical material was filled by a mixture of pagan and distorted Christian notions and methods--in particular the sermon. Independent teachers in the church became less significant and were effectively removed by the 4th century although laymen preached occasionally as late as the 5th century.[49] The modern distinction between clergy and laity is virtually unknown in the New Testament and probably made its first tentative appearance in the writings of Clement of Rome (1:40:5), probably towards the end of the 1st century,[50] and became firmly established towards the end of the 2nd century.[51] (Some see the distinction in 1 Cor. 14:16, Eph. 4:11f and the Pastoral Epistles, but this is unlikely.[52])

The teaching function devolved onto the newly emerging monarchical bishops and their presbyters, who formerly had only limited teaching duties.[53] Thus church leaders acquired teaching responsibilities for which they were seldom prepared and the 'laity' were left gifts and skills, which could neither be developed nor fitted into the existing ecclesiastical structure. This structure became increasingly rigid and resistant to independent thought and action with regard to ecclesiastical expression as the gap between clergy and 'laity' widened, especially from the 3rd century onwards.[54]

The maturing of the individual in a community and the preservation of an organization are often mutually opposed. As religious organizations expand, there tends to be a certain amount of goal displacement as routinization sets in, and what began as a group begins to take on the character of an institution. The original emphasis of the founder on the person as well as the group tends to be displaced in favor of a one-sided emphasis upon the growth and development of the organization. Religious practices and beliefs become standardized by ecclesiastical specialists and hierarchical structures may proliferate. Consequently, the individual member is likely to take on the subordinate role of an instrument to serve the greater needs of the organization, which then functions in ways not necessarily in the best interests of the movement. Institutionalization is a common phenomenon in religion throughout the ages and most of its major elements can be discerned in Christianity by the 4th century or even earlier. In Christianity, however, spiritual reformers are recurring figures—as were the prophets in Israel—and they can assist in mitigating the worst evils of institutionalization.[55]

The institutionalization of the church is sometimes regarded as the inevitable outworking of known social or historical laws. But, as R.H. Trigg, A.G.N. Flew and others have demonstrated, there are no known laws of social behavior or of history and there is, therefore, no justification for regarding institutionalization as inevitable.[56] At every point in the life of the church, alternative responses have been possible.

AN INCREASE IN CHURCH NUMBERS

Persecution had been common, if intermittent, from the earliest days of the church and yet the number of Christians had steadily increased. Sometimes this very increase was itself the cause of persecution.[57] But this ever-present threat, combined with the fact that becoming a Christian was not a route to social or political advancement, allowed the church to cope with its own modest expansion. When persecution finally ceased and Christianity was tolerated and protected by the emperors, membership was widened and there came into the church large numbers of people who were by Christian standards poorly instructed, or barely converted folk. They brought with them a wide variety of pagan ideas. This development influenced the conduct of Christian gatherings in a variety of ways because the new converts often appreciated rhetoric and religious architecture, were grossly superstitious and held false views of God as well as a worldview generally hostile to Christianity. The sheer numbers involved made these problems virtually insoluble.[58] In addition, when these Christians, freed from the restrictions of persecution, took a more active part in the public and social life of the community and the wider world, they often compromised their faith still further. Soon enough the church itself followed the organizational patterns of the city and the province and incorporated state ceremonial, a complex hierarchical structure, an expanded canon law and the use of force to suppress opposition.[59]

THE RISE OF THE CHURCH BUILDING

From the late 2nd century onwards, the New Testament practice of meeting in private homes gradually declined and was replaced at first by meetings held in houses perhaps owned by private persons, but kept for the use of the Christian community and converted for Christian purposes. This type of building is usually known as the *domus ecclesiae* or meetinghouse. Meetings in private houses might be resumed in times of persecution (*cf.* Tertullian, *De fuga in persec* 14:1), but even private houses were not always secure when persecution was in the air (Acts 8:3; Eus *HE* 6:41:5).[60] Subsequently, Christian communities met in purpose-built 'church' buildings based initially on the pattern of simple halls and then a basilican design—usually known as the *domus dei* or house of God.[61] Numerous Christians in this period were wealthy and owned houses, which might have been used as meeting places for the church (see below). The more elaborate of these may have influenced Christian ecclesiastical architecture in its formative period.[62]

The exact origin of Christian ecclesiastical architecture is difficult to pinpoint. In Edessa, the Christians had a church building by about 200AD;[63] there may even have been a structure specially built for meetings of the church as early as 123-136AD[64] although both of these were possibly renovated meetinghouses.[65] References by Clement of Alexandria may indicate something similar or just that Christians commonly met at one particular place (*Strom* 7:5; *Paed* 3:11).[66] Eusebius also mentions church buildings before the time of Constantine (*HE* 8:1:5 and perhaps 7:30: 19, 8:13:13),[67] but these too may have been adapted meetinghouses. They might be substantial buildings.[68] Praying 'in church'—possibly an adapted house—is mentioned by Hippolytus (*Apost Const* 18)[69] probably in the first half of the 3rd century. The house at Dura-Europus was probably converted for Christian use as a meeting place between 232-256AD.[70] The so-called 'house of Peter' at Capernaum is appreciably earlier. Here a large room appears to have been converted from private to some kind of public use before 100AD, but its use as a meetinghouse (*domus ecclesiae*) at this period cannot be established with certainty.[71]

The conventional explanations given for the initial lack of church buildings usually refer to the smallness of the Christian community, its lack of resources, its uncertain legal status, preference for charitable acts rather than buildings, widespread belief in the imminence of the Second Coming and the risk of persecution.[72] (Similar reasons have been given for the initial lack of Christian schools and ecclesiastical dress for church leaders).[73] But such explanations are inadequate because they fail to take account of three commonly, and often unconsciously, held assumptions: that the early Christians would have had purpose-built church buildings in the first and second centuries had circumstances been more favorable; that such buildings represent a fulfillment of that which is implicit in the teaching of the New Testament; and that the spread of church buildings had some significance apart from mere accommodation to external pressure or an adaptation to the cultural milieu in which the church happened to find itself.

In examining the validity of these assumptions it will be helpful to survey the role of religious buildings in the surrounding pagan culture and in Judaism.

The pagan home served to introduce the main elements of religion and was a primitive miniature of public worship. Some homes and gardens were equipped like little temples.[74] Often the home was also the scene of more formal instruction, particularly that given by sophists.[75] Religious buildings were, nonetheless, an integral part of Greco-Roman religion. Even so, devotees did not need to spend much time there for the duties of attendance and sacrifice were very limited. Meetings for fellowship were similarly restricted since the creation and growth of small communities was no more than a by-product of the occasional use of religious buildings as dormitories for priests and pilgrims, restaurants and meeting places.[76] Even the mystery religions generated little fellowship or community spirit comparable with that of the Christian congregation.[77] Some of the philosophers did better; the Epicureans formed communities of friends.[78]

In the Old Testament, buildings were significant but not central to the day-to-day life of faith for, as with pagan temples, the devotees of both the Tabernacle and the Temple were required to visit only occasionally. There were, however, differences in the Jewish and pagan attitude to religious buildings. First, the Tabernacle was not an ordinary building for it was portable, indicating that God's presence was 'a Presence on the move'.[79] Second, the position of the Temple in the Jewish economy was disputed. The first temple had been instituted at the request of David. The making of the Tabernacle was commanded by God and the instructions concerning its planning were extensive (Exod. 36-40). In contrast, there was nothing comparable in connection with the planning and execution of the Temple where divine involvement seems to have been minimal.[80] The design of the Temple, although in many ways similar to that of the Tabernacle, appears to have been inspired by the longroom temples commonly found in the Near East.[81] It included numerous elements not particularly characteristic of Israel, which is hardly surprising given Solomon's propensity to absorb ideas from the surrounding cultures.[82]

The extent to which the Temple represents a departure from earlier ideals is unclear. Most Jews held the Temple in high regard but there was some opposition culminating in the criticism of Stephen (Acts 7:47-50), although the latter has been variously interpreted.[83] Jesus' attitude to the Herodian Temple is complex[84] but the essence of it seems to be that God could utilize and purify the Temple—even though it employed pagan forms, ceremonials and architecture;[85] even with the High Priest a Roman or Herodian appointee;[86] even though it was built by an enemy who had himself built pagan temples;[87] even though, as F.V. Filson puts it, 'the Temple never corresponded to the distinctive features of the religion of Israel';[88] and even though the Temple was ultimately to become redundant (John 4:21-24).

By the time of Jesus, the synagogues in Palestine had achieved prominence as major teaching and community centers. Initially they may have been no more than large rooms in private houses or in what had been private houses.

These were subsequently adapted for synagogue use and finally the purpose-built synagogue emerged probably before 70AD. The synagogue of the Diaspora developed in a broadly similar way.[89]

The extent of pagan architectural influence is difficult to determine precisely.[90] Of all the institutions of the ancient world, the synagogue most closely resembled the gatherings of the primitive church and thus it is possible that in resorting to ecclesiastical architecture the church was following Jewish rather than pagan practice. If, however, the architectural inspiration for the synagogue was pagan, then the church would ultimately have been indebted to paganism for its earliest buildings. But, as L.M. White points out, 'In many ways...the development of a normative synagogue architecture through the 4th century paralleled—rather than preceded—that of Christian church building.'[91]

We now turn to the question of whether the rise of church buildings represents a development in accordance with the principles and practices of the New Testament, or whether it amounts to little more than cultural accommodation.

First, church buildings were not a natural progression from the religious buildings of the Old Testament for, in the New Testament, architectural terms such as 'temple' and 'house' are applied to the church, the Christian community (1 Cor. 3:16f, 6:19; 2 Cor. 6:16; Eph. 2:19-22; 1 Peter 2:5).[92] No thought of the necessity of religious buildings to replace those of the Old Testament appears in the New

Testament. This attitude is echoed in the writings of some of the Fathers (Min Fel, *Oct.* 32:1; Origen *CC* 8:17; Clement Alex *Strom* 7:5).[93]

Second, the house church was in full accord with the teaching of Jesus and his followers and was admirably suited to dealing with human problems and maximizing spiritual growth (see below). House churches should not be regarded as an unfortunate necessity, which cramped the effectiveness of the early church.[94] The New Testament gives no support for the view that church buildings are either necessary or desirable; its emphasis throughout is on a living community.[95] Adolf Harnack, referring to the lack of church buildings early in the 2nd century, makes this point explicitly:

> One thing is clear—the idea of a special place for worship had not yet arisen. The Christian idea of God and of divine service not only failed to promote this, but excluded it, while the practical circumstances of the situation retarded its development.[96]

Third, although we do not know the precise extent to which Christians of the first and second centuries desired to be like the non-Christians around them in the possession of rich ecclesiastical architecture, it appears that by the third and fourth centuries the old objections had lost their power and there was a desire in the church for specialized ecclesiastical buildings. The collapse of persecution removed the final obstacle. The new attitude is well expressed by Eusebius of Caesarea, who early in the 4th century compared the building of the then new church at Tyre with the building of the Tabernacle and the Temple of Solomon (*HE* 10:4:1-4). Many Christians must have seen the extensive church building program of the 4th century from the perspective of the Old Testament.[97] They failed to understand biblical attitudes to ecclesiastical architecture and tended to see Christian and pagan approaches to the subject as essentially similar. As in rabbinic Judaism, ideas derived from paganism were often made acceptable by attributing them to an origin in the Old Testament.[98]

Fourth, as the church gained legitimacy in the Roman world in the 4th and 5th centuries, the western bishops found themselves the custodians of considerable new wealth—more than could be disposed of easily by charitable giving. In pagan society, wealth of this kind would normally be bestowed in public benefactions. As the bishops had little perception of biblical principles of finance or church growth, building presented itself as a conventional solution to the problem.[99]

Fifth, the use of the synagogue by Jesus and Paul hardly indicates the desirability of comparable buildings for the church. It shows, rather, that each of them made maximum use of *existing* social structures to facilitate the mission.[100] In any given locality, the synagogue would be the center of Jewish life and held in high esteem by the Jewish community and perhaps even by the gentile community where Jews and gentiles were well integrated.[101] Few Jews would voluntarily separate themselves from their fellows as loneliness and isolation were alien to Jewish thinking and few were expelled from the community. Jews of questionable standing, like Bar-Jesus (Acts 13:6), might be the exception although he may still have enjoyed synagogue fellowship.[102] Consequently, the synagogue would provide access to virtually all the Jews of any given area, which made it a convenient starting point in the mission.

It thus appears that the early building program of the church owed little to a clear understanding of biblical principles and was probably the result of following pagan patterns—a conclusion which will be reinforced as we examine the effects of church buildings on the early church.

EFFECTS OF CHURCH BUILDINGS ON THE EARLY CHURCH

Several practical consequences followed on the change from the use of house churches to church buildings.

1. *Congregation size* could be increased without dividing into smaller groups. Archaeological discoveries in Corinth and Pompeii indicate that the largest rooms in even the most substantial private houses could seldom hold more than fifty people[103] although on occasion the much larger colonnaded garden or courtyard (peristyle) might have been used, which could have held a congregation of perhaps up to two hundred.[104] The early church included patrons of wealth and distinction who might have owned substantial houses offering this kind of facility in many Christian communities.[105]

Unfortunately, our knowledge of early church membership figures is virtually non-existent, apart from Jerusalem, so we cannot know if a limiting figure of perhaps fifty was a problem. At Jerusalem it might have been, given the considerable number of converts (Acts 2:41,4:4).[106] Sometimes converts met in the Temple (Acts 5:12) but the weather just after Pentecost was usually good and open air meetings in the early days would have eased the problem. Open-air meetings would seldom have been a viable option except for rural areas and areas of lax administration because of the official suspicion frequently aroused by almost any kind of large private assembly (Suet *Aug* 32; Pliny *Epp* 10:34, 93, 96).[107] Even in what we might guess to be the largest Christian communities Antioch, Ephesus,[108] Corinth and Rome[109]—it is not obvious that size was a problem although the Corinthian church may have had a hundred or more members.[110]

There are indications that there were several house groups in some of the larger cities and that these worked in fellowship with each other (Rom. 16:5, 10f, 14f; 1 Cor. 11:20, 14:23; Phil. 1:1; 1 Thes. 5:27; Heb. 13:24).[111] Occasionally, they may have come together for large-scale meetings but this does not appear to have been common and would have been risky (1 Cor. 11:18-20, 14:23).[112]

Meeting in small groups may have been the result of an awareness of the efficiency of the small group but such a keen and critical awareness seems out of character for the majority and the New Testament writers make no reference to it. More likely, this method was followed simply for lack of an alternative and without realizing its full significance. But whatever the thinking of the early Christians on the question of group size, circumstances prior to the rise of the church building ensured that groups remained small and groups multiplied as the community expanded, although the forms which this multiplication took are unknown.[113] Mutual ministries (see below), therefore, would always have been applicable irrespective of the total number in any given Christian community. Consequently, it would be wrong to suggest that the church building program of the third and fourth centuries was an inevitable or necessary response designed to cope with expanding congregations as small-scale alternatives could usually be found.

2. As church buildings and congregations increased in size, the *character of church meetings* changed. The informal approach, characteristic of the earlier period, gradually disappeared. Many who might have spoken before a small group of beloved friends would be uneasy at attempting the same thing in front of a large assembly of acquaintances for, in the ancient world (as now), even trained orators could be nervous at the prospect of speaking before a large audience.[114]

And yet, at the time, no method of communication would have appeared more natural, when faced with a large congregation in a large building, than the sermon delivered by a rhetorician/leader.

The architecture of any building necessarily imposes numerous constraints upon the activities, which occur within it.[115] The needs of congregations vary and the forms of meeting, therefore, need flexibility—but church buildings are inflexible.[116] The larger the building (even when the congregation is not commensurate in size with the building) the more difficult it becomes to conduct meetings on a New Testament pattern and a more dominant form of leadership becomes almost inevitable. This type of leadership appeared early in the history of the church for a variety of reasons (1 Pet. 5:1-3; 3 John 9f).[117] The church building provided greater opportunities for the exploitation of this particular human weakness. This problem was exacerbated by further architectural developments. For example, in Northern Europe, benches and later pews, were introduced from about the 13th century onwards.[118] These changes may have reduced fellowship among church members still further.[119]

The atmosphere of many church buildings today conforms uncomfortably closely to R. Sommer's description of sociofugal space (where people tend to avoid personal contact with one another) as tending:

To be large, cold, impersonal, institutional, not owned by any individual, over concentrated rather than overcrowded, without opportunity for shielded conversation; providing barriers without shelter, isolation without privacy, and concentration without cohesion.[120]

The same problem may well have arisen early in the history of ecclesiastical architecture rather than later. They could have been mitigated had small group meetings continued in parallel with building-based meetings. This happened initially[121] but they soon diminished due to the increasing scarcity of teachers, fear of schism,[122] lack of understanding and volume of converts. Even so, the house church has continued throughout the history of the church albeit with varying fortunes.[123]

3. The cost of maintaining an extensive ecclesiastical empire has always been high and the church has frequently needed to enlist the *aid of the wealthy*, Christian or otherwise. The independence of the church has thus been compromised and it has frequently identified with the rich and powerful and their political systems.[124]

4. The use of church buildings *diminished the role of women in the church*. Many non-Christians in the towns and cities of the Roman Empire, particularly those who lived in overcrowded conditions with limited facilities, were not home-lovers and preferred to spend their free time socializing at markets, shops, taverns, baths, the forum, the theatre or the games.[125] The church, however, was centered in the home and so this previously undervalued secular institution was given new vitality and significance. Moreover, the home was the particular province of women. But as the locus of Christian activity gradually shifted from the home, where women often had a significant role, to the church building, where they had little place, so the status of women, already under pressure, declined still further.[126]

The position of women in Judaism varied. At times women shared tasks with men, undertaking considerable responsibilities in the home and the cultus. But by New Testament times, women were subordinate to their husbands and suffered lower status legally and socially. They had little part to play in society beyond the home and endured an equally circumscribed role in the religious sphere.[127] In the early church, following on the reforming work of Jesus,[128] supplemented by that of Paul,[129] the position of women was more favorable and some attained the status of leaders although most leaders were still men, particularly in the East.[130] Christianity seems to have provided a rich and full life for many women and this was particularly the case in the home and the house church although their position and authority in the two were different.[131] But in some cases, where a woman was the head of the household, she might also be a leader of the church that met in her home.[132]

In the Greco-Roman world, women were generally held in low esteem but in the 1st century there was a modest liberalizing process at work.[133] This, combined with the New Testament views expounded by Jesus and Paul, might have been expected to ensure for women approximately equal standing with men in the church. But from as early as the 2nd century, these ideas gradually faded. Women came to be seen as inferior to men and capable of only very limited Christian service. The reasons for this change are complex but were probably the consequence of a failure to appreciate the richness and novelty of the biblical picture. This opened the way to an uncritical acceptance of Jewish and pagan notions of woman and her role. The problem was compounded by the behavior of women leaders in heretical sects which prompted the church to set even more restrictive bounds for women. Consequently, under the influence of the church, the liberalizing process was halted.[134] The contribution of the church building to the problem is difficult to assess but I suggest that in this area, as in others, it helped the church to abandon biblical patterns and embrace those of paganism and Judaism.

The church is still influenced adversely by secular attitudes to women and their role—although perhaps with some improvement of late as pressure from feminist groups has helped to persuade some Christians to rethink their position and to adopt a more biblical, less sexist stance.[135] Even so, as Mary Hayter argues, the current emphasis on these issues has resulted in many conventional theologians and ecclesiastics reacting negatively towards any idea of female leadership in the church.[136]

5. A further consequence was a *changed understanding of the sacred.* The people of God in the Old and New Testaments, as well as the church of the first two centuries, thought of themselves primarily as a people. As persecution waned and the church expanded, it began to develop the organizational patterns of the city and the province. The Christian community then tended to see itself as an organization.[137] This view was buttressed, from about the beginning of the 3rd century, by a spurious theology of the church building, incorrectly designated 'the house of God[138] and imbued with Jewish and pagan notions of the sanctity of religious places.[139] As we have already seen, the New Testament writers applied the terminology of buildings to the Christian community, not to ecclesiastical architecture; and they showed little interest in sacred places.

Following and developing the thought of the Old Testament, reality in general was not divided into secular and sacred for as A.F. Holmes notes, 'The basic Biblical distinction is not between sacred and secular but between God and his creation.[140] Christians initially followed biblical teaching and set their faces against treating created objects and rituals as sacred. They were concerned to desacralize the world in the light of the implications of the doctrines of creation and incarnation.[141] Within a few centuries, however, the church had reverted to pagan patterns and had recreated a plethora of sacreds (or idols) within the church itself—places, objects, times, dress, rituals, techniques, func-tionaries, Saints and political structures. All these helped to distance believers from God.[142]

6. Given that the church had been heavily influenced by the spirit of the age, it would be remarkable had it remained free

from the anxiety, insecurity and pessimism which was always characteristic of the Roman Empire.[143] But how could such an influence relate to the rise of sermons and buildings? Perhaps a guess is in order. In the early days, problems besetting church order could he resolved in a manner approximating to biblical forms because church order roughly followed New Testament patterns. As ecclesiastical forms gradually hardened into a hierarchical structure fashioned after a bureaucratic organization, biblical solutions became increasingly unworkable and the clergy turned to pagan patterns for inspiration. The answer to insecurity lay, therefore, not in the security characteristic of the mature Christian in a mature Christian community but in a more efficient ecclesiastical organization—tighter controls and an increasing reliance upon hierarchical structures, sermons and buildings. Weber's ideal type of bureaucracy provides an uncomfortably good description of church organization both in the 4th century and today.[144]

CONCLUSION

In this chapter we have reviewed some significant ways in which the apostolic church developed. We have mentioned the decline of the charismatic gifts; changes in teaching techniques; failure to understand the Scriptures; unthinking absorption of both pagan ideas and unconverted pagans; the rise of the church building; and a reconstitution of the sacred. It was as a result of all these things that the sermon triumphed and took its place among an extensive battery of pagan and semi-pagan ideas and practices, which were passed off by the church as integral elements of Christian faith and practice. The sermon has not always held a dominant place in Christian gatherings—particularly from the days of Augustine to Luther—but it still remains and so do most of the other developments we have described.[145]

ENDNOTES

1.   W.H.C. Frend, 'Early Christianity and Society: A Jewish Legacy in the Pre-Constantinian Era', *HTR*, 76, 1983, 55-71; G.N. Stanton, 'Aspects of Early Christian-Jewish Polemic and Apologetic', *NTS*, 31, 1985, 377f; L.H. Schiffman, 'At the Crossroads: Tannaitic Perspectives on the Jewish-Christian Schism' in E.P. Sanders et al (eds), *Jewish and Christian Self-Definition*, 1981, II, 152-156

2.   E. Schweizer, *Church Order in the New Testament*, 1961, p. 16 (section 1c); E. von Dobschütz, *Christian Life in the Primitive Church*, 1904, pp. 287f; L. Goppelt, *Apostolic and Post-Apostolic Times*, 1970, p. 120

3.   F. Gabrieli, 'Islam in the Mediterranean World' and C.C. Anawati, 'Philosophy, Theology and Mysticism' in J. Schacht and C.E. Bosworth (eds), *The Legacy of Islam*, ²1974, pp. 86-100, 382-389; G.G. Polton, 'Diversity in Post-Biblical Judaism' in R.A. Kraft and G.W.E. Nickelsburg (eds), *Early Judaism and its Modem Intepreters*, 1986, pp. 57-59; B. Gerhardsson. *Memory and Manuscript: Oral Tradition and Written Transmission in Rabbinic Judaism and Early Christianity*, Sweden, Gleerup, 1961, p. 27; M. Hengel, *The 'Hellenization' of Judaea in the First Century after Christ*, 1989, p. 19

4.   *HJP*, II, 78; D. Daube, 'Rabbinic Methods of interpretation and Hellenistic Rhetoric', *HUCA*, 22, 1949, 239-264; idem, *The New Testament and Rabbinic Judaism*, 1956, pp. 151-157; A. Marmorstien, 'The Background of the Haggadah', *HUCA*, 6, 1929, 182-204

5.   B. Gerhardsson, *Memory and Manuscript*, Sweden, Gleerup, p. 89

6.   *HJP*, II, 452f; S. Safrai, 'The Synagogue', *Compendia* I:2, 930f; I.M. Goldman, *Lifelong Learning Among Jews: Adult Education in Judaism from Biblical Times to the Twentieth Century*, 1975, p. 18

7.   D.A. Russell, *Criticism in Antiquity*, 1981, pp. 114, 119, 121

8.   A.D. Litfin, *St Paul's Theology of Proclamation: 1 Corinthians 1-4 and Greco-Roman Rhetoric*, 1994, pp. 119-124; S.M. Pogoloff, *Logos and Sophia: The Rhetorical Situation of 1 Corinthians*, 1992, pp. 113-121, 129-153

9.   H.I. Marrou, *A History of Education in Antiquity*, 1956, pp. 194-200, 204; idem, 'Education and Rhetoric' in M.I. Finley (ed), *The Legacy of Greece: A New Appraisal*, 1981, pp. 195-197; M.L. Clarke, *Rhetoric at Rome: A Historical Survey*, 1966, pp. 20-22, 36; G.A. Kennedy, *The Art of Persuasion in Greece*, 1963, pp. 13, 25; C. Gempf, 'Public Speaking and Published Accounts', *BAFCS*, I, 259-262

10. M.L. Clarke, *Rhetoric at Rome*, pp. II , 63; G.A. Kennedy, *The Art of Rhetoric in the Roman World*, 1972, p. xv

11. E. Hatch, *The Influence of Greek Ideas and Usages Upon the Christian Church*, 1897, pp. 91-99

12. H.I. Marrou, *History of Education*, pp. 204f; E.A. Judge, 'Paul's Boasting in Relation to Contemporary Professional Practice', *ABR*, 16, 1968, 43f

13. D.A. Russell, *Criticism in Antiquity*, 1981, p. 119

14. G. A. Kennedy, *The Art of Persuasion in Greece*, London, Roudedge & Kegan Paul PLC., 1963, p. 23

15. G. A. Kennedy, *The Art of Persuasion in Greece*, London, Roudedge & Kegan Paul PLC., 1963, p. 23

16. E.J. Kenney, 'Books and Readers in the Roman World' in idem (ed) , *The Cambridge History of Classical Literature*, 1982, II, 9

17. W. W. Tarn and G.T. Griffith, *Hellenistic Civilization*, ³1952 repr 1974, p. 281

18. G.A. Kennedy, *Art of Persuasion*, p. 24; M. L. Clarke, *Rhetoric at Rome: A Historical Survey*, 1966, p. 59

19. M.L. Clarke, *Higher Education in the Ancient World*, 1971, p. 38; idem, *Rhetoric at Rome: A Historical Survey*, 1966. pp. 160, 164; G.A. Kennedy, *Art of Persuasion*, pp. 24f

20. M.L. Clarke, *Rhetoric at Rome*, pp. 160f; A.D. Litfin, *St Paul's Theology of Proclamation: An Investigation of 1 Cor 1-4 in the Light of Greco-Roman Rhetoric*, D Phil Thesis (Oxford University), 1983, p. 348; B.W. Winter, 'The Entries and Ethics of Orators and Paul (1 Thessalonians 2: 1-12)', *Tyn B*, 44, 1993, 63f; G.B. Kerferd, *The Sophistic Movement*, 1981, pp. 62f

21. M.L. Clarke, *Higher Education in the Ancient World*, 1971, pp. 44f; B.W. Winter, 'Entries and Ethics', 61-63

22. M.L. Clarke, *Rhetoric at Rome*, pp. 88f

23. W.W. Tarn and G.T. Griffith, *Hellenistic Civilization*, London, Arnold (Edward) (publishers) Ltd., p. 281

24. E. Hatch, *The Influence of Greek Ideas*, pp. 86-115. Similarly J.A. Overman, 'Homily Form', *ABD*, III, 280-282. See also GA Kennedy, 'Rhetoric' in R. Jenkyns (ed), *The Legacy of Rome: A New Appraisal*, 1992, pp. 282f

25. A. Cameron, *Christianity and the Rhetoric of Empire: The Development of Christian Discourse*, 1991, p. 86

26. E. Hatch, *Influence of Greek Ideas*, p. 113; M.L. Clarke, *Higher Education*, p. 124; R . Browning, 'Oratory and Epistolography' in E.J. Kenney (ed), *The Cambridge History of Classical Literature*, 1982, II, 761; F. van der Meer. *Augustine the Bishop*, 1961, pp. 409-432; G.W. Doyle, 'Augustine's Sermonic Method', *WTJ*, 39, 1977, 219, 233

27. J.J. Murphy, Rhetoric in the Middle Ages: *A History of Rhetorical Theory from Saint Augustine to the Renaissance*, 1974. pp. 55f, 298f

28. W. Jaeger, *Early Christianity and Greek Paideia*, 1962, p. 16; B. Smalley, 'The Bible in the Medieval Schools', *CHB*, II, 209

29. A.H. Armstrong, 'The Self-Definition of Christianity in Relation to Later Platonism' in E.P. Sanders (ed), *Jewish and Christian Self-Definition*, 1980, I, 83f

30. There seems to be no systematic distinction between philosophy and theology at this period (F.C. Copleston, *A History of Philosophy*, 1950, II, 14f; W. Jaeger, *Early Christianity*, p. 130 n10)

31. A.M. Wolters, *Our Place in the Philosophical Tradition*, 1975, p. 11; G.L. Bray, *Holiness and the Will of God*, 1979, pp. 35-37; E. Hatch, *Influence of Greek Ideas*, pp. 133f

32. E.A. Judge, 'Paul's Boasting in Relation to Contemporary Professional Practice', *ABR*, 16, 1968, 37-50; idem, 'The Reaction Against Classical Education in the New Testament', *JCE* Papers 77, July 1983, 7-14; C. Forbes, 'Comparison, Self-Praise and Irony: Paul's Boasting and the Conventions of Hellenistic Rhetoric', *NTS*, 32, 1986, 22-24; B. Witherington III, *Conflict and Community in Corinth*, 1995; C.C. Black II, 'The Rhetorical Form of the Hellenistic Jewish and Early Christian Sermon: A Response to Lawrence Wills', *HTR*, 81, 1988, 1-18

33. A.D. Litfin, *St Paul's Theology of Proclamation*, 1994, pp. 198-201; S.M. Pogoloff, *Logos and Sophia*, p. 121; E.A. Judge, 'Reaction', 10-14

34. R.F. Hock, *The Social Context of Paul's Ministry: Tentmaking and Apostleship,* 1980, pp. 37-42; E.F.F. Bishop, *Apostles of Palestine,* 1958, p. 97; A. Wallace-Hadrill, 'The Social Structure of the Roman House', *PBSR,* 56, 1988, 84-86; M. Peskowitz, '"Families" in Antiquity: Evidence from Tannaitic Literature and Roman Galilean Architecture' in S.J.D. Cohen (ed), *The Jewish Family in Antiquity,* 1993, pp. 28-31

35. On the self-confidence of the rhetorician see Philostratus *Vit Soph* 519; *cf.* 1 Cor. 2:3

36. J.J. Murphy, *Rhetoric in the Middle Ages: A History of Rhetorical Theory From Saint Augustine to the Renaissance,* 1974, p. 282

37. In the biblical literature, right action is a frequent characteristic of wisdom (F.D. Kidner, *The Proverbs,* 1964, pp. 36f; G. Fohrer, *TDNT,* VII, 480f, 484f

38. See the discussion in A.D. Litfin, *St Paul's Theology of Proclamation,* 1983, pp. 279-302, 352, 366; idem,*St Paul's Theology of Proclamation,* 1994, pp. 191f; J.J. Murphy, *Rhetoric in the Middle Ages,* p. 282

39. F. van der Meer, *Augustine the Bishop,* 1961 , pp. 140f

40. Quoted in T.R. Glover, *The Jesus of History,* London, Hodder & Stoughton Ltd., 1917, p. 81

41. G.D. Fee, *The First Epistle to the Corinthians,* 1987, pp. 65f, 89f; W.F. Orr and J.A. Walther, *1 Corinthians,* 1976, pp. 151 f; A.D. Litfin, *St Paul's Theology of Proclamation,* 1983, pp. 274f; B.W. Winter, 'Entries and Ethics', 55-74

42. J.I. Durham, *Exodus,* 1987, pp. 249-253; J. Ruffle, 'The Teaching ofAmenemope and its connection with the Book of Proverbs', *Tyn B,* 28, 1977, 29-68; K.A. Kitchen, 'Proverbs and Wisdom Books of the Ancient Near East', *Tyn B,* 28, 1977,69-1 14; idem, 'The Tabernacle-A Bronze Age Artefact', *Eretz-Israel,* 24, 1993,1 19-129

43. J. Pedersen, *Israel: Its Life and Culture,* ²1959, III-IV , 466-476; Th C. Vriezen, *An Outline of Old Testament Theology,* ²1970, pp. 38, 41-44, 358, 426-429; S. Sumithra, 'Syncretism, Secularization and Renewal' in D.A. Carson (ed), *The Church in the Bible and the World,* 1987, pp. 261-268

44. These and other views are examined in B.B. Warfield, *Counterfeit Miracles,* 1918 repr 1976, pp. 3-31; V. Edmunds and C.G. Scorer, *Some Thoughts on Faith Healing,* ³1979; S. Fowler, 'The Continuance of the Charismata', *EQ,* 45, 1973, 172-183; J.S. McEwen, 'The Ministry of Healing', *SJT,* 1954, 133-145; J.I. Packer, *Keep in Step with the Spirit,* 1984, pp. 211-219; R.A.N. Kydd, *Charismatic Gifts in the Early Church,* 1984; M.M.B. Turner, 'Spiritual Gifts Then and Now', *VE,* 15, 1985, 41-50; W.A. Grudem, *The Gift of Prophecy in the New Testament and Today,* 1988, pp. 227-252

45. G. Friedrich, *TDNT,* VI, 860

46. H. von Campenhausen, *Ecclesiastical Authority and Spiritual Power in the Church of the First Three Centuries,* 1969, p. 208

47. J. Bright, *The Authority of the Old Testament,* 1967, pp. 79-83; J.N.D. Kelly, 'The Bible and the Latin Fathers' in D.E. Nineham, *The Church's Use of the Bible,* 1963, pp. 45-54; R.P.C. Hanson, 'Biblical Exegesis in the Early Church', *CHB,* 1970, I, 412-433

48. G.E. Wright, 'The Old Testament: A Bulwark of the Church Against Paganism', *IRM,* 40, July 1951, 265-276; G.T. Purves, 'The Influence of Paganism on Post-Apostolic Christianity', *Presbyterian Review,* 36, October 1888, 534-546; E. Brunner, "The

Significance of the Old Testament for Our Faith' in B.W. Anderson (ed), *The Old Testament and Christian Faith,* 1964, pp. 243-264

49.   W.H.C. Frend, 'The Church of the Roman Empire 313-600' in S.C. Neill and H.-R. Weber (eds), *The Layman in Christian History,* 1963, pp. 59f; J.K. Coyle, 'The Exercise of Teaching in the Postapostolic Church', *Église et Théologie,* 15, 1984, 22-43

50.   *1 Clement* is usually dated around 95-96AD but this may be too precise. J.AT. Robinson dates *1 Clement* as early as 70AD (*Redating the New Testament,* 1976, pp. 327-335). L.L. Welborn and B.B. Bowe place *1 Clement* between 80 - 140AD (B.E. Bowe, *A Church in Crisis: Ecclesiology and Paraenesis in Clement of Rome,* 1988, pp. 2f, 8)

51.   A. Harnack, *The Constitution and Law of the Church in the First Two Centuries,* 1910, pp. 112-114; G.H. Williams, 'The Ancient Church, AD30-313' in S.C. Neill and H.-R. Weber, *The Layman,* p. 30; A. Faivre, *The Emergence of the Laity in the Early Church,* 1990, pp. 15-40; G Bornkamm, *TDNT,* VI, 673

52.   H. Köster, *TDNT,* VIII, 205; G.D. Fee, *The First Epistle to the Corinthians,* 1987, pp. 672f; M. Barth, *Ephesians,* 1974, II, 478-481

53.   A. Harnack, *The Mission and Expansion of Christianity in the First Three Centuries,* [2]1908, I, 360-362; G.H. Williams, 'The Ancient Church' and W.H.C. Frend, 'The Church of the Roman Empire 313-600' in S.C. Neill and H.-R. Weber, *The Layman,* pp. 40-44, 59f

54.   H. von Campenhausen, *Tradition and Life in the Church,* 1968, pp. 123-140; W.H.C. Frend, 'The Church', pp. 57-66; A Faivre, *The Laity,* pp. 43-104, 129-132; J.N.D. Kelly, *Early Christian Creeds,* [3]1972, pp. 98f

55.   B.R. Wilson, *Religion in Sociological Perspective,* 1982, pp. 121f; T.F. O'Dea and J. O'Dea Aviad, *The Sociology of Religion,* [2]1983, pp. 56-58; D.J. Tidball, *An Introduction to the Sociology of the New Testament,* 1983, pp. 123-136; S.C. Barton, 'Social-Scientific Approaches to Paul', *DPL,* p. 899

56.   R.H. Trigg, *Understanding Social Science: A Philosophical Introduction to the Social Sciences,* 1985, pp. 178-184; A.G.N. Flew, *Thinking About Social Thinking: The Philosophy of the Social Sciences,* 1985, pp. 97-109; T.K. Seung, *Structuralism and Hermeneutics,* 1982, pp. 1-20, 157-163, 176f, 214f; A.F. Holmes, *Faith Seeks Understanding: A Christian Approach to Knowledge,* 1971, pp. 60-84; D.W. Bebbington, *Patterns in History,* 1979, pp.145-157

57.   W.H.C. Frend, *Martyrdom and Persecution in the Early Church,* 1981, p. 258

58.   K.S. Latourette, *A History of the Expansion of Christianity,* 1937, I, 319-328; G.A Kennedy, *Classical Rhetoric and its Christian and Secular Tradition from Ancient to Modern Times,* 1980, pp. 145f; A.H.M. Jones, *The Later Roman Empire,* 284-602, 1973, II, 957-964; R. MacMullen, *Christianizing the Roman Empire (AD100-400),* 1984, pp. 74-101, 106f, 114-118

59.   A.H.M. Jones, *Later Roman Empire,* II, 875, 938-950; J.H.W.G. Liebeschuetz, *Continuity and Change in Roman Religion,* 1979, pp. 298f; R. MacMullen, *Christianizing,* pp. 86-101, 118f

60.   B.B. Blue, 'Acts and the House Church', *BAFCS,* II, 127; idem, *In Public and in Private: The Role of the House Church in Early Christianity,* PhD Thesis (University of Aberdeen), 1989, p. 70

61.   H.W. Turner, *From Temple to Meeting House,* 1979, pp. 159-162; J.G. Davies, *The*

Secular Use of Church Buildings, 1968, pp. 6-9; L.M. White, *Building God's House in the Roman World,* 1990, pp. 102-148

62. A. Biéler, *Architecture in Worship,* 1965, pp. 22-24
63. J.B. Segal, *Edessa 'The Blessed City',* 1970, pp. 24, 62
64. J.G. Davies, *The Origin and Development of Early Christian Church Architecture,* 1952, p. 14; G.F. Snyder, *Ante-Pacem: Architectural Evidence of Church Life Before Constantine,* 1985, p. 67
65. L.M. White, *Building God's House,* p. 118
66. A. Nesbitt, *DCA,* I, 366; similarly Tertullian *De Spect* XXV
67. R.M. Grant, *Early Christianity and Society,* 1978, pp. 149f
68. L.M. White, *Building God's House,* pp. 123f, 127f, 141, 146
69. G.J. Cumming, *Hippolytus: A Text for Students,* 1976, p. 16; G. Dix and H. Chadwick, *The Treatise on the Apostolic Tradition of St Hippolytus of Rome,* ³1992, p. lvi
70. G.F. Snyder, *Ante-Pacem,* p. 69; M. Rostovtzeff, *Dura-Europus and its Art,* 1938, p. 130
71. E.M. Meyers and J.F. Strange, *Archaeology, the Rabbis and Early Christianity,* 1981, pp. 59f, 114f, 128-130; J.H. Charlesworth, *Jesus Within Judaism,* 1989, pp. 109-115; J. McRay, *Archaeology and the New Testament,* 1991, pp. 164-166
72. R.M. Grant, *Early Christianity,* p. 146
73. W. Barclay, *Educational Ideals in the Ancient World,* 1959, p. 238; J. Mayo, *A History of Ecclesiastical Dress,* 1984, p. 11
74. R.M. Ogilvie, *The Romans and Their Gods,* 1969, pp. 100-105; M.P. Nilsson, 'Roman and Greek Domestic Cult', *Opuscula Romana,* 18, 1954, pp. 77-85; W.F. Jashemski, *The Gardens of Pompeii, Herculaneum and the Villas Destroyed by Vesuvius,* 1979, pp. 115-140
75. S.K. Stowers, 'Social Status, Public Speaking and Private Teaching: The Circumstances of Paul's Preaching Activity', *Nov T,* 26, 1984, 65-73; J.D.G. Dunn, 'The Responsible Congregation (1 Cor. 14:26-40)' in L. De Lorenzi (ed), *Charisma und Agape,* 1983, pp. 203f; B.B. Blue, *In Public and in Private,* pp. 225-230; G.B. Kerferd, *The Sophistic Movement,* 1981, p. 30
76. W.D. Gray, 'The Rôle Played by the Classical Temple in Secular Life', *Classical Journal,* 38,1942-3, 325-330; J.E. Stambaugh, 'The Functions of Roman Temples', *ANRW,* II:16:1, 1978, 587-591
77. E.R. Dodds, *Pagan and Christian in an Age of Anxiety,* 1965, pp. 136-138; W. Burkert, *Ancient Mystery Cults,* 1987, pp. 30f, 43-53; G.E. Wright, *The Biblical Doctrine of Man in Society,* 1954, pp. 77-79; S.C. Barton, 'Paul, Religion and Society' in J. Obelkevich et al (eds), *Disciplines of Faith,* 1987, pp. 169f
78. A.J. Malherbe, *Paul and the Thessalonians,* 1987, pp. 84-87, 102, 104
79. J.I. Durham, *Exodus,* Word Publishing, USA, 1987, p. 373
80. But, *cf.* 1 Chron. 28:11-19: H.G.M. Williamson, *1 and 2 Chronicles,* 1982, pp. 182, 183; idem, 'The Temple in the Books of Chronicles' in W. Horbury (ed), *Templum Amicitiae: Essays on the Second Temple Presented to Ernst Bammel,* 1991, p. 26; M.J. Selman, *1 Chronicles,* 1994, pp. 248f
81. C.J. Davey, 'Temples of the Levant and the Buildings of Solomon', *Tyn B,* 31,1980, 131-137,140-143
82. M. Noth, *The History of Israel,* ²1960, pp. 210, 214-216, 218f; H.H. Rowley, *Worship in Ancient Israel,* 1967, pp. 79-87

83. M.O. Wise, 'Temple', *DJG*, pp. 813-816; H.W. *Turner, Temple to Meetinghouse,* pp. 68-78; R. de Vaux, *Ancient Israel: Its Life and Institutions,* 1965, pp. 329f; C.K. Barrett, *A Critical and Exegetical Commentary on the Acts of the Apostles,* 1994, I, 373f; E.P. Sanders, *Judaism: Practice and Belief 63BCE-66CE,* 1992, pp. 52-54. For the view that in Acts 7:47-50 Stephen is not condemning the Temple as such but the false attitudes that grew up around it see F.F. Bruce, *The Book of the Acts,* [2]1988, p. 149; J. Calvin, *The Acts of the Apostles,* 1965, I, 208-210; D.G. Peterson, *Engaging with God: A Biblical Theology of Worship,* 1992, p. 141

84. A.S. Peake and W.O.E. Oesterley, *DCG,* 1908, II, 13f, 711-713; Y.M.J. Congar, *The Mystery of the Temple,* 1962, pp. 112-119; C.A. Evans, *Jesus and His Contemporaries: Comparative Studies,* 1995, pp. 352-365

85. E.E. Urbach, *The Sages: Their Concepts and Beliefs,* [2]1979, I, 581; *HJP,* II, 57f; W.F. Stinespring, *IDB,* IV, 550, 558

86. *HJP,* II, 228-232

87. Caesarea (Jos *BJ* I:414; II:266); Sebaste (*BJ* I:403)

88. F.V. Filson, 'The Significance of the Temple in the Ancient Near East', *BA,* 7, 1944, 77, *cf.* 82f

89. E.M. Meyers and J.F. Strange, *Archaeology, the Rabbis and Early Christianity,* 1981, p. 141; E.P. Sanders, *Jewish Law from Jesus to the Mishnah,* 1990, pp. 341-343; idem, *Judaism: Practice and Belief 63BCE-66CE,* 1992, pp. 199-201; S.J.D. Cohen, *From the Maccabees to the Mishnah,* 1987, p. 114; R.E. Oster, 'Supposed Anachronism in Luke - Acts Use of ΣΥΝΑΓΩΓΗ,' *NTS,* 39, 1993, 191-196; L.M. White, *Building God's House,* pp. 60-101; R. Riesner, 'Synagogues in Jerusalem', *BAFCS,* IV, 179-210

90. A. Ovadiah and T. Michaeli, 'Observations on the Origin of the Architectural Plan of Ancient Synagogues', *JJS,* 38, 1987, pp. 234-241; R. Milburn, *Early Christian Art and Architecture,* 1988, p. 83; E.M. Meyers and J.F. Strange, *Archaeology,* pp. 145-147

91. L.M. White, *Building God's House,* Johns Hopkins University Press, p. 8

92. R.J. McKelvey, *The New Temple: The Church in the New Testament,* 1969, pp. 92f, 179-187; H.N. Ridderbos, *Paul: An Outline of His Theology,* 1975, pp. 429-432; D. Guthrie, *New Testament Theology,* 1981, pp. 747-749, 782f; O. Michel, *TDNT,* V, 125-128

93. These passages are discussed in P.C. Finney, 'Early Christian Architecture: The Beginnings (A Review Article)', *HTR,* 81:3, 1988, 327f

94. H.W. Turner, *Temple to Meetinghouse,* pp. 153f, 158; J.A.T. Robinson, *On Being the Church in the World,* 1969, pp. 102-106; B.B. Blue, 'Acts and the House Church', *BAFCS,* II, 121

95. H.W. Turner, *Temple to Meetinghouse,* p. 323; J.G. Davies, *The Secular Use of Church Buildings,* 1968, pp. 1-9

96. A. Harnack, *Mission,* II, 86, *cf.* L.M. White, *Building God's House,* Williams & Norgate, p. 19; R. Krautheimer, *Early Christian and Byzantine Architecture,* 1965, p. 2

97. P. Schaff, *History of the Christian Church: Nicene and Post-Nicene Christianity, AD311-600,* [5]1893 repr 1989, III, 544; J.G. Davies, *The Secular Use of Church Buildings,* 1968, pp. 16f. This attitude continues to the present day (Davies, pp. 96-99)

98. G.G. Porton, 'Diversity in Post-Biblical Judaism' in R.A. Kraft and G.W.E. Nickelsburg (eds), *Early Judaism and its Modern Interpreters,* 1986, p. 59; M. Smith, 'The Image of God', *HTR,* 40,1957-8, 473f

99. R.M. Grant, *Early Christianity and Society,* 1978, pp. 150-163; P.R.L. Brown, *The Cult of the Saints,* 1981, pp. 39-41; P. Veyne, *Bread and Circuses: Historical Sociology and Political Pluralism,* 1990, pp. 26-28

100. C.S. Hill, *The Sociology of the New Testament Church to AD62,* PhD Thesis (Nottingham University), 1972, p. 222

101. W. Schrage, *TDNT,* VII, 827; S. McKnight, *A Light Among the Gentiles: Jewish Missionary Activity in the Second Temple Period,* 1991, pp. 14f, 26f; P.R. Trebilco, *Jewish Communities in Asia Minor,* 1991, pp. 173-180; S. Mitchell, *Anatolia: Land, Men, and Gods in Asia Minor,* 1993, II, 36f

102. H.J. Zobel, *TDOT,* I, 479; H.W. Wolff, *Anthropology of the Old Testament,* 1974, pp. 216-219; E.P. Sanders, *Judaism: Practice and Belief 63BCE-66CE,* 1992, pp. 144f, 236f; D.F. Flusser, 'Paganism in Palestine', *Compendia* I:2,1091f

103. J. Murphy-O'Connor, *St Paul's Corinth: Texts and Archaeology,* 1983, pp. 153-158 R.J. Banks estimates thirty people could be accommodated in comfort in a moderately well-to-do house and perhaps forty-five in an emergency (*PIC,* pp. 41t)

104. E.E. Ellis, *Pauline Theology: Ministry and Society,* 1989, pp. 139-141, 144, cf. L.M. White, *Building God's House,* p. 107

105. Luke 1:1-4; Acts 12:12, 16:31-35,17:4-12,18:17; Rom. 16:23; 1 Co.r 1:14-16,6:1; Eph. 6:9; Phil. 4:22; Col. 4:1; 1 Tim. 6:1f; Philemon; James 1:9-11, 2:2; *1 Clem.* 38:2; *Did.* 4:10f; *Ep Barn* 19:7, 21:2; Herm *Shep Vis* 3:6:5-7; *Mand* 10:1:4-6; *Sim* 8:9:1; Tation *Ad Graec* 32; Tert *Apol* 1:7; *Ad Scap* 5; *Ad Ux* 2:8; Origen *CC* 8:75; Hipp *Ap Trad* 16:18 (E.A.Judge, *The Social Pattern of Christian Groups in the 1st century,* 1960, pp. 49-61; A.J. Malherbe, *Social Aspects of Early Christianity,* ²1984; W.A. Meeks, *The First Urban Christians,* 1983, pp. 51-74; D.J. Tidball, *An Introduction to the Sociology of the New Testament,* 1983, pp. 90-103; G. Hamel, *Poverty and Charity in Roman Palestine, First Three Centuries CE,* 1990, pp. 224-238)

106. These figures, which are high, are often regarded with suspicion but for no adequate reason. See I.H. Marshall, *The Acts of the Apostles,* 1980, p. 82; R.P.C. Hanson, *The Acts,* 1967, pp. 76f; R. Longenecker, *The Acts of the Apostles,* EBC, 1981, IX, 287; W. Reinhardt, 'The Population Size of Jerusalem and the Numerical Growth of the Jerusalem Church', *BAFCS,* IV, 237-265

107. A.N. Sherwin-White, *The Letters of Pliny,* 1968, pp. 608f

108. There may have been several local congregations in Ephesus. See the discussion in C.E. Arnold, *Ephesians: Power and Magic. The Concept of Power in Ephesians in Light of its Historical Setting,* 1989, p. 6

109. Antioch: Acts 11:21,24; Ephesus: Acts 19:10,17-20; 1 Cor. 16:8-9; Corinth: 1 Corinthians as a whole; Rome: Rom. 16. I assume Romans 16 was originally part of Paul's letter to the Romans (C.E.B. Cranfield, *The Epistle to the Romans,* 1980, I, 9-11; D. Guthrie, *New Testament Introduction,* ⁴1990, pp. 412-417

110. B.E. Bowe, *A Church in Crisis,* 1988, pp. 12f

111. D.J. Tidball, *An Introduction to the Sociology of the New Testament,* 1983, pp. 82f; W.L. Lane, *Hebrews 9-13,* 1991, p. 570

112. G.D. Fee, *The First Epistle to the Corinthians,* 1987, p. 683; R.J. Banks, *PIC,* pp.

38f. On the advantages of occasional large scale meetings see R. Pointer, *How Do Churches Grow?*, 1984, pp. 53, 74f; E. Gibbs, *I Believe in Church Growth*, [3]1990, pp. 193-198

113. For examples of the multiplication process in action in house churches today see L. Barrett, *Building the House Church*, 1986, pp. 147-154; R.J. and J. Banks, *The House Church*, 1986, pp. 163-167

114. Pliny *Ep* 7:17:8-13; Philostratus, *Vit Soph*, 541

115. P.A. Andersen and J.K. Burgoon in R.S. Cathcart and L.A. Samovar (eds), *Small Group Communication: A Reader*, [4]1984, pp. 272, 279f; P.G. Cobb, 'The Architectural Setting of the Liturgy' in C.Jones, G. Wainwright and E. Yarnold (eds), *The Study if Liturgy*, 1978, pp. 473-480

116. H. W. Turner, *Temple to Meetinghouse*, 1979, p. 326; H.A. Snyder, *The Problem of Wineskins*, 1977, pp. 61-65

117. Party strife may have been fostered by differences between house groups (F.V. Filson, 'The Significance of the Early House Churches', *JBL*, 58, 1939, 110). Certain functions within the body of the church were of high status from the beginning, but beyond the sphere of the church, clerical office was not a route to prestige and the favor of the nobility until the 3rd century and beyond (P.H. Davids, *The Epistle of James*, 1982, p. 136; H. von Campenhausen, *Ecclesiastical Authority and Spiritual Power in the Church of the First Three Centuries*, 1969, pp. 252-254)

118. G.D.W. Randall in J.G. Davies (ed), *A New Dictionary of Liturgy and Worship*, 1986, p. 432; J.G. Davies, *The Secular Use of Church Buildings*, 1968, p. 138

119. On the connection between communication and seating see P.A. Andersen and J.K. Burgoon in R.S. Cathcart and L.A. Samovar, *Small Group Communication*, pp. 270, 272, 279-283; C.A. Insko and J. Schopler, *Experimental Social Psychology*, 1972, pp. 383-386; J. Rogers, *Adults Leaming*, [3]1989, pp. 83-86; L. Barrett, *Building the House Church*, 1986, p. 45

120. R. Sommer, 'Sociofugal Space', *American Journal of Sociology*, 72, 1967, 655. See further A.P. Hare, *Handbook of Small Group Research*, [2]1976, pp. 219, 221. Large spaces can still be conducive to human interaction-sociopetal (Sommer, 659).

121. A. Harnack, *The Mission and Expansion of Christianity in the First Three Centuries*, [2]1908, II, 88; idem, *Bible Reading in the Early Church*, 1912, pp. 63f, 112

122. Not an idle fear: S.L. Greenslade, *Schism in the Early Church*, [2]1964

123. H. Hargreaves, 'The Wycliffite Versions', *CHB*, II, 414; D. Birkey, *The House Church*, 1988, pp. 65-71; R.J. and J. Banks, *The Home Church*, 1986, pp. 60-65; D.F. Durnbaugh, 'Intentional Community in Historical Perspective' in A.L. Foster (ed), *The House Church Evolving*, 1976, pp. 14-29

124. M. Paget-Wilkes, *Poverty, Revolution and the Church*, 1981, pp. 37-66, 105, 110f; A. Storkey, *A Christian Social Perspective*, 1979, pp. 113-115; H. Feldman, *Some Aspects of the Christian Reaction to the Tradition of Classical Munificence with Particular Reference to the Works of John Chrysostom and Libanius*, D Phil Thesis (Oxford University), 1980, p. 126

125. J.E. Packer, 'The Insulae of Imperial Ostia', *Memoirs of the American Academy in Rome*, 31, 1971, 73f. The attitude of wealthy Romans to their homes was different (A. Wallace-Hadrill, 'The Social Structure of the Roman House', *PBSR*, 56, 1988, 46)

126. C.S. Hill, *New Testament Church*, p. 242 n2; E.S. Fiorenza, *In Memory of Her*, 1983, pp.176-178, 286-288

127. L.J. Archer, *Her Price is Beyond Rubies: The Jewish Woman in Greco-Roman Palestine*, 1990, pp. 207-250; J. Jeremias, *Jerusalem in the Time of Jesus*, 1969, pp. 359-376

128. B. Witherington III, *Women in the Ministry of Jesus*, 1984, pp. 125-131; J.B. Hurley, *Man and Woman in Biblical Perspective*, 1981, pp. 79-112; M. Evans, *Woman in the Bible*, 1983, pp. 44-57; G. Bilezikian, *Beyond Sex Roles*, [2]1991, pp. 79-118

129. R.J. Banks, 'Paul and Women's Liberation', *Interchange*, 18, 1976,81-105; C. Kroeger, 'The Apostle Paul and the Greco-Roman Cults of Women', *JETS*, 30:1,1987,25-38; B. Witherington III, *Women in the Earliest Churches*, 1988, pp. 73-75, 125-127; G.B. Caird, 'Paul and Women's Liberty', *BJRL*, 54, 1971-2,268-281

130. M. Evans, *Woman in the Bible*, pp. 122-133; G. Bilezikian, *Beyond Sex Roles*, pp. 193-206

131. J.B. Hurley, *Man and Woman*, pp. 116-124; M. Evans, *Woman in the Bible*, pp. 126-130; S.C. Barton, 'Paul's Sense of Place: An Anthropological Approach to Community Formation in Corinth', *NTS*, 32, 1986, 230f

132. B. Witherington III, *Conflict and Community in Corinth*, 1995, pp. 35, 149f

133. J.P.V.D. Balsdon, *Roman Women: Their History and Habits*, 1962, pp. 45-62; L.P. Wilkinson, *Classical Attitudes to Modern Issues*, 1979, pp. 69-78

134. B. Witherington III, *Women in the Earliest Churches*, 1988, pp. 183-210; I. Maclean, *The Renaissance Notion of Woman*, 1980, pp. 6-27; R.B. Edwards, *ISBE*, IV, 1096f; R.A. Tucker and W. Liefeld, *Daughters of the Church: Women and Ministry from New Testament Times to the Present*, 1987, p. 100 (*cf.* p. 275); C. Osiek, 'The Church Fathers and the Ministry of Women' in L. and A. Swidler (eds), *Women Priests*, 1977, pp. 75-80

135. R.S. Kraemer, 'Women in the Religions of the Greco-Roman World', *RSR*, 9:2, 1983, 127; E. Storkey, *What's Right with Feminism*, 1985, pp. 46-53,113-120; R.A. Tucker and W. Liefeld, *Daughters of the Church*, pp. 15-17, 130f

136. M. Hayter, *The New Eve in Christ*, 1987, pp. 49f

137. G.E. Wright, *The Biblical Doctrine of Man in Society*, 1954, pp. 77-88; H. Strathmann, TDNT, IV, 34f, 52-57; E. Schweizer, *Church Order in the New Testament*, 1961, pp. 160-162 (section 19a-c)

138. A. Harnack, *Mission*, II, 86

139. H.W. Turner, *Temple to Meetinghouse*, 1979, p. 180; J.E. Taylor, *Christians and the Holy Places: The Myth of Jewish-Christian Origins*, 1993, pp. 81-83, 154, 333-341; cf. P.E. Finney, 'Early Christian Architecture', 319-338

140. A.F. Holmes, *All Truth is God's Truth*, Eerdmans Publishing Co., USA, 1977, p. 28

141. J. Ellul, *The Subversion of Christianity*, 1986, pp. 54-60; A. Storkey, *A Christian Social Perspective*, 1979, pp. 116-118, 384; J.A. Walter, *A Long Way from Home*, 1979, pp. 152-158

142. J. Ellul, *Subversion*, pp. 61-68, 134; J.E. Taylor, *Holy Places*, pp. 333-341; P.R.L. Brown, *The Cult of the Saints*, 1981; H.W. Turner, *Temple to Meetinghouse*, pp. 180-184

143. P.R.L. Brown, *The Making of Late Antiquity*, 1978, pp. 4-6

144. A summary of Weber's conclusions is provided in A. Giddens, *Sociology,* ²1993, p. 288 and see further below

145. G.J. Laing, 'Roman Religious Survivals in Christianity' in J.T. McNeill, M. Spinka and H.R. Willoughby (eds), *Environmental Factors in Christian History,* 1939 repr 1970, pp. 72-90

3 Quest for Maturity in the New Testament[1]

Many Christians apparently find it difficult to imagine what the early Christians could have done together in their meetings and how they could have grown up to maturity in Christ if the sermon were not the centerpiece of their gatherings. But the New Testament provides us with detail enough to build up a realistic picture of early Christian groups at work. We can see something of how Jesus lived and worked with the Twelve and how the Pauline churches functioned or were expected to function. We shall find here a guide not merely to church life but to the training of Christian leaders. We shall also see the extent to which Christian maturity, as presented in the New Testament, was (or was not) dependent upon the sermon and the preacher.

THE GROUP LIFE OF THE TWELVE

TWELVE MEN

The number twelve corresponds to the number of tribes and to the number of princes in Israel. The selection of twelve disciples may, therefore, be a symbolic, prophetic action concerned with salvation history. It further suggests that Jesus had messianic pretensions.[2] But the significance of the number twelve is by no means exhausted by such considerations. The choice of twelve followers also relates to the requirements of efficient working in a group. Recent studies in small group theory are insufficient to prove beyond doubt that twelve is the ideal number for a group such as the apostolic band, yet there is some evidence to suggest that twelve or thirteen may be the optimum size in terms of effective working and use of resources, stability, growth, learning, intimacy, friendliness and satisfaction although some would suggest that the optimum number may be as low as five.[3] There are dangers in applying modern group studies to an ancient Semitic culture, but the results obtained suggest that the procedure is not wholly worthless, particularly as it entails no violence to the gospel texts.

The apostolic band was entirely male as were similar fellowship groups in the Old Testament and later Judaism.[4] An all-male team might be more productive than a mixed group although recent psychological studies on the relative effectiveness of mixed and non-mixed groups yield conflicting results.[5] Given the status of women at the time, an all-male group was probably the most sensible arrangement although some argue that women were excluded on principle.[6] There was also an outer group of disciples which travelled about with Jesus. Some of them must have been very close to him and almost formed a part of the Twelve: men such as Cleopas, Joseph and Matthias (Luke 24:18; Acts 1:21-23); the relatives of the Twelve (Mark 1:30) and also a number of women who may have travelled as a distinct group under the aegis of a well-known figure such as Joanna, the wife of Herod's steward (Mark 15:40f; Luke 8:1-3).[7] Many of the Twelve were already known to one another before their selection for the apostolate. Some had been disciples of John the Baptist (John 1:35-40; Acts 1:22) and there were two pairs of brothers (Matt. 10:2). Possibly some of the apostles were related to Jesus.[8] Such friendships might also increase productivity.[9]

The relationship between Jesus and the Twelve was in some ways comparable with that of a rabbi and his disciples for Jesus was a master and indeed more than a master to them. As their teacher he was also their 'father'.[10] The group was always twelve plus one rather than thirteen. The Twelve frequently shared problems with each other although not so frequently with Jesus, who at times was on the fringe of the group with his own thoughts (Mark 9:33, 10:32). But Jesus was no detached leader and revealed to the Twelve a wide range of his emotions (Mark 8:33; John 11:15, 33, 12:27). Paul acted similarly (2 Cor. 1:8f; Phil. 1:12-26; 1 Thes. 2:7f).

STRENGTHS AND WEAKNESSES OF THE PAIRING SYSTEM

The group was divided into pairs when out on mission (Mark 6:7). This may have been a natural development from the Jewish requirement for at least two witnesses in law (Deut. 17:6, 19: 15) and further reflects the Jewish dislike of isolation. Pairing of messengers is unknown in the Old Testament though common in later Judaism. In the early church, both orthodox and unorthodox teachers worked in pairs.[11] Paul often worked in groups of three or more (Acts 13:13, 16:17, 18:5, 19:22, 29, 20:4; Gal. 2:1; 1 Thes. 1:1; 2 Thes. 1:1). The advantages of pairing were numerous:

1. There was *increased talking time*. Talking time decreased as group size increased, especially for the more reserved members of the group who may have been in the majority. Conversations in the group as a whole usually give the impression of a tiny vocal minority surrounded by a group of silent observers which is characteristic of groups of this size.[12] Only eight of the apostles are directly recorded as saying anything to the group although silence in a group is not necessarily an indicator of non-involvement or powerlessness. Even so, one might expect the most able to speak more in group discussion.[13] Not surprisingly, a higher proportion seemed willing to engage in discussion at the end rather than the start of Jesus' ministry for by then they were more at home in the group.[14] During the Last Supper, Peter, John, Judas, the other Judas (probably = Thaddaeus), Thomas and Philip all spoke either to Jesus or to one another and on one occasion all the disciples commented (Matt. 26:25, 35; John 13:6 - 14:22). Andrew and James the brother of John spoke earlier on (Luke 9:54; John 6:8). Those for whom we have no recorded conversations are Matthew, James of Alphaeus, Simon the zealot and possibly Bartholomew—unless he is to be identified with Nathanael (John 1:45-49).[15] The gospel material here is, however, thin and we should not press these and the following conclusions too far.

2. *Decisions and conclusions may have been arrived at more quickly* in pairs than in the larger group, although the answer

was more likely to be wrong (Luke 9:54).[16] The whole group could be wrong in unison too (Matt. 14:15, 15:23, 16:6-12, 19:13f; Acts 1:6).

3. There was *increased responsibility* in a pair because, when faced with a task, neither member could easily fade into the background. This reduced to a minimum that dependency and deskilling, which the disciples were liable to feel in the presence of Jesus;[17] although he counteracted it where possible, since he called the disciples to be, not unthinking slaves, but active participants in the work of the kingdom (John 15:15). Decisions had to be made. When there was no arbiter (as, for example, on missions when Jesus was unavailable for consultation and had given little instruction beforehand) these decisions had to be unanimous. Few two-person decisions are mentioned but all indicate agreement (Mark 10:35-41; Luke 9:54; John 12:22).[18]

4. There was possibly *freer exchange of opinions and suggestions* than in the larger group. In pairs there is often a higher rate of asking for opinions than for giving them.[19] There is, however, another side to this issue since a larger group allows for greater anonymity. In the larger group dissatisfaction might be more freely vented because the consequences of alienating one person in a pair are generally greater than those, which might arise from the alienation of one person in a larger group. But as the pair got to know each other well, disagreements might have been aired without destroying the relationship.[20] Jewish bluntness[21] would have helped to keep misunderstanding at bay but critical assessment of the work of fellow group members was apparently absent. Jesus alone provided criticism and assessment (Luke 9:10, 10:17-20). Similarly, competition was not encouraged between individuals or sub-groups—their attention was focused quite differently (Luke 10:17-20).

5. There are *variations* in the pairings given in the several lists of apostles (Matt. 10:2-4; Mark 3:16-19; Luke 6:13-16; Acts 1:13). The reasons for this are unknown but one conjecture, in

the light of group theory, may be helpful. In order to function effectively, a group must be flexible and recognize the available resources, which promote growth. It is dangerous for groups and group members to become locked in fixed roles.[22] There is no reason for assuming that pairings in the Twelve, once made, would continue unchanged throughout Jesus' ministly. Our knowledge of the apostles and of Jesus' intentions for them is insufficient to enable us to appreciate what pairing adjustments would be required as the ministry progressed. However, we can speak more confidently of one disciple—Matthew (= Levi). As a toll collector, his social standing would have been low. He would have been suspected of dishonesty (Luke 3:12f)[23] and his testimony in a Jewish court of law might have been invalid.[24] Even his alms might not have been acceptable on the assumption that it had been obtained by robbery.[25] In general, toll collectors were ranked with gentiles, prostitutes, murderers and robbers (m Ned 3:4; Matt. 18:7, 21:31).[26] Even Jesus spoke disparagingly of them although his objections centered on abuses rather than the job itself (Matt. 5:46,18:17, cf. Mark 12:17 and also John the Baptist, Luke 3:12f).

The presence of an outcast in the apostolic band may have caused problems initially. That there is no mention of any conflict between Matthew and the others or between Hebrew and Hellenistic elements probably means that such conflict was minimal. Other apostolic failings are clearly revealed throughout the gospels and there is no obvious reason for silence on this point. Even so, Jesus' emphasis on love for the brethren may have had Matthew as its focus (John 13:34, 15:12). But working in a common cause, in which both parties are necessary for success, frequently promotes harmony even between erstwhile enemies.[27]

The main problem caused by Matthew's membership of the Twelve was probably the antagonism he aroused among fellow Jews. Given the widespread attention to Matthew's abandonment of his occupation (Matt. 9:9-11), his background could hardly be concealed and he was liable to be the object of hatred by his audience. The taint of his former calling might still have remained and his witness would have been compromised.[28] The problem of accepting the gospel from a member of a despised social group is well known.[29]

Thomas may have found that his partner, Matthew, created problems unknown to the other pairs. The end of Jesus' ministry had paired Matthew with another disciple—Bartholomew (Acts 1:13).

6. The presence of a pair of witnesses rather than a single individual would help to iron out idiosyncrasies, provide mutual encouragement, make travelling safer and, in a small way, reveal to their audience *the practical meaning of Christian fellowship.*[30]

STRUCTURE, STRENGTHS & WEAKNESSES LARGER GROUPS

The larger group of twelve was similarly rich in advantages such as the stimulus of a wider range of ideas, greater absorptive power of controversial material, greater anonymity for shy persons, more extensive development of leadership potential, wider scope for friendship and greater use of gifts. There was adequate changing of roles and considerable flexibility, sufficient to cope with the defection of one member (who was replaced) and the death of another (who was not replaced).[31] Most significantly, even after the crucifixion of Jesus, when the group was at its lowest ebb and facing the apparent disintegration of its hopes (Luke 24:21), its effective community life helped it to survive (John 21:3).[32] The group was also able to cope with the great expansion which followed Pentecost (Acts 2:41,4:4) as well as a fresh structure and a new set of functions requiring the ability to absorb new ideas and assume new responsibilities.[33] Members of the group were given adequate scope for the development of their skills.

On the negative side, even groups of twelve can develop factions. Splits occurred, but these were counterbalanced by the personal authority of Jesus, which prevented the formation of disaffected subgroups. Group cohesion was developed early on and maintained in spite of the differences in outlook of its members; it was demonstrated by occasional acts of hostility toward outsiders (Luke 9:49f, 54). Such acts are not surprising, as increased affection for members of one's own group is often accompanied by increased hostility for those outside it.[34] Cohesion was further strengthened by the constant threat of persecution,[35] by occasional successes (Matt. 14:13-21; John 4:38), [36] by Jesus' insistence that interpersonal disputes be settled quickly (Matt. 5:22-24), by ensuring that all had direct access to Jesus and by spending a great deal of time together working, eating, relaxing and building personal relationships (Mark 6:31f). The work done was considerable but Jesus preserved the group from busyness and a rigid timetable so that all were available for the important and not just the immediate task. All this would have helped to unify the group.[37]

DIVISIONS IN THE GROUP

1. The first cause of division was *the squabble over precedence.* This was characteristic of Jewish society[38] and, in the case of the Twelve, continued throughout the ministry of Jesus right up to the Last Supper (Mark 10:35-41; Luke 9:46, 22:24). In an ordinary group of twelve young men, we might expect this problem to be resolved, in early days, with the establishment of a pecking order[39]—which might be revised as the group matured. Jesus' policy of ensuring that all answered directly to him, without being under the authority of any other member of the apostolic band, ensured that the question of internal leadership was never resolved. Jesus was the only leader in the group and he appointed no deputy. Peter gives the impression of being a leader in the group or at least 'first among equals' but it was a position unacknowledged by the others until after the resurrection (Mark 9:33f, 10:35-41; Luke 22:24). After that, Peter assumed the position for which he had been prepared (Matt. 16:18f; Luke 22:31f; Acts 1:15-26, 5:1-9).[40]

   If the pairs and quaternions (groups of four) in the lists of the apostles correspond with their working arrangements on mission, then, as far as we can tell, the abler disciples regularly worked together as a group of four or in two pairs (Matt. 10:2-4; Mark 3:16-19; Luke 6:14-16; Acts 1:13).[41] In all four New Testament lists of the apostles, the first, fifth and ninth names are constant (Simon Peter, Philip and James of Alphaeus) and, although the pairings vary, the quaternions remain constant. M.J. Wilkins suggests that each quaternion had its own group leader.[42] This may be so but there is no further evidence for it or any suggestion that apostles worked in pairs comprising a senior and junior member. Each appears to have answered directly to his Lord and not another apostle. Whenever Peter forgot this arrangement and attempted to dominate others, he was rebuked (Mark 8:32f; John 21:20-22). There is a parallel here with the Old Testament prophets, all of whom answered directly to God and not to another prophet. Some prophets had assistants but these assistants were not then prophets and had other duties.[43]

However well this system worked, the successful execution of some tasks may have been impaired by the non-resolution of the ranking issue within the Twelve.[44] Matters would have been complicated further had members of the group previously been assigned status by family members who were also in the Twelve or on its fringes. Certainly there was friction and Jesus' emphasis on love for the brethren (John 13:34, 15:12) may suggest that they had to overcome some indifference or mutual hostility.[45] The reasons behind Jesus' actions, however, are clear enough. He intended the apostles to transcend the spirit of their age and adopt a view of leadership defined in terms of service rather than an hierarchical structure (Mark 10:42-45).

2. The second cause of division concerned the group's *experience of failure, fear, bewilderment or false optimism which was set in opposition to Jesus* (Mark 4:41, 8:14-16, 10:32, 14:31; John 4:27, 13:22).[46] The group seldom showed itself in real sympathy with Jesus and frequently contributed unhelpful remarks and suggestions (Matt. 19:13; Mark 1:37, 5:31, 6:35f, 8:32f, 9:5; Luke 9:54; John 11:8). The Gospels reveal little trace of intelligent suggestions made to Jesus by the Twelve (Mark 14:12; Luke 11:1; John 6:8f).[47] These problems, however, did not prove crucial for the apostles were at that time only apprentices.

The threat of division within the apostolic band never reached a crisis point and the group was sufficiently stable to admit within it the presence of two distinct sub-groups. These were the pairs already mentioned and a group comprising what appears to be the three or four most responsive disciples—Peter, James the son of Zebedee, John and occasionally Andrew. This sub-group undertook various activities including instruction and discussion (Mark 5:37, 9:2, 14:33; with Andrew: Mark 13:3, *cf.* Luke 22:8 (Peter and John).[48] It did not form a separate power block or committee guiding the activities of the rest. Rather its existence suggests Jesus' concern to develop the potential and individuality of each disciple to the fullest possible extent. This is in line with the strong individualistic strain running throughout the teaching and actions of Jesus (Matt. 10:21, 35f; Mark 10:29f; Luke 14:26, 17:34; John 3:1-5, 14:21-24).[49] This was based on the thinking of the Old Testament.[50]

Apart from the two sub-groups the larger group had little formal structure. Judas acted as treasurer (John 12:6, 13:29) but otherwise the group members showed little specialization other than gifts in the making. This may have been an advantage, given the unstructured nature of the apostolic task and the need for adaptability.

CONCLUSION

The methods used by Jesus in maturing the apostolic band certainly contain material to guide the church in the art of training leaders but is there also guidance for nurturing the church as a whole? In fact, these methods are fully congruent with the ideals and practices of the primitive church in Jerusalem and with those developed by Paul.

THE PRIMITIVE CHURCH IN JERUSALEM

It is widely accepted that temple ritual contributed little, directly, to early Christianity, but many take it for granted that the form of early Christian meetings owed a great deal to that of the synagogue, not least because most of the early converts were Jews familiar with the synagogue pattern.[51] There is some truth here but we have little evidence to suggest that the first Christians attempted to perpetuate the style of the synagogue.[52] The fledgling Christian gatherings were sometimes regarded by Jews and non-Jews as synagogues of a kind and many Christians may have so regarded themselves in the early days.[53] However, the fact that the new communities met in the houses of members facilitated the maturing of their own forms. These centered on the teaching of the apostles, prayers and the breaking of bread. All this was conducted amid a set of relationships constituting fellowship which included the exercise of mutual kindness, the sharing of hospitality and perhaps goods (Acts 2:42).[54]

It would have been possible for the apostles to have turned to the synagogue for inspiration in establishing the infant Christian community, but several arguments can be raised against such an approach:

- Jesus has more in common with the prophetic tradition of the Old Testament than with the traditions of the contemporary teachers of Israel or the later rabbis.[55]
- Although Jesus is the fulfillment of Judaism as seen in the law, writings and prophets this is not necessarily the same as being the fulfillment of specific manifestations of Judaism in the 1st century (Matt. 5:17; Rom. 10:4). The first Christians, therefore, had no duty to build upon the foundations of 1st century Judaism. Rather they were to build on the Old Testament as interpreted by Jesus, who was himself to be the sufficient foundation (1 Cor. 3:9-11; Eph. 2:19-22).[56] A commonly ignored source of inspiration for the early church is Jewish domestic religion with its Old Testament emphasis on family devotions, instruction and ritual meals.[57] Jesus had grown up under its influences and, in his ministry, involved himself and his disciples in various aspects of it, particularly prayers, instruction and meals (Luke 10:38f, 14:1, 24:30).[58]
- Jesus often attended synagogue (Mark 1:21, 3:1; John 18:20) and it might seem that he thus set his seal of approval on the institution and, by implication, offered its forms for emulation by the early church. There is, however, little to indicate that his attendance was anything other than part of his mission. Primarily, Jesus seems to have used the synagogue as a means of reaching the people of Israel—just as he utilized the Temple—without implying that the disciples should copy its forms.
- The synagogue, no doubt in conjunction with parents and local

leaders, had been less than successful in educating the apostles. Their biblical understanding was deficient in many areas but particularly in understanding the writings and prophets. This is suggested by the following points:

1. Some disciples, possibly including apostles, followed contemporary Jewish teaching and assumed a direct and inevitable connection between individual sin and suffering (Luke 13:1-5; John 9:1-3).[59] The Old Testament teaches no such doctrine and offers numerous examples from Abel and Joseph onwards which militate against such an idea.[60] Jewish teaching on this point involved misunderstanding not just the later parts of the Old Testament but the Law itself, the understanding of which was a primary goal of Jewish education (m Ab 1:1, 6:1).[61]

2. The apostles' apparent identification of wealth with the blessing of God (Matt. 19:24f) is characteristic of the earlier Old Testament period and some of the wisdom literature but hardly of the prophets.[62]

3. When confronted by scribal teaching on the coming of Elijah, the inner circle of apostles referred to it exclusively in terms of its scribal origins (Mark 9:11, cf. mBM 1:8, 2:8; m Eduy 8:7), seemingly oblivious of its prophetic background (Mal. 4:5) . The point should not be pressed as the question may turn on the scribal interpretation rather than the origin of the passage.[63]

4. The general failure of the apostles and other disciples to understand so much of Jesus' teaching was in part a consequence of their lack of understanding of the prophets and writings. This failure persisted beyond Jesus' earthly ministry (Luke 24:25; Acts 1:6; Gal. 2:11-21).

- Some synagogues had turned against Jesus with the result that his ministry there was hampered. Jesus accordingly warned the disciples against the corruption of the synagogue (Matt.

23:34; Mark 13:9). Significant figures from the synagogues, including Pharisees (Mark 2:6; Luke 6:7),[64] were opposed to Jesus and may have been associated with those denounced by both Jesus and John the Baptist as 'a brood of vipers' (Matt. 3:7, 12:34). Much of this material is commonly assumed to be anachronistic—the product of the early church's ignorance, error and anti-Jewish tendency. In reality, the alleged anachronisms and other errors are easy to assume but difficult to demonstrate; and the problems with the view that the gospels accurately reflect the relationship between the Jewish leaders and Jesus are not as formidable as is frequently claimed.[65]

Although it is possible, therefore, that Judaism in the time of Jesus was supplying an adequate system of instruction, worship and community growth, which might have provided a pattern for the meetings of the emerging Christian community, this is certainly not obvious. There is nothing to suggest that it was obvious to the Twelve. After the Ascension, when virtually all doubts about Jesus had evaporated, it must have been almost instinctive for them to apply Jesus' teaching methods to their new circumstances. They had spent three years or more in the finest of schools; it is difficult to imagine their rejecting our Lord's methods in favor of the methods of contemporary Judaism.[66]

We return to the question: would the apostles have used sermons in nurturing the Christian community? There is little evidence of this in Acts 1-12 but, the absence of any pattern of regular sermons is not necessarily decisive. If the apostles did follow the methods of Jesus on this point then sermons might have been used initially among the faithful to be replaced subsequently by more personal and discriminating methods.

THE METHODS OF PAUL

INTRODUCTION

When we examine the communities established by Paul, as revealed in his epistles and the latter part of Acts, theory and practice can be examined together.[67] (The Epistles of Peter, James and John will not be studied separately. The communities to which they were addressed may or may not have functioned in the same ways as the Pauline communities, but in any case they furnish only modest material on our chosen themes—the church in Jerusalem certainly had a different flavor from that of the Pauline communities (Acts 21:17-26).[68] Hence they will be cited only occasionally and for illustrative purposes.

Following Jesus, Paul's ultimate aim was that God might be glorified and in particular glorified by his people (1 Cor. 10:31, 15:28; Eph. 1:5f, 12; 2 Thes. 1:10-12). From a different perspective, Paul's primary aim was that every person should be sanctified and mature—complete in Christ (Eph. 4:13; Col. 1:28)—a great being in the making, not a falsely humble, static 'little person'.[69] Paul's concern for Christian maturity is expressed in some form in all his epistles (and in the general epistles).[70] It relates not only, or even primarily, to individual maturity, but to the maturity of members in community resulting in a mature community (Eph. 2:22, 4:13; 1 Thes. 5:11).[71] The inspiration for this may derive from the Old Testament,[72] the teaching and practice of Jesus, particularly as seen in his dealings with the Twelve, pagan philosophy[73] or direct revelation (Gal. 1:11f) although these need not be mutually exclusive. The means for achieving this aim are directly related to the way in which the church functioned and may be broken down into inter-connected units: worship, participation, mutual ministries, development of gifts and skills, knowledge of scripture and the world. In this essay, no hard and fast distinction is intended between spiritual gift and natural skill. Some spiritual gifts are distinct from natural abilities but sometimes it appears that God reinforces natural talents or social skills.[74] The distinction between means and ends may not be clearly defined. For example, I.H. Marshall suggests that the growth and maintenance of the Christian family, the church, may be an end in itself; and the same may be true of worship.[75]

However, the emphasis on organizational structure, in the material under consideration, is so slight that it would be difficult to provide a detailed analysis from that viewpoint. Instead, we shall examine the New Testament understanding of Christian leadership, which pervades all the interconnected units listed above.

As we examine these units, we should bear in mind that if the sermon is as crucial to the growth of the kingdom of God as many today would maintain, then although regular sermons do not appear in the New Testament, it should at least be possible to construct a theoretical New Testament framework into which the sermon might fit comfortably.

WORSHIP, PARTICIPATION AND MUTUAL MINISTRIES

The New Testament contains only one extended description of a Christian gathering in the New Testament, apart from the Lord's Supper[76] (1 Cor. 14:23-40) and even this is a brief, partial account, since the activities mentioned do not include corporate prayer (cf. 1 Cor. 14:16), the reading of Scripture (cf. 1 Tim. 4:13) and perhaps other items.[77] Furthermore, it says what Paul would like to happen and not necessarily what did happen.

We need not assume that 1 Corinthians 14:23-40, provides an order of service.[78] But this description agrees well with practices and recommendations elsewhere in the New Testament—the group life of the Twelve, the treatment of mutual ministries by Paul and in Hebrews 3:13, 10:24f[79] and in 1 Peter 4:7-11.[80] Indeed, the New Testament provides no alternative pattern. As J.D.G. Dunn suggests, it is likely that other New Testament churches operated similarly.[81]

We may assume that many or all of the Christians in the Corinthian congregation had a gift or gifts of some kind, (1 Cor. 12:4-11, cf. 1 Pet. 4:10)[82] and may have been in the process of seeking or developing more gifts (1 Cor. 12:31, 14:1),[83] but it does not follow that all members had an obvious contribution to make during the meetings. Some might never say anything but might contribute by their intercession, listening and faith.[84] But all were seen as potential ministers to their fellows. There was no limitation on contributing save peace, order and concern for others. Outside the meetings, a similar diversity was expected, with gifts being used to the full in group or individual activities (Rom. 12:6-8; 1 Cor. 12:1-31). This is the essence of mutual ministry: that all practice their gifts and ministries among the congregation for the benefit of individuals or the group as a whole, with the result that all benefit and, in particular, grow to maturity as they both receive the blessings of God and serve as agents in disseminating them.

Many Christians at the lowest levels of society would have needed to use most of their energy merely to exist, for a substantial proportion of the population of the Roman Empire lived at or near subsistence level, but the church endeavored to lighten their burdens rather than increase them.[85] Unfortunately, this pattern was not followed in later centuries and those least able to look after themselves tended to be bound with 'heavy burdens and grievous to be borne' (Matt. 23:4 AV). E. Grubb lists the following factors which he believes militated against the spirit of true philanthropy in the early church: absorption in defining the creed, the rise of the church as an organization, asceticism (which is self-regarding and tends to displace the spirit of love) and a loveless approach to alms giving.[86]

At Corinth, as elsewhere, not all those in attendance seem to have been Christians (1 Cor. 5:11; 2 Cor. 11:13, 26; 1 John 2:19; Rev. 3:1-6, 14-22), but nominal Christians were not a major problem until the time of Origen and Cyprian.[87] Their numbers were kept to a minimum by discipline and a concern for the purity of the church, combined with the regular practice of mutual ministries such as encouragement and admonition and the maintenance of a spiritual atmosphere which unbelievers would have found disturbing. [88]

Paul emphasized the need for mustering the entire church for welfare, discipline and growth and expected the church as a whole to make intelligent godly decisions.[89] Unanimity in decision-making does not seem mandatory in New Testament thinking, but being of one mind was an ideal frequently requested, if less frequently attained (Acts 1:14, 2:46, 4:24, 5:12, 6:5, 15:22, 25; Rom. 12:16, 15:5f; 2 Cor. 13:11; Phil. 2:2). Although more autocratic methods were apparently present, particularly in connection with major doctrinal issues, the main emphasis in day-to-day church matters seems to have been on consensus. Consensus preserves the solidarity of the group without rejecting the views of the minority or the minority itself.[90] Reaching a true consensus takes time but this represents a good investment in terms of morale and group satisfaction.[91] Majority decisions are not found in the New Testament and first appear in the writings of Clement of Rome (1 *Clem* 54:2).[92]

At the heart of early Christian meetings was fellowship, comprising the mutual ministries of upbuilding, admonishing, discipline, edification, service, instruction and reconciliation.[93] Not all these terms necessarily refer to ministries exercised in Christian gatherings but, given their significance in the life of the community, there is no obvious reason to think they were not included. To what extent these demanding obligations were practiced in the New Testament churches is unknown.[94]

Participation was essential for growth but also very much in line with the spirit of the age, for men and women generally, especially Jews and Greeks, wanted to take a more active part in their religion than that of the passive observer.[95] This may be yet another example of the preparation of this particular era for the coming of Christ—a thought well expressed by S. Angus, who writes:

> The more one studies this era the more will he be persuaded that the Christ came in the fullness of time; that all its activities, political, social, moral and religious, were converging toward His appearing.[96]

In its desire to participate, the 1st century is rather like our own.

Little is said about the leadership of meetings. Perhaps they were spontaneous and unstructured, with everyone expected to show some responsibility under the guidance of the Holy Spirit, but it seems more likely that there was a president although not necessarily the same person on every occasion. In some churches, the host may have acted as president.[97] We should not assume, with H. von Campenhausen, that the disorganized worship at Corinth implies an absence of leaders.[98] The options are wider. The disorganization may indicate that there were no leaders or equally that they were ineffective, perhaps dominated by secular ideals. No 'real' leadership need not imply no leaders at all. Confusion and frustration, as seen in the Corinthian church, are typical results of laissez-faire leadership in small groups.[99] Paul was pleased to see leaders appointed in at least some and perhaps all of the churches he planted (Acts 14:23) and expected Christians to recognize leaders as such (1 Cor. 16:15-18; Phil. 1:1; 1 Thes. 5:12; 1 Tim. 5:17).[100] There is no reason to assume that their leadership functions were exercised exclusively outside Christian gatherings or that the guidance of the Holy Spirit and human leadership were seen as mutually exclusive.[101] In both Testaments, God's word, guidance and leadership frequently come through human agency.[102] What does seem clear is that, however the Pauline churches were led, the gathering was not divided into one speaker and a passive congregation; such a picture is, as E. Schweizer observes, 'completely foreign to the New Testament'.[103]

Much of what is said above refers to gatherings often described today as 'services of worship' but, like the synagogue,[104] the early church was not primarily concerned with worship in its meetings. The major emphasis was on activities directed towards members of the congregation for their mutual growth and upbuilding, although worship was involved here as in every other sphere of life.[105]

DEPENDENCE ON LEADERS

The New Testament provides many illustrations of apostolic activity and leadership, but examples of local church leadership are scarce. Furthermore, the New Testament contains no comprehensive statement of the duties of leaders or even a detailed description of what any given leader actually did in a local congregation. Occasional duties are mentioned in passing but these probably represent only a part of the leader's total work. They include guarding, ruling, teaching, equipping the saints for ministry, praying for the sick, helping the weak, administering funds and being an example to those within and without the church, but there is little evidence to show how these duties were to be implemented (Acts 15:2, 6, 22-29, 16:4, 20:28, 35; 1 Cor. 9:7; Eph. 4:11f; 1 Tim. 3:5, 5:17; Jam. 5:14f).[106] The exercise of discipline does not appear to have been a distinct function of the local leadership but the responsibility of the church as a whole, although the leaders would often play a major role.[107] Given the differences between the churches and between leaders and given the relative independence of churches, it seems likely that the duties varied somewhat from one church to the next.

Whatever local leaders were required to do, Christians were to be persuaded by and submit to them (1 Cor. 16:16; Heb. 13:17; 1 Pet. 5:5; cf. Phil. 2:29; 1 Thes. 5:12f). Taken out of context, this element of New Testament teaching might seem to imply an authoritarian leadership upon which the church was highly dependent. Other evidence, however, counterbalances this interpretation.

First, Jesus insisted that leaders should be as servants (Matt. 20:25-28) and this point is taken up by Peter in the very passage where he urges subjection to elders (1 Pet. 5:1-5).

Second, throughout the epistles of Paul, we find an emphasis on mutual submission[108]—and there is little evidence to suggest that leaders are exempted from this requirement.[109]

Third, following Old Testament and later Jewish teaching, Christians were instructed to submit to the governing authorities (Rom. 13:1-7; Titus 3:1; 1 Pet. 2:13-17). The verb used for submission here is *hupotasso*, the same as in 1 Corinthians 16:16 and 1 Peter 5:5 where submission to Christian leaders is in mind.[110] The precise limits to this yeilding are not worked out, but the early Christians knew that, in the event of a conflict between their duty to God and to the state, they should obey God rather than men (Acts 4:19f, 5:29; Heb. 11:23; *cf.* Matt. 22:21). Here too they followed Old Testament precedent and later Jewish practice (Exod. 1:17; Dan. 3:13-18, 6:10; 1 Macc. 2:22).

Fourth, in some cases leaders were likely to defer to others:

i. Not all elders taught regularly (1 Tim. 5:17). Where a plurality of elders existed, any elder(s) not teaching would *submit to the teaching of the elder*(s) presenting—or even to the presentation of one who was not an elder, if such a situation existed.

ii. Leaders would be required to *acknowledge the gifts of others* in their congregations and respond appropriately to those gifts when exercised. For example, E.E. Ellis suggests that '...the role of the prophet may overlap that of the elder as it does that of the apostle and the teacher, especially in certain teaching functions.'[111]

iii. Leaders were required to *defer to the authority of their wives* on occasion (1 Cor. 7:4).

iv. Elders might have to *answer criticisms* brought by members of the congregation (1 Tim. 5:19f).

It is thus clear that submission and obedience to leaders in the New Testament is not absolute. Something approaching the absolute authority of leaders first appeared in 1 Clement and the epistles of Ignatius.[112]

Paul sees submission as connected with work done in building up the church, and Christians are to submit to all who work on their behalf. But given that all Christians were likely to be gifted in some way that might benefit the community (1 Cor. 12:7; Eph 4:7; 1 Pet. 4:10), this might suggest the submission of everyone to everyone else in some sense. In what areas, therefore, do church leaders receive a submission above that due to other Christians? It is, I suggest, in the area of gifts. Leaders may have any of the gifts possessed by other Christians but, in place of, or in addition to them, leaders may well have specific gifts appertaining to leadership. The gift of leading (*proistemi*) is mentioned several times by Paul (Rom. 12:8, 16:1-2; 1 Thes. 5:12; 1 Tim. 5:17) and is used in a non-technical sense elsewhere (Tit- us 3:8,14). There is some disagreement as to whether, in essence, the term suggests leadership,[113] caring[114] or protection[115] although these three need not be mutually exclusive.[116] The occurrence at 1 Timothy 5:17 is more generally assumed to refer to ruling[117] but even this is disputed.[118] Paul mentions a second gift of leadership (*kubernesis*, 1 Cor. 12:28) which seems to refer to directing, administering or guiding the local congregation, although the precise function is not clear. It does not appear to include teaching.[119] L. Coenen suggests that the term involves 'keeping order within the whole life of the church'.[120] In particular, it may involve ensuring that gifts are not used in any way which might create chaos—in this respect, and perhaps in this respect only, gifts of leadership would out rank other gifts. But leadership gifts were not seen as different in kind from other gifts nor were they seen as creating a separate clerical class.[121]

In some Christian communities, such as those at Corinth and perhaps Thessalonica, members of higher social status and wealth appear to have been acknowledged as leaders in virtue of their standing as protectors and patrons; they were sometimes the hosts of house churches. This reflects something of the social patterns of the day as seen in the Diaspora synagogues and Greco-Roman society generally.[122] Just how this form of leadership relates to spiritual gifts is not clear but it may indicate the reinforcement of natural gifts with spiritual gifts.

P.H. Davids offers another perspective on New Testament leadership. Commenting on 1 Peter 5:3 he says:

Rather than dominating his house church, then, the elder is to lead by example: 'being examples to the flock'. This concept of leadership is common in the NT. Jesus often presented himself as an example (Matt. 10:24-25; Mark 10:42-45; Luke 6:40; John 13: 16; 15:20). Paul could write, 'Walk according to the example you had in us' (Phil. 3:17) and 'We gave an example to you so that you might imitate us' (2 Thes. 3:9), or even 'Be imitators of me, as I am of Christ' (1 Cor. 11:1; *cf.* Acts 20:35). Other leaders were also expected to be examples (1 Thes. 1:6-7; 1 Tim. 4:12; Titus 2:7; James 3:1-2). In fact, one could well argue that, following the pattern of the ancient world and especially of Judaism, teaching and leading was for the NT basically a matter of example rather than of lecture or command. Being an example fits well with the image of 'flock', for the ancient shepherd did not drive his sheep, but walked in front of them and called them to follow.[123]

Whatever we are to understand by local leadership in the New Testament, there are at least one and probably two gifts of leadership. And it is, I suggest, as leaders exercised these gifts that Christians were to submit to those leaders. This should not have resulted in an unhealthy form of dependence because little or no competition was involved. Even when Christians had the same gifts as their leaders, such trainee leaders could then be prepared for posts of leadership in their own or another house church. The system could fail, and did fail, for Corinth was not the only church with leadership problems (2 Thes. 3:6-15; 1 Pet. 5:1-3; 3 John 9f). But if all submitted to the gifts and skills of others in a spirit of mutual humility (1 Cor. 10:24; Eph. 5:20f; Phil. 2:3f), it had the potential to work well.[124]

THE DEVELOPMENT OF GIFTS

The Old Testament expresses a concern that all God's people should have a part to play in the life of the community (Exod. 19:6; Num. 3-4, 11:29). The New Testament echoes this thought and consequently one of the major responsibilities of Christian leaders is to ensure that all members can utilize their gifts effectively (without being valued by others solely in terms of those gifts).[125] Members may thus be delivered from both the domination of the church and the domination of ignorance, in order that the church may be built up. Paul may have known the Mishnaic tradition that there are 248 bones in the body but, even if not, he would probably have known that the body contains hundreds of different elements, particularly as about eighty parts of the body are named in the Old Testament. He used and developed the figure, common in ancient literature, of the body as a unity composed of various elements and compared the church with the human body in terms of variety of functions within it (Rom. 12:4-8; 1 Cor. 12:12-30).[126] He believed Christians should rejoice in that variety because the church would be both blessed and balanced by the correct exercise of a multiplicity of gifts. We may note here the similar richness and diversity of the twelve tribes of Israel (Gen. 49:3-27), the original creation (Gen. 1-2; Ps. 104) and the New Jerusalem (Rev. 21:10-27), all of which are partial parallels to the church.

Paul emphasized diversity and difference in gifts just as much as unity. As E.F. Scott points out, it is precisely the practice of harmonious diversity which creates unity—as in the human body;[127] but this is achieved through the unifying and loving practice of gifts rather than the independent fulfillment of a self-chosen personal destiny.[128] The balancing of this unity and diversity has always been one of the great tests of leadership. E.K. Simpson adds the thought that this kind of variegated unity is attractive—much more so than the drab uniformity sought and achieved in so many churches over the centuries.[129] Failure on this point is a consequence of the rejection of the social implications of Paul's teaching on the body of Christ. On the other hand, this attractiveness is, to some extent, inevitable if a Christian community reflects something of the beauty of God. Without it and without the richness, life and power, which emanate from a community exercising the skills or gifts given by the Holy Spirit, then the church has little to offer those within or without.

Just how gifts were developed is not clear but the standard method of training in technical skills throughout the ancient world was apprenticeship.[130] In the Old Testament, this kind of training for the leadership of God's people was provided for Joshua by Moses, Samuel by Eli and Elisha by Elijah (Exod. 17:9-13, 24:13; Num. 11:28, 27:15-23; 1 Sam. 3:1; 1 Kings 19:16-21; 2 Kings 2:1-12). In the New

Testament, even Jesus cast himself in the role of apprentice (John 5:19f) and also trained the disciples in a kind of apprenticeship scheme. Paul recognized gifts quickly, especially gifts of leadership[131] and trained a number of fellow Christians who travelled round with him in mission. Training Christian leaders in apprenticeship schemes was widely followed in the early church and has continued up to the present day.[132] For a number of gifts, the apprenticeship scheme could be applied in meetings where gifts might be discovered, recognized and then developed (inside or outside the meeting) by more experienced possessors of similar gifts. This system would function best with plenty of mature Christians and with a wide range of gifts freely operating. The New Testament provides little detail here but, like Jesus, Paul frequently set himself up as a pattern to be imitated (1 Cor. 4:15-17, 11:1f; Phil. 3:17, 4:9; 1 Thes. 1:6-8; 2 Thes. 3:6-12).[133] This would apply to all significant areas of the Christian life. The idea of finding one whose life was worthy of emulation in whole or in part, whether for living or in the perfection of an art, was common in Judaism and the Greco-Roman world.[134]

It would not have been possible for Paul to operate such a system as this if he had permanently dominated meetings for, had he done so, it would have been difficult for leaders to emerge and Paul would have found it difficult to move on.[135] Equally, this system requires small groups with a friendly atmosphere in which all feel able to contribute as they wish. In larger groups, many members feel inhibited.[136] Another essential requirement is understanding. Thin as it is, the evidence suggests that very few Christians of the first and second centuries had a clear grasp of Paul's teaching.[137] Perhaps the extent of his activities was too wide, his teaching in most communities too brief, learning aides too sparse and false teaching too pervasive to permit more than a few to enter deeply his motivation and thought, but something similar might be said of Jesus and other great teachers. In the area of gifts, ignorance has been remarkably persistent.

BIBLICAL KNOWLEDGE

As we have seen, teachers are somewhat shadowy figures in the New Testament and their precise activities are difficult to assess, but teaching is a prominent feature of early Christian gatherings and the New Testament writers were conscious of passing on a corpus of Christian teaching which in turn was to be passed on to others.[138]

As in the Old Testament and later Judaism, so in the New Testament, teaching was aimed primarily at adults[139]—what E.A. Judge calls '...a kind of higher education in Christ, which is the complete development of men.'[140]

The knowledge gained should have been sufficient (a) not merely to enable the Christian to give a reason for the hope within (1 Pet. 3:15) but sufficient to understand local and world affairs as Paul, John and the prophets had done; (b) to be able to refute error and communicate the gospel; (c) to combat doubt—so frequently a by-product of poor teaching; (d) to develop and maintain a consistent Christian worldview; (e) to understand the emotions and learn how to direct them properly;[141] (f) to live effectively as a Christian in the Christian community and the wider world, and (g) to live, in short, in a way pleasing to God. Not all Christians would have been brought to the same level of learning and many favored ignorance, but there was placed before the community the desirability of aiming at a high standard. The intellectually less able might seem to have been at a disadvantage here, but there is nothing in the New Testament to suggest that teaching was restricted to formal academic instruction of a kind which the less able might have found beyond them since the principal emphasis was not on the acquisition of knowledge but on how to live a godly life—a theme common to both Old and New Testaments. Even if members did not excel in all these areas, the general development of individual gifts, combined with the sense of honor and worth which was due to all Christians from their fellows (Rom. 12:10; Phil. 2:3) should have helped to diminish any sense of failure resulting from a self-perceived deficiency in any single area. But where teaching functioned effectively all should have been able to achieve their potential. Also many new converts joined the church with very restricted Christian knowledge (Acts 1:6, 8:27-38, 18:24f and perhaps 19:1-3) so the teachers should have been busy. Their work was supplemented at various levels by the mutual ministry of instruction, which was encouraged by Paul and others, but the distinction between official and unofficial teaching was not clear-cut (Rom. 15:14; Col. 3:16; Heb. 5:12). Sometimes teaching may have been done by those with very limited teaching abilities.[142]

In some communities teachers were probably highly valued (Acts 17:11; Gal. 6:6; 1 Tim. 5:17; James 3:1) whereas in others, such as Corinth, the gift of teaching must have seemed drab in comparison with the more spectacular gift of prophecy.[143]

Prophecy, however, often extended to areas that were the province of other gifts such as teaching, encouraging and exhorting with the result 'that, at times, the distinction between these gifts must have seemed slight.'[144] Prophecy was exercised in the context of Christian gatherings but its regularity and frequency are unknown. There is little evidence to suggest that it was exalted to the detriment of teaching. Equally, there is little evidence to indicate that prophecy was, or was seen as, an alternative route to biblical knowledge, if we may judge by the meager content of the early Christian prophecies recorded in the New Testament.[145] At any rate, the anti-intellectualism so prevalent in our own day, particularly in England and America, and which has so often been a product of Christian non-thinking, does not seem characteristic of the church, at least up to the time of Justin Martyr and perhaps beyond.[146]

How was biblical and related material acquired? This is difficult to say. Since the starting point for Christian understanding was what God had done in Christ, an understanding of the Old Testament was desirable as a foundation although not adequate in itself (Luke 24:25-27; Acts 8:26-35; 1 Cor. 15:3f; 2 Tim. 2:15, 3:16f).[147] Although there is little direct evidence that Christians systematically read from the Old Testament in their meetings it is likely that they did So.[148] It may have been read aloud to the group (cf. 1 Tim. 4:13) and perhaps even learned by heart, although this is not stressed in the New Testament.[149] The Old Testament was not the only written material available. Paul's letters were to be read aloud in Christian gatherings (Col. 4:16; 1 Thes. 5:27) as perhaps were the writings of other worthies (Rev. 1:3; Justin 1 Apol 67; Eus HE 4:23:11) and some of these, possibly including expanded notes of apostolic speeches and events, were probably available in writing from the earliest days of the church.[150] Reading aloud before a group was a standard Jewish practice,[151] which was readily taken over by the church. Private reading also occurred in Jewish[152] and Christian circles (Acts 8:28; Aug Conf 6:3) but seems to have been less common and apparently was not seen in Christianity as a necessity for the majority, particularly as most Christians were probably illiterate. But enthusiastic readers might wish to read Christian material without the aid of a public reader. Wealthy converts might have slaves read to them. The early fathers stressed the need to read and understand the Scriptures but their exhortations may have been aimed primarily at those who were already well educated.[153]

Memorization was common as an educational technique with Jews and gentiles, not least because of the shortage of written materials.[154] The use of memorization techniques became common in the early church so that knowledge of Christian tradition was not necessarily dependent upon literacy.[155] Precise details of how these methods were used by the first Christian communities are lacking but techniques might include repetition, rote learning (not necessarily accompanied by understanding),[156] questions and answers, discussion and encouragement—all designed to help members to understand the meaning of Christian life and to assist the learner to change in accordance with what had been learned. Additionally, scriptural material might have been interpreted and applied to relevant issues or, following Paul, the group might have started with the problem and worked back to the Scriptures and subsequently developed principles of action.[157] No doubt in teaching and learning, as in other areas, the impress of founders and subsequent leaders caused the local churches of the 1st century to emphasize different subject areas and techniques. The activities of the Christian communities resemble, in some respects, those of the contemporary lecture room and philosophical school.[158]

Teachers may have worked consistently with the whole group or perhaps spent extra time with potential leaders, although Paul stressed that no aspect of Christian teaching was to be reserved for an élite (Col. 1:28). Even so, it would hardly have been surprising had Paul given extra time to the most responsive (just as Jesus spent extra time with Peter, James and John; and as the rabbis did with their most gifted pupils).[159] These might then have taken up positions of leadership in the local church or accompanied Paul on mission. Teaching 'on the job' may have been common, especially for potential leaders. Paul also emphasized his care for individual converts (Col. 1:28; 1 Thes. 2:11) and did so in connection with their instruction but precisely how this was done is not known.[160] The aim, at least, is clear: what Paul did for them initially, they were to do for one another subsequently (Col. 3:16; 1 Thes. 5:11, 14). Furthermore, teachers were to be reflections of Christ in their lives and work, thus becoming models fit for imitation by the congregation.[161]

There is no clear evidence in the New Testament of separate instruction for those awaiting baptism or for the newly converted aside from what might more accurately be termed evangelism (Acts 8:30-38, 16:27-33). Baptism and church membership followed immediately after conversion and any deficiencies in knowledge might be remedied afterwards. Separate instruction for intending members arose soon after the New Testament period but records are scanty before about 200AD. A fully developed catechism appeared during the 3rd and 4th centuries. For some catechumens such instruction might last years.[162]

Christian teachers do not emerge clearly as a distinct class in the New Testament. They are not necessarily to be identified with pastors although there was a close connection between teaching and pastoral care. Teaching may have been the duty of leaders who had other functions and all church members might teach on occasion (Rom. 15:4; Col. 3:16),[163] How many teachers were there in any given congregation? Some congregations appear to have had several teachers (Acts 13:1; 1 Tim. 5:17) and this could facilitate a multiform presentation of Christian truth and minimize the depressing possibility of becoming subject to the truth of one idea. But given the presence of several house churches in anyone town, each group may still have had only one teacher. Even in this case the possibility of variety existed through the practice of mutual ministries and the emergence of trainee teachers (1 Tim. 4: 14; 2 Tim. 1:6, 2:2)—the absence of which in mature congregations was a matter worthy of censure (Heb. 5:12). It may be that each house church had one or more elders and could thus function independently, but the house churches together in any given town would still be regarded as making up one congregation.[164]

There is no evidence to suggest that teachers divided groups on the basis of age or sex. The responsibility for the child's early education and, in particular, religious education lay with the parents. In this the church followed the pattern of Judaism and the ancient world generally.[165] No special arrangements seem to have been made for children by the early church. The Christian school was a long way off (around 372AD)—the Sunday school even more so.[166]

LIVING THE CHRISTIAN LIFE

In the writings of Paul and in early Christian literature generally, there is considerable emphasis on the Christian life lived in and before the world.[167] This is not distinct from the other aspects of Christian discipleship, all of which materially help to build life in the family and the church. The elements already discussed, such as worship, gifts and knowledge, enable human beings to retain and develop their humanity in personal relationships. They further help to maintain a biblical balance between individual and social concerns both inside and outside the Christian community. Christians can achieve these goals without being dominated by the individualism characteristic of Christian pietism and of modern society generally, especially the middle classes.[168]

Problems in day-to-day living force the Christian back to prayer, the Scriptures and the support of the group. The group provides encouragement, counsel, correction (Heb. 3:12f), the possibility of conversation, communal prayer, a guide to the interpretation of Scripture, knowledge and gifts—all of which help the Christian to become Christ-like and to tackle problems in a Christ-like manner. As God seldom comforts his people directly, the group becomes God's agent for the mediation of strength and comfort and should thus enable the Christian to live more effectively than would be possible in isolation.[169] Regular actions in and with the group reinforce Christian attitudes, enable appropriate behavior patterns to be internalized, develop Christian character and strengthen beliefs.[170] Face-to-face encounters increase the possibility of accurate self-understanding and self-identity and can frequently aid in the correction of emotional and psychological difficulties.[171] The ideal here is that truth is presented in the context of close personal relationships because this maximizes growth to maturity.[172] The group should thus be a tangible expression of the character of God and, in conjunction with the Christian family, was probably a significant factor in the early expansion of the church. Such groups provided a pattern of Christian living to challenge paganism and these spiritually self-sufficient and self-reproducing communities were ideally suited to survival in a hostile environment.[173] The point is underlined by the judgment of the secular psychologist and former President of the American Psychological Association, O. Hobart Mowrer, that 'the early Christian church was the most powerful therapeutic community that ever existed'.[174]

ENDNOTES

1. For thoughts on the nature of maturity see J.D. Carter, 'Maturity: Psychological and Biblical', *JPT*, II, 1974, 89-96; D .M. Wulff, *Psychology of Religion: Classic and Contemporary Views*, 1991, pp. 337, 582-586; R.W. Crapps, *An Introduction to Psychology of Religion*, 1986, pp. 355-369; W. Popkes, 'New Testament Principles of Wholeness', *EQ*, 64:4,1992,319-332

2. G. Lohfink, *Jesus and Community: The Social Dimension of Christian Faith*, 1985, p. 10; W. Horbury, 'The Twelve and the Phylarchs', *NTS*, 32, 1986, 503-527

3. E.J. Thomas and C.F. Fink, 'Effects of Group Size', *Psychological Bulletin*, 60, 1963, 371-377; M.E. Shaw, *Group Dynamics: The Psychology of Small Group Behaviour*, [2]1976, p. 156. J. Garnett suggests a maximum of 15 for a working group (*The Work Challenge: Leaders at Work*, [5]1988, pp. 22-24)

4. G.E. Wright, *The Biblical Doctrine of Man in Society*, 1954, p. 47 n2

5. R.W. Napier and M.K. Gershenfeld, *Groups: Theory and Experience*, [2]1981, p. 215; M.E. Shaw, *Group Dynamics*, pp. 222-225

6. G. Bilezikian, *Beyond Sex Roles*, [2]1991, p. 273 n14; M. Hayter, *The New Eve in Christ*, 1987, pp. 156-159; W. Neuer, *Man and Woman in Christian Perspective*, 1990, pp. 98f, 144, 152f, 173

7. J. Koenig, *New Testament Hospitality—Partnership with Strangers as Promise and Mission*, 1985, p. 33

8. J.W. Wenham, 'The Relatives of Jesus', *EQ*, 47, 1975, 6-15; R.J. Bauckham, *Jude and the Relatives ofJesus in the Early Church*, 1990, p. 18

9. R.W. Napier and M.K. Gershenfeld, *Groups*, p. 215

10. J. Neusner, *A Life of Yohanan Ben Zakkai Ca 1-80CE*, [2]1970, p. 97. The rabbinic school is not an exact parallel as the emphasis there was on learning rather than service (T.W. Manson, *The Teaching of Jesus*, [2]1935, pp. 239f; M. Hengel, *The Charismatic Leader and His Followers*, 1981, pp. 2, 53, 57, 80f)

11. J. Jeremias, *New Testament Theology*, I, 1971, p. 235; W. Schmithals, *The Office of Apostle in the Early Church*, 1969, pp. 53f, 227f

12. A.P. Hare, *Creativity in Small Groups*, 1982, pp. 144f; M.E. Shaw, *Group Dynamics*, pp. 156f

13. J. McLeish, W. Matheson and J Park, *The Psychology of the Learning Group*, 1973, pp. 113f; R.T. Stein and T. Heller, 'An Empirical Analysis of the Correlations Between Leadership Status and Participation Rates Reported in the Literature', *Journal of Personality and Social Psychology*, 37:11, 1979, 1993-2002

14. L. Morris, *The Gospel According to John*, 1972, p. 654; R.W. Napier and M.K. Gershenfeld, *Groups*, p. 216

15. See the discussions in M.J. Wilkins, *DJG*, p. 180; E.P. Blair, *IDB*, I, 359; A. Plummer, *DCG*, 1,172

16. A.P. Hare, *Handbook of Small Group Research*, [2]1976, p. 222; cf. D.G. Myers, *Social Psychology*, [3]1990, p. 298

17. B.W.M. Palmer, 'Dependence' in C.L. Mitton (ed), *The Social Sciences and the Churches*, 1972, pp. 32, 34

18. Andrew and Philip are a pair in Mk 3:18 but not in the parallel lists

19. A.P. Hare, *Small Group Research*, p. 226

20. R.F. Bales and E.F. Borgatta, 'Size of Group as a Factor in the Interaction Profile' in A.P. Hare, E.F. Borgatta and R.F. Bales (ed), *Small Groups: Studies in Social*

Interaction, [2]1965, pp. 500-502; E.J. Thomas and C.F. Fink, 'Group Size', 372-375; P.E. Slater, 'Contrasting Correlates of Group Size', Sociometry, 21, 1958,134f

21.   Num. 11:10-15; 2 Sam. 19:1-7; Job 3:3-26; Ps. 137:7-9; Jer. 20:7-18; Amos 4:1; Mark 5:30f; John 8:55, 11:49; Gal. 1:6, 3:1, 5:12; Rev. 2-3

22.   R.W. Napier and M.K. Gershenfeld, Groups, p. 217

23.   Taxes in Galilee were under the supervision of Herod Antipas and, therefore, the toll collectors responsible for them would probably not have been regarded as traitors in the service of Rome, as were their Judaean counterparts (J.R. Donahue, 'Tax Collectors and Sinners', CBQ, 33, 1971, 45f; O. Michel, TDNT, VIII, 102)

24.   J.R. Donahue, 'Tax Collectors', p. 51, referring to a later period

25.   mBK 10:1 with attached note in H. Danby, The Mishnah, 1933, p. 346

26.   J.R. Donahue, 'Tax Collectors', p. 52

27.   A.P. Hare, Handbook of Small Group Research, [2]1976, pp. 161-163; D.G. Myers, Social Psychology, 31990, pp. 504-506

28.   J. Jeremias, Jerusalem in the Time of Jesus, 1969, p. 311; A. Edersheim, The Life and Times of Jesus the Messiah, [3]1887, I, 517

29.   D.J. Hesselgrave, Communicating Christ Cross-Culturally, 1978, pp. 336-338,377f

30.   R.A. Guelich, Mark 1-8:26, 1989, p. 321; H.A. Snyder, The Community of the King, 1977, p. 124; B. Witherington III, The Christology of Jesus, 1990, p. 134

31.   Acts 1:15-26, 12:1f. On the possible replacement of James see R.A. Campbell, 'The Elders of the Jerusalem Church', JTS, 44, 1993, 517f; R.N. Longenecker, The Acts of the Apostles, EBC, 1981, IX, 266f; P.H. Menoud, 'The Additions to the Twelve Apostles According to the Book of Acts' in idem, Jesus Christ and the Faith, 1978, pp. 133-148

32.   D.C. Dunphy, The Primary Group: A Handbook for Analysis and Field Research, 1972, pp.24-27

33.   T.M. Mills, The Sociology of Small Groups, 1967, pp. 19, 111

34.   A.P. Hare, Handbook of Small Group Research, 1976, pp. 158-161; C.A. Insko and J. Schopler, Experimental Social Psychology, 1972, p. 503; D. Cartwright, 'The Nature of Group Cohesiveness' in D. Cartwright and A. Zander (eds), Group Dynamics: Research and Theory, [3]1968, pp. 104

35.   R.A. Baron and D. Byrne, Social Psychology: Understanding Human Interaction, [6]1991, p 443

36.   R.A. Baron and D. Byrne, Social Psychology, p. 443

37.   R.J. Banks, The Tyranny of Time, 1983, pp. 168-199; D.C. Dunphy, The Primary Group, 277; J.H. Neyrey, 'Ceremonies in Luke-Acts: The Case of Meals and Table Fellowship' in idem (ed), The Social World of Luke-Acts, 1991, p. 375

38.   W. Grundmann, TDNT, IV, 532; J.D.M. Derrett, Jesus' Audience: The Social and Psychological Environment in Which He Worked, 1973, pp. 38-45

39.   C.A. Insko and J. Schopler, Experimental Social Psychology, 1972, pp. 406

40.   O. Cullmann, Peter: Disciple, Apostle, Martyr, [2]1962, p. 32

41.   J. Morison, A Practical Commentary on the Gospel According to St Matthew, 1902, p. 155; W. Patrick, DCG, I, 104a

42.   DJG, p. 178

43.   K.H. Rengstorf, TDNT, IV, 428, 430; J. Lindblom, Prophecy in Ancient Israel, 1963, pp. 160-165; T.R. Hobbs, 2 Kings, 1985, pp. 25-27

44.   C.A. Insko and J. Schopler, Experimental Social Psychology, 1972, p. 407

45. L. Morris suggests that the emphasis on love in the New Testament may indicate a lack of love among believers (*Testaments of Love: A Study of Love in the Bible*, 1981, p. 227)

46. R.H. Lightfoot, *St. John's Gospel*, 1956 repr 1972, pp. 68-73

47. B.L. Melbourne, *Slow to Understand: The Disciples in Synoptic Perspective*, 1988, pp. 46f, 48, 61f, 77, *cf.* 159f. See also J. Dewey, 'Oral Methods of Structuring Narrative in Mark' in R.L. Eslinger (ed), *Intersections: Post-Critical Studies in Preaching*, 1994, pp. 35

48. A.P. Hare observes that 'The optimum size for a small discussion group may be five members' (*Creativity in Small Groups*, 1982, p. 142). L. Button thinks three or four may be better (*Discovery and Experience: A New Approach to Training, Group Work, and Teaching*, 1971, p. 122)

49. J. W. Oman, *DCG*, I, 814-816, 819-821; E. Schweizer, *Church Order in the New Testament*, 1961, pp. 122-124 (section 11f-i); C.F.D. Moule, 'The Individualism of the Fourth Gospel', *Nov T*, 5, 1962, 182-186

50. H.H. Rowley, *The Faith of Israel*, 1956, pp. 99-109; Th C. Vriezen, *An Outline of Old Testament Theology*, [2]1970, pp. 386f, 418-420

51. The 'celebration' meeting is sometimes given a biblical basis by reference to large gatherings in the Old Testament including, those in the Temple, particularly during the major feasts. Some aspects of Roman Catholic ritual may derive from Temple ritual (F.V. Filson, 'The Significance of the Temple in the Ancient Near East', *BA*, 7, 1944, 88). A. Cabaniss argues that Temple worship left a considerable mark upon early Christian worship (*Pattern in Early Christian Worship*, 1989, pp. 28-31, 41)

52. L. Morris, *The New Testament and the Jewish Lectionaries*, 1964, pp. 35-40; W.A. Meeks, *The First Urban Christians*, 1983, pp. 80f; R.J. Banks, *PIC*, pp. 111f

53. W. Schrage, *TDNT*, VII, 840f; D.E. Aune, 'Worship, Early Christian', *ABD*, VI, 979

54. I.H. Marshall, *The Acts of the Apostles*, 1980, pp. 83, 85f; R.J. Banks, *PIC*, pp. 110-112; T.W. Manson, *Ethics and the Gospel*, 1960, pp. 77-86; J.L. Gonzalez, *Faith and Wealth*, 1990, pp. 79-83; B. Capper, 'The Palestinian Cultural Context of Earliest Christian Community of Goods', *BAFCS*, IV, 323-356

55. R.P. Meye, *Jesus and the Twelve: Discipleship and Revelation in Mark's Gospel*, 1968, pp. 56f; C.K Barrett, *The Holy Spirit and the Gospel Tradition*, [2]1966, pp. 94-99; C.H. Dodd, 'Jesus as Teacher and Prophet' in G.K.A. Bell and D.A. Deissmann (eds), *Mysterium Christi: Christological Studies by British and German Theologians*, 1930, pp. 53-66; D. Hill, *New Testament Prophecy*, 1979, pp. 48-69; Matt. 16:13f, 23:29-31; Mark 1:22,6:14, 7:5; John 9:17

56. O.S. Rankin, 'The Extent of the Influence of the Synagogue Service Upon Christian Worship', *JJS*, 1, 1948, 30f

57. L.H. Marshall in J.G. Davies (ed), *A New Dictionary of Liturgy and Worship*, 1986, p. 389b; E.P. Sanders, *Judaism: Practice and Belief 63BCE-66CE*, 1992, pp. 196f; A.E. Millgram, *Jewish Worship*, 1971, pp. 289-319

58. J. Jeremias, *The Prayers of Jesus*, 1967, pp. 66-81; S. Safrai, *Compendia* I:2, 800f; S.S. Bartchy, 'Table Fellowship', *DJG*, pp. 796-800

59. Jewish attitudes to reward and punishment are discussed in E.E. Urbach, *The Sages: Their Concepts and Beliifs*, [2]1979, I, 436-444

60. H.H. Rowley, *The Faith of Israel*, 1956, pp. 103-116

61. *HJP*, II, 332; M. Hengel, *Judaism and Hellenism*, 1974, I, 82

62. F. Hauck, W. Kasch and E. Bammel, *TDNT*, VI, 323-326, 890; W.F. Albright and C.S. Mann, *Matthew*, 1971, p. 233; L.E. Keck, *IDBS*, pp. 672

63. W.L. Lane, *The Gospel According to Mark*, 1974, pp. 324f; R.H. Gundry, *Mark: A Commentary on His Apology for the Cross*, 1993, pp. 463f, 483f

64. Pharisees kept a watchful and influential eye on some (perhaps all) synagogues but the precise extent of this influence is disputed. See the discussions in A.J. Saldarini, *Pharisees, Scribes and Sadducees*, 1989, pp. 52, 193, 196f; E.P. Sanders, *Jewish Law from Jesus to the Mishnah*, 1990, p. 80; idem, *Judaism: Practice and Belief 63BCE-66CE*, 1992, p. 398; M. Hengel and R. Deines, 'E.P. Sanders "Common Judaism," Jesus and the Pharisees', *JTS*, 46:1,1995, 32-35,60-62; S. Mason, 'Pharisaic Dominance Before 70CE and the Gospels' Hypocrisy Charge' (Matt. 23:2-3), *HTR*, 83:4, 1990, 363-371

65. D.A. Carson, 'The Jewish Leaders in Matthew's Gospel: A Reappraisal', *JETS*, 25, 1982, 161-174; idem, *Matthew*, EBC, 1984, VIII, passim; R.T. France, *Matthew: Evangelist and Teacher*, 1989, pp. 218-223, 238-241; B. Witherington III, *The Christology of Jesus*, 1990, pp. 59-63; S. Mason, 'Pharisaic Dominance', 371-381

66. On the duration of Jesus' ministry see H.W. Hoehner, *Chronological Aspects of the Life if Christ*, 1977, pp. 45-63

67. I take all thirteen epistles in the New Testament from Romans to Philemon to be by Paul.

68. P.H. Davids, *The Epistle of James*, 1982, pp. 28-34

69. J.V. Langrnead Casserley, *Christian Community*, 1960, pp. 82-85

70. D.J. Tidball, *Skilful Shepherds*, 1986, pp. 135-143

71. G. Lohfink, *Jesus and Community: The Social Dimension of Christian Faith*, 1985, pp. 102-106; K. Barth, *Church Dogmatics*, 1958, IV:2, 626f; R.J. Banks, *PIC*, pp. 71f. Note that Paul's concept of the maturity of the individual was very different from the corresponding Greek concept (E.A. Judge, 'St Paul as a Radical Critic of Society', *Interchange*, 16, 1974, 193-195).

72. G.E. Wright, *The Biblical Doctrine of Man in Society*, 1954, pp. 18-29,46-52,96-101; Th C. Vriezen, *An Outline of Old Testament Theology*, [2]1970, pp. 382-388

73. A.J. Malherbe, '"Pastoral Care" in the Thessalonian Church', *NTS*, 36, 1990, 375-391; idem, *Paul and the Thessalonians*, 1987, pp. 81-88

74. M.M.B. Turner, 'Spiritual Gifts Then and Now', *VE*, 15, 1985, 33; R.J. Banks, *PIC*, p. 100; L.P. Barnes, 'Miracles, Charismata and Benjamin B. Warfield', *EQ*, 67:3, 1995, 224f

75. L.H. Marshall, 'How Far Did the Early Christians Worship God?', *Churchman*, 99:3, 1985, 226; D.G. Peterson, *Engaging with God: A Biblical Theology of Worship*, 1992, p. 221

76. The Lord's Supper (1 Cor. 11:23-34) is mentioned separately from the meeting of 1 Cor 14:23-40 and may have been held separately at Corinth and elsewhere— and in a variety of forms. The evidence is insufficient to be certain. See further L. Goppelt, *Apostolic and Post-Apostolic Times*, 1970, pp. 210-212 and I.H. Marshall, *Last Supper and Lord's Supper*, 1980, pp. 144f (suggesting separate meetings); O. Cullinann, *Early Christian Worship*, 1953, pp. 26-30 (suggesting one meeting); G. Bornkamm, *Early Christian Experience*, 1969, p. 176 n2 and R. Bultmann, *Theology of the New Testament*, 1952, I, 144f (suggesting there is no fixed rule)

77. G.D. Fee, *The First Epistle to the Corinthians*, 1987, pp. 690f; D.A. Carson,

Showing the Spirit: A Theological Exposition of 1 Corinthians 12-14, 1987, pp. 135f

78. G.D. Fee, *Corinthians*, p. 690; G. Delling, *Worship in the New Testament*, 1962, p. 42; R.A. Campbell, *The Elders: Seniority within Earliest Christianity*, 1994, pp. 105f

79. The latter verses refer to exhortation at the Christian gathering but the former verse is unspecific.

80. Where these mutual activities are to be practiced is unspecified but there is no obvious reason for excluding all of them from the regular gatherings of the church. See further G. Lohfink, *Jesus and Community*, pp. 99-106; J.R. Michaels, *1 Peter*, 1988, pp. 244, 250; W.A. Grudem, *1 Peter*, 1988, p. 175; P.H. Davids, *The First Epistle of Peter*, 1990, pp. 157, 161f; cf. J.H. Elliott, *A Home for the Homeless*, 1981, pp. 64, 69, 145-148, 203

81. J.D.G. Dunn, 'The Responsible Congregation (1 Co 14, 26-40)' in L. De Lorenzi (ed), *Charisma and Agape*, 1983, pp. 235f

82. G.D. Fee, *Corinthians*, p. 589; W.A. Grudem, *1 Peter*, p. 175; M.M.B. Turner, 'Spiritual Gifts', 31f; C.E.B. Cranfield, *Commentary on the Epistle to the Romans*, 1983, II, 619; H.H. Esser, *NIDNTT*, II, 121f

83. R.J. Banks, *PIC*, p. 98

84. E. Schweizer, *Neotestamentica*, 1963, p. 335

85. R. MacMullen, *Roman Social Relations: 50BC to AD284*, 1974, pp. 32-38, 92f; G. Hamel, *Poverty and Charity in Roman Palestine, First Three Centuries CE*, 1990; D.A Fiensy, *The Social History of Palestine in the Herodian Period*, 1991, pp. 104f, 167f; D.E. Oakman, *Jesus and the Economic Questions of His Day*, 1986, pp. 18,57-80

86. *ERE*, IX, 839a

87. A. Harnack, *Bible Reading in the Early Church*, 1912, pp. 69f

88. H. Ridderbos, *Paul: An Outline of His Theology*, 1975, pp. 470-473; S.L. Greenslade, *Shepherding the Flock*, 1967, pp. 70-105; D.G. Peterson, 'The Ministry of Encouragement' in P.T. O'Brien and D.G. Peterson (eds), *God Who is Rich in Mercy*, 1986, pp. 238, 240-246

89. R.J. Banks, *PIC*, pp. 139-141; R. Allen, *Missionary Methods: St Paul's or Ours?*, 1912 repr 1962, pp. 151f; J.D.G. Dunn, *Unity and Diversity in the New Testament*, [2]1990, pp. 113f; G. Bilezikian, *Beyond Sex Roles*, [2]1991, pp. 104-118

90. L.A. Richards, *A New Face for the Church*, 1970, pp. 122-127; E. Schweizer, *Church Order in the New Testament*, 1961, pp. 211f (section 26a)

91. Examples of consensus in action are given in A.P. Hare, *Creativity in Small Groups*, 1982, pp. 148f, 163-174; R.J. and J. Banks, *The Home Church*, 1986, pp. 143-146; L. Barrett, *Building the House Church*, 1986, pp. 104-107

92. E. Schweizer, *Church Order*, p. 147 (section 16c)

93. Rom. 14:19, 15:14; 1 Cor. 12:7,25, 14:1-19,26; Gal. 5:13, 6:2; Eph. 4:15, 25f, 29, 32, 5:19-21; Phil. 2:1; Col. 3:13,16; 1 Thes. 4:9, 18, 5:11, 14; similarly Heb. 3:13, 5:12, 10:24f; James 5:19f; 1 Pet. 4:10, 5:5; James adds mutual confession and intercession to the list; James 5:16, cf. Acts 19:18: G. Bornkamm, *Early Christian Experience*, 1969, p. 163; J.T. McNeill, *A History of the Cure of Souls*, 1951 repr 1977, pp. 85-87; R.J. Banks, *PIC*, pp. 139-141, 150f

94. J.T. McNeill, *Cure of Souls*, pp. 86f

95. J.B. Skemp, *The Greeks and the Gospel*, 1964, pp. 28-36

96. S. Angus, *The Environment of Early Christianity*, Duckworth (Gerald) & Co. Ltd., 1914, pp. 109f, 111

97. K.N. Giles, *Patterns of Ministry Among the First Christians*, 1989, pp. 29-40

98. H. von Campenhausen, *Ecclesiastical Authority and Spiritual Power in the Church of the First Three Centuries*, 1969, p. 66

99. M.A. Thung, *The Precarious Organisation: Sociological Explorations of the Church's Mission and Structure*, 1976, p. 259

100. The account of the appointment of elders at several churches of Pauline foundation (Acts 14:23) is commonly regarded as contrary to the picture presented in the undisputed Pauline epistles. This is not necessarily so. Leadership of some kind is implied in 1 Cor 16:15-18, Phil 1:1 and 1 Thess 5:12. The precise functions of these leaders and the elders of Acts 14:23 are unknown. We are dealing here with first generation leaders and their roles may not have been clearly defined. The use of the term *presbuteros* in Acts 14:23 need not imply all that was intended in its later use and patterns of leadership probably varied to suit local needs. See further C.A. Wanamaker, *The Epistles to the Thessalonians*, 1990, pp. 191-194; D. Wenham, 'The Paulinism of Acts Again: Two Historical Clues in 1 Thessalonians', *Themelios*, 13:2, 1988, 54f; A.L. Chapple, *Local Leadership in the Pauline Churches: Theological and Social Factors in its Development: A Study Based on 1 Thessalonians, 1 Corinthians and Philippians*, PhD Thesis (Durham University), 1984, pp. 43, 45, 391-393; C.K. Barrett, *Church, Ministry and Sacraments in the New Testament*, 1985, pp. 32-38, 52; R.A. Campbell, *The Elders: Seniority Within Earliest Christianity*, 1994, pp. 165-167

101. C. Buchanan, *Leading Worship*, 1981, pp. 4-7; P. Bradshaw, *Liturgical Presidency in the Early Church*, 1983, pp. 6-8; R.Y.K. Fung, 'Charismatic Versus Organized Ministry?', *EQ*, 52,1980,195-214; K.N. Giles, *Patterns of Ministry*, pp. 14-19

102. For example, in Exod. 3:7-10 the deliverance from Egypt is both the work of God (v. 8) and of Moses (v. 10)

103. E. Schweizer, 'Worship in the New Testament', *Reformed and Presbyterian World*, 24, 1957,205, *cf.* 199

104. On the synagogue as a center of instruction more than worship, particularly prior to AD70 see L. Morris, *The New Testament and the Jewish Lectionaries*, 1964, pp. 35f; *HJP*, II, 424f; J.W. Bowker, 'Speeches in Acts', *NTS*, 14, 1967,97f

105. R.J. Banks, *PIC*, pp. 91-93; I.H. Marshall, 'How Far Did the Early Christians Worship God?', *Churchman*, 99:3, 1985,216-229; D.G. Peterson, *Engaging with God: A Biblical Theology if Worship*, 1992, pp. 150f, 195f, 214, 219-221, 247f; P.T. O'Brien, 'Church', *DPL*, p. 130

106. See the discussion in B. Holmberg, *Paul and Power*, 1978, pp. 99-102, 112f

107. H.N. Ridderbos, P*aul: An Outline of His Theology*, 1975, p. 473; R.L. Saucy, *The Church in God's Program*, 1972, pp. 121f

108. Rom. 12:10; 1 Cor. 12:12-27; Eph. 5:21; Col. 3:16; and, cf. Poly *Phil* 10:2 (R.J. Banks, 'The Early Church As a Caring Community and Some Implications for Social Work Today', *Interchange*, 30, 1982, 42f; G.C. Berkouwer, *The Church*, 1976, pp. 214f). Mutual dependence, particularly at Christian meetings, soon became unpopular (Ign *Mag* 4:1; *Trall* 2:2: W.R. Schoedel, *Ignatius of Antioch*, 1985, pp. 109, 141; G. Bornkamm, *TDNT*, VI, 674f; cf. B.E. Bowe, *A Church in Crisis*, 1988, pp. 110f)

109. Exemption for leaders is, however, argued for by S.B. Clark, *Man and Woman in Christ*, 1980, pp. 74-76; W. Neuer, *Man and Woman in Christian Perspective*,

1990, p. 126. Against this see G. Bilezikian, *Beyond Sex Roles*, [2]1991, pp. 153-171, 189-193; M. Barth, *Ephesians 4-6,*1974, pp. 609-611, 708-715

110. New Testament usage of *hupotasso* is discussed in M. Barth, *Ephesians*, p. 710; G. Delling, *TDNT*, VIII, 41-45

111. E.E. Ellis 'The Role of the Christian Prophet in Acts' in W. W. Gasque and R.P. Martin (eds), *Apostolic History and the Gospel,* Carlisle, Paternoster Press 1970, p. 66

112. E. Schweizer, *Church Order in the New Testament*, 1961, section 17d (p. 154), 16c (p. 148), *cf.* 7i (p. 99)

113. I.H. Marshall, *1 and 2 Thessalonians*, 1983, pp. 147f; L. Coenen, *NIDNTT*, I, 197

114. J.D.G. Dunn, *Romans 9-16,*1988, p. 731; E. Best, *A Commentary on the First and Second Epistles to the Thessalonians*, 1972, pp. 224f

115. J.D.G. Dunn, *Romans 9-16*, p. 731; C.E.B. Cranfield, *A Critical and Exegetical Commentary on the Epistle to the Romans*, II, 1983, 626f; C.A. Wanamaker, *Thessalonians*, pp. 192f

116. I.H. Marshall, *1 and 2 Thessalonians*, p. 148; F.F. Bruce, *1 and 2 Thessalonians*, 1982, p. 119; B. Reicke, *TDNT*, VI, 701-703

117. D. Guthrie, *The Pastoral Epistles*, 1990, p. 117; R. St J. Parry, *The Pastoral Epistles*, 1920, p.34.

118. G.W. Knight III, *The Pastoral Epistles*, 1992, pp. 231f; *cf.* B. Reicke, *TDNT*, VI, 702

119. H.W. Beyer, *TDNT*, III, 1036

120. C. Brown, *NIDNTT*, I, Carlisle, Paternoster Press 1986

121. E. Hatch, *The Organization of the Early Christian Churches*, 1892, pp. 121f, *cf.* pp. 143-168; P. Beasley-Murray, 'Ordination in the New Testament' in idem (ed), *Anyone for Ordination?*, 1993, pp. 4f, 6, 12f

122. W.A. Meeks, *The First Urban Christians: The Social World of the Apostle Paul*, 1983, pp. 78, 118f, 134; C.A. Wanamaker, *Thessalonians*, pp. 193-195; A.D. Clarke, *Secular and Christian Leadership in Corinth*, 1993; R.A. Campbell, *The Elders*, pp. 117f, 126f

123. P.H. Davids, 71, *First Epistle of Peter*, Eerdmans Publishing Co., USA 1990, pp. 180f

124. J.N.D. Kelly, *The Epistles of Peter and of Jude*, 1976, p. 203

125. Eph. 4:11-13: L.O. Richards and C. Hoeldtke, *A Theology of Church Leadership*, 1980, p. 53, *cf.* J. Garnett, *The Work Challenge: Leaders at Work*, [5]1988, p. 11

126. *m Ohol* 1:8: J. Preuss, *Biblical and Talmudic Medicine*, 1911, *ET*, 1978, pp. 60f. Paul shows some familiarity with ancient physiology at Eph. 4:16 and Col. 2:19.

127. E.F. Scott, *Man and Society in the New Testament*, 1946, p. 124

128. O. O'Donovan, *Resurrection and Moral Order: An Outline for Evangelical Ethics*, 1986, p. 222

129. E.K. Simpson and F.F. Bruce, *Commentary on the Epistles to the Ephesians and the Colossians*, 1957, p. 95

130. N. Drazin, *History of Jewish Education from 515BCE to 220CE*, 1940, pp. 14f; W. Barclay, *Educational Ideals in tihe Ancient World*, 1959, pp. 100-102; H.I. Marrou, *A History of Education in Antiquity*, 1956, p. 191; K.R. Bradley, *Discovering the Roman Family: Studies in Roman Social History*, 1991 , pp. 106-117

131. D.S. Gilliland, *Pauline Theology and Mission Practice*, 1983, pp. 214-222

132. G. Hodgson, *Primitive Christian Education*, 1906, pp. 39-44; L. Millar, *Christian Education in the First Four Centuries*, 1946, pp. 16-18; H.H. Rowdon, 'Theological Education in Historical Perspective', *VE*, 7, 1971, 75-87

133. G.F. Hawthorne, *Philippians*, 1983, pp. 159-162; P.T. O'Brien, *The Epistle to the Philippians*, 1991, pp. 444-450, 510f

134. B. Gerhardsson, *Memory and Manuscript*, 1961, pp. 184-187; D.L. Clark, *Rhetoric in Greco-Roman Education*, 1957, pp. 144-176; A.J. Malherbe, *Paul and the Thessalonians*, 1987, pp. 52-60

135. A.L. Chapple, *Local Leadership in the Pauline Churches*, p. 184. Given that Paul exercised considerable influence over the churches of his foundation even after he had left them, truly autonomous leadership could hardly emerge until after Paul's death (K.N. Giles, *Patterns of Ministry*, pp. 30f).

136. A.P. Hare, *Handbook of Small Group Research*, [2]1976, pp. 221, 341; J. Rogers, *Adults Learning*, [3]1989, pp. 82f; D. Legge, 'Discussion Methods' in M.D. Stephens and G.W. Roderick (eds), *Teaching Techniques in Adult Education*, 1971, p. 83

137. F.C. Burkitt, 'The Debt of Christianity to Judaism' in E.R. Bevan and C. Singer (eds), *The Legacy of Israel*, 1928, p. 76; F.F. Bruce, *Paul: Apostle of the Free Spirit*, 1977, pp. 465-467; M.F. Wiles, *The Divine Apostle: The Interpretation of St Paul's Epistles in the Early Church*, 1967, pp. 3f, 132-139

138. M.E. Boring, *Sayings of the Risen Jesus: Christian Prophecy in the Synoptic Tradition*, 1982, pp. 78-80; J.N.D. Kelly, *Early Christian Creeds*, [3]1972, pp. 6-13; C. Brown, *NIDNTT*, III, 61f

139. I.M. Goldman, *Lifelong Learning Among Jews: Adult Education in Judaism from Biblical Times to the Twentieth Century*, 1975, pp. 1-5, 11,43, 69f

140. E.A. Judge, 'The Conflict of Educational Aims in New Testament Thought', *JCE*, 9, 1966, 35

141. R.P. Philipchalk, *Psychology and Christianity: An Introduction to Controversial Issues*, [2]1988, pp. 112-118; J.M. Frame, *The Doctrine of the Knowledge of God*, 1987, pp. 335-340; P.D. Meier et al, *Introduction to Psychology and Counseling: Christian Perspectives and Applications*, [2]1991, pp. 73-84; D.M. Lloyd-Jones, *Spiritual Depression: Its Causes and Cure*, 1965

142. W.A. Grudem, *The Gift of Prophecy in the New Testament and Today*, 1988, p. 207

143. A.C. McGiffert, *A History of Christianity in the Apostolic Age*, 1897, p. 530

144. D. Hill, *New Testament Prophecy*, 1979, pp. 129f; E.E. Ellis, 'The Role of the Christian Prophet in Acts' in W.W. Gasque and R.P. Martin (eds), *Apostolic History and the Gospel*, 1970, pp. 58f, 62-64, 66; W.A. Grudem, *Gift of Prophecy*, p. 152, cf. p. 166; J.D.G. Dunn, *Romans 9-16*, 1988, p. 729

145. W.A. Grudem, *Gift of Prophecy*, pp. 153f, 160f, 166

146. A. Harnack, *Bible Reading*, pp. 62f, 130-134; R. Hofstadter, *Anti-Intellectualism in American Life*, 1964, pp. 3-141; M.A. Noll, *The Scandal of the Evangelical Mind*, 1994. 1 Thes. 4:9 and 1 John 2:27 do not necessarily amount to the rejection of human teachers (E. Best, *The First and Second Epistles to the Thessalonians*, 1972, pp. 172f; I.H. Marshall, *The Epistles of John*, 1978, pp. 162f; S.S. Smalley, *1,2,3 John*, 1984, p. 125)

147. C.F.D. Moule, *Worship in the New Testament*, 1977, p. 4

148. J.A. Lamb, 'The Place of the Bible in the Liturgy', *CHB*, 1970, I, 564-566

149. C.F.D. Moule, *The Birth of tlhe New Testament*, [3]1981, p. 241; R. Riesner, 'Jesus as Preacher and Teacher' in H. Wansbrough (c d), *Jesus and the Oral Gospel*

Tradition, 1991, pp. 203-208

150. C.P. Thiede, *Simon Peter: From Galilee to Rome*, 1986, p. 109; E.E. Ellis, 'New Directions in Form Criticism' in G. Strecker (ed), *Jesus Christus in Historie und Theologie*, 1975, pp. 304-309; D. Guthrie, *New Testament Introduction*, [4]1990, pp. 1034f; G. Kennedy, 'Classical and Christian Source Criticism' in W.O. Walker, Jr (ed), *The Relationships Among the Gospels*, 1978, pp. 130f, 136, *cf.* Pliny; Ep 6: 16:10; Eus *HE* 6:36:1.

151. B. Gerhardsson, *Memory and Manuscript*, 1961, pp. 165f; C. Perrot, 'The Reading of the Bible in the Ancient Synagogue', *Compendia* II:1, 1988, 149; H.T. Strack and G. Sternberger, *Introduction to the Talmud and Midrash*, 1991, pp. 10f

152. B. Gerhardsson, *Memory and Manuscript*, p. 166

153. A. Harnack, *Bible Reading*, pp. 53-70; S.L. Greenslade in *CHB*, 1963, III, 489-491; W.V. Harris, *Ancient Literacy*, 1989, pp. 221, 304f, 319-322

154. E. Ebner, *Elementary Education in Anciet Israel During the Tannaitic Period* (10-220CE), 1956, pp. 90-93; B. Gerhardsson, *Memory and Manuscript*, pp. 62-65, 123-127, 164-166, 203; C.L. Blomberg, *Interpreting the Parables*, 1990, pp. 95-97; S. F. Bonner, *Education in Ancient Rome*, 1977, pp. 81, 177, 212, 262, 330; *cf.* K.E. Bailey, 'Middle Eastern Oral Tradition and the Synoptic Gospels', *Exp T*, 106, 1995, 363-367; idem, 'Informal Controlled Oral Tradition and the Synoptic Gospels', *AJT*, 5:1, 1991, 34-54

155. A. Harnack, *Bible Reading*, pp. 83f, 122, 125f; W.V. Harris, *Ancient Literacy*, p. 301; C.L. Blomberg, *The Historical Reliability of the Gospels*, 1987, pp. 27f; R.S. Kraemer, *Her Share of the Blessings*, 1992, pp. 144f

156. In Hellenistic and rabbinic schools it was standard practice to memorize a text before understanding it (B. Gerhardsson, *Memory and Manuscript*, pp. 126t)

157. R.J. Banks, 'The Early Church as a Caring Community and Some Implications for Social Work Today', *Interchange*, 30, 1982, 45

158. W. Jaeger, *Early Christianity and Greek Paideia*, 1962, pp. 29-32; W.A. Meeks, *The First Urban Christians*, 1983, pp. 81-84; S. Mason, 'Chief Priests, Sadducees, Pharisees and Sanhedrin in Acts', *BAFCS*, IV, 130-156

159. N. Drazin, History of Jewish Education from 515BCE to 220CE, 1940, pp. 40f

160. Later Jewish teachers gave their pupils individual attention and Ignatius of Antioch recommended dealing with Christians on an individual or 'by name' basis (E. Ebner, *Elementary Education*, p. 76; Ign *Ep* to *Poly* 4:2: W.R. Schoedel, *Ignatius of Antioch*, 1985, p. 270.

161. K.N. Giles, 'Teachers and Teaching in the Church', Part 2: *JCE* Papers 71, July 1981, 54f

162. A. Hamman, 'Catechumen, Catechumenate', *EEC*, I, 151f; S.L. Greenslade, *Shepherding the Flock*, 1967, pp. 53-70; C.F.D. Moule, *The Birth of the New Testament*, [3]1981, pp. 179, 181-186

163. K.N. Giles, *Patterns of Ministry*, pp. 111-118

164. G.S.R. Cox, 'The Emerging Organization of the Church in the New Testament and the Limitations Imposed Thereon', *EQ*, 38, 1966, 35f; A.J. Malherbe, *Social Aspects of Early Christianity*, 1983, p. 101; Justin Martyr 1 *Apol* 67: G.T. Purves, *The Testimony of Justin Martyr to Early Christianity*, 1888, p. 261; *cf.* K.N. Giles, *Patterns of Ministry*, p. 40

165. E.A. Judge, 'The Conflict of Educational Aims in New Testament Thought', *JCE*, 9, 1966, 43f; W. Barclay, *Educational Ideals in the Ancient World*, 1959, pp. 14-17,

234-238; H.I. Marrou, *A History of Education in Antiquity*, 1956, p. 143
166. H.I. Marrou, *Education*, pp. 325f
167. Matt. 5:16; 1 Cor. 10:23-33, 14:23-25; 2 Cor. 8:20f; Phil. 2:15; 1 Thes. 4:12; 1 Tim. 6:1; Titus 2:8; 1 Pet. 2:12-15, 3:1f,16; 2 Pet. 2:1f; 2 *Clem* 13:1-4; Ign *Eph* 10:1-3; *Trall* 8:2; Poly *Phil* 10:2f
168. G.E. Wright, *The Biblical Doctrine of Man in Society*, 1954, pp. 21, 47, 51; J.A. Walter, *A Long Way from Home*, 1979, pp. 89-102; idem, *The Human Home*, 1982, pp. 36-56
169. O. Schmitz and G. Stahlin, *TDNT*, V, 790, 792, 797-799, 822f; R.J. Banks, *PIC*, pp.91-93
170. D.G. Myers, 'Social Psychology and Christian Faith' in M.A. Jeeves (ed), *Behavioural Sciences: A Christian Perspective*, 1984, pp. 103-113; B. Mitchell, *The Justification of Religious Belief*, 1973, pp. 130f
171. L.J. Crabb, *Effective Biblical Counseling*, 1977, pp. 163-165; M. and D. Bobgan, *Psychoheresy: The Psychological Seduction of Christianity*, 1987, pp. 169-171, 182-186, 224
172. L.J. Crabb and D. Allender, *Encouragement*, 1986, pp. 83-91; L.O. Richards, *Expository Dictionary of Bible Words*, 1988, pp. 589f, 592
173. W. Burkert, *Ancient Mystery Cults*, 1987, pp. 51-53
174. Quoted in R.F. Hurding, *Roots and Shoots: A Guide to Counselling and Psychotherapy*, London, Hodder & Stoughton Ltd., 1986, pp. 301f

4 Interim Conclusion

Having examined the biblical material relating to our theme, it may be useful to summarize the results so far obtained. In this essay, the sermon has been defined as follows: a speech, essentially concerned with biblical, ethical and related material, designed to increase understanding and promote godly living among the listening congregation, delivered by one in good standing with the local community of God's people and addressed primarily to the faithful in the context of their own gatherings. Such sermons occur in the Old Testament, the New Testament and the sub-apostolic literature in the context of special occasions or in order to deal with specific problems. But there is no evidence to suggest that such sermons were common.

The regular sermon, as used today, is one of a series of sermons which takes place at most of the major meetings of the whole local church. The regular sermon cannot be detected in the Judaism of the Old Testament, the ministry of Jesus, the life of the primitive church or the church of the apostolic fathers. We shall discover evidence for it only as the church came increasingly under the influence of a variety of non-Christian ideas from the surrounding culture, frequently ideas which, like the sermon, were inimical to New Testament practice. The regular sermon was common by the 3rd century and became the norm by the fourth, taking its place among a wide variety of ecclesiastical practices which owed little to the teaching, patterns and principles of the New Testament. Many of these practices continue to this day as wide sections of the church remain imprisoned by the limitations of their forbears.

In New Testament times spiritual growth was achieved by a variety of means, all designed to help produce mature Christians in mature Christian communities. There is nothing to suggest that these means included the regular sermon.

If we acknowledge that the regular sermon has no biblical basis, that it utilizes pagan methods hostile to New Testament practice and that it appears to have had no part in early Christian growth, we are forced to ask how the use of the regular sermon today can be justified. One answer would be tradition. But, as we have seen, behind that tradition lies an even older tradition, which knows nothing of regular sermons. This renders the argument from tradition difficult, if not untenable. A better approach might be to rely on purely pragmatic considerations: if the sermon 'works' we may possibly conclude that the Holy Spirit is using an old method of questionable origin in a new and effective way.

The next chapter will therefore be devoted to estimating the value of the regular sermon in developing maturity today.

Sermon and the Quest for Maturity

Our analysis of the general means of achieving spiritual maturity in the New Testament did not touch upon the regular sermon as a necessary ingredient for it does not appear in that light. We now approach the problem from a different angle by trying to assess the current role of the regular sermon in achieving these aims today.

The substance of the present chapter is based upon the material cited in the endnotes supplemented by my own knowledge derived from working in and observing a wide range of English churches, particularly Anglican, Baptist and Methodist.

We shall refer to a variety of defects in church life today. Some readers may believe that their churches lack most of the faults outlined below. May it often be so. Two comments are in order. First, there is no suggestion here that *every* church exhibits *all* the defects listed below—only that such defects are common in English churches as a whole. Second, notwithstanding the self-critical tendencies of both the Old and New Testaments, many English Christians show little critical understanding concerning the traditions of their own Christian communion. I hope that what follows may stimulate greater awareness.

SERMONS IN RELATION TO WORSHIP, PARTICIPATION AND MUTUAL MINISTRIES

Regular sermons do not, in theory, preclude audience participation, particularly before and after the sermon. But in practice such participation is almost non-existent aside from Pentecostal circles and Black preaching, except for the occasional 'Amen' or other reinforcing response.[1] Christian liturgies may also tend to repress participation and the growth of community.[2]

The structure of the church building is similarly seldom conducive to any fellowship save that between God and the congregation via the leader. Even the Lord's Supper has been reduced in most churches to a one-sided and formal activity. This contrasts sharply with what appears to be the original form which was celebrated in the context of an ordinary shared meal involving the mutual fellowship of believers in a Christian home.[3] Mutual ministry today may exist in prayer and song but is often restricted by the structure and is usually a secondary consideration. As R.J. Banks has pointed out:

> The concentration of local church activities around a large central service, generally formal in character, and around other intermediate-sized organizations defined according to age, *gender* and interest, means that the possibility of small, enduring inter-generational and *gender*-mixed groups, in which the members are fully committed to each others' welfare and openly sharing their abilities with one another, either does not exist or is low down the scale of priorities... The related problem in churches today stems from the influence of attitudes derived from the Anglo-Saxon cultural ethos, according to which private matters are not the concern of others, not even one's fellow Christians, or stemming from the Pietist-Evangelical outlook which encourages openness at the so-called 'spiritual' level, but not in other aspects of one's life, leads to a contraction in Christians' vision of community life and in the responsibility they take for one another.[4]

CONSEQUENCES OF IMPAIRED PARTICIPATION

If Christians cannot have real fellowship in their meetings then it is likely that Christian beliefs and activities will be distorted and that life as a whole will suffer. Here are three examples of the problems, which occur, I suggest, as a combined result of inadequate fellowship and poor teaching.

A. When church life is particularly divisive or poverty stricken and centered on large-scale formal church building-based meetings, without the support of small-scale activities, the *personal problems of church members*, which ought to be and can be solved, are not solved. The problem is worsened when the clergy create a distance between themselves and the congregation,[5] discourage feedback and allow people to think that answers to their problems will come principally via the sermon.[6] In some cases, the church not only fails to help the troubled but can create problems in those who were previously without them. Typical of such problems are false guilt, depression, frustration, stress and alienation. Even maintaining one's own faith becomes more difficult in the absence of warm fellowship. This social dimension of belief has been sadly neglected by the church.[7] J.M. Barnett maintains that:

Most Christians today seem to have little sense of being an integral and important part of a community—a caring, loving family—which needs each one in all of his or her uniqueness to be whole. This means among much else that far fewer people are actively participating in the Church's work. Much of the Church's ministry goes undone. This lack of community also is probably the principal cause for the high rate of dropouts among adult converts experienced by the major churches in America in recent times.[8]

B. If Christians do not develop a sense of community in a church context then *they are unlikely to work together outside their own meetings* aside from church-arranged activities. Alan Storkey argues that English Christians, especially those from the middle class, tend to live individualist, conformist, home-centered, privatized lives[9] and find it difficult to act Christianly outside the context of the local church in any but an individual capacity. He says:

For example, it is assumed that Christ's precept, 'You are the salt of the earth...' is to be taken individualistically. It talks of the Christian in industry, politics, the teaching profession, the trade union or elsewhere as an *individual*. To suggest that Christians act together in industry, housing, banking or any other sociological economic activity is to talk of something strange. Although, for example, the letters of Peter, Paul and John are full of exhortations about various forms of Christian communal activity, this is still seen as something that is mildly heretical. Yet, Christians supported this individualism in a society where, outside marriage and family life, nearly all-important decisions are made within corporate or institutional structures. To approach these structures individualistically is to be automatically ineffective, to fail to be salting salt. The individual manager rarely touches company policy, the individual Christian MP depends on the party and effects nothing of importance, and the single Christian teacher often finds what he teaches compromised by others on the staff. If this explanation has validity, and if the pattern is both unbiblical and ineffective, then the obvious conclusion is that we should break away from it, and Christians should learn to work, pray and think together in all these so called secular situations.

After considering the possibility of establishing a wide range of Christian institutions, Storkey concludes:

The alternative to this kind of corporate action is sobering. Without this kind of development it is inevitable that many Christians will live essentially secular and humanist lives for most of the week. In many important ways their lives will be compromised by non-Christian practices and policy. When they shed their secular coats at the end of the week to worship God, their faith will have been weakened and assaulted. It therefore seems that corporate social responses of faith are important if Christians are to confront the dominant faith of our era in a realistic and consistent way.[10]

The New Testament shows the church encouraging both individual and group activity. Group activities include:

1. *Mission.* Jesus' disciples went out in pairs (Mark 6:7; Luke 10:1) and Paul usually had one or more co-workers with him. There were also missionary couples (Rom. 16:3-7; 1 Cor. 9:5). Group witness played a significant part in Christian advance. It may be that Christian witness was seen more in group than in individual terms (John 13:34f; Acts 5:12-14; 1 Cor. 14:23 and perhaps Matt. 5:13).

2. *Teaching.* This is seen in the instruction of Apollos by Priscilla and Aquila (Acts 18:26). The teachers at Antioch (Acts 13:1) may have worked together.

3. *Hospitality.* Some homes were often given over to looking after the saints (particularly those travelling) or for use as meeting places. Some homes may have been used very frequently, for example, in Jerusalem in the early days of the church when converts met on a daily basis (Acts 2:42-47, 5:42). Daily meetings may also be in mind at Hebrews 3:12f.[11]

4. *Service.* Examples of service rendered by groups include the ministry of women disciples to Jesus (Mark 15:40f; Luke 8:1-3), the work of the seven (Acts 6: 1-6) and the involvement of the Philippian Christians in the work of Paul (Phil. 4:10-16).

5. *Writing.* Many New Testament letters were written in conjunction with others either as joint writers or amanuenses.[12]

6. *Earning a Living.* Many of the apostles worked together in the same trade and a number of them were related. Family ties played an important role in the business life of Palestine and the ancient world generally.[13] Paul and Aquila shared the same occupation and worked together (Acts 18:1-3).

C. A third result concerns the problem of *communicating the faith to others.* Many Christians, individually and in communities, relate poorly to outsiders and give an inaccurate impression of what Christianity really is. European Christians, especially from the north, find difficulty in making strangers welcome to their gatherings—a problem felt most keenly perhaps by those of low self-esteem and those living in large cities, particularly where the environment is unpleasant.[14] Christians should be able to bear witness to a love for one another which results in unity—a unity effected by God and based on love for and devotion to Jesus and his word (John 13:34f, 17:21,23; 1 John 3:14). From this springs a richness and fullness of community life capable of making its own impact on the surrounding world. Evangelism is then a natural consequence of the spiritual maturity, loyalty, devotion and godly living of Christians in community.[15] A Christian community appears directly as such to the world only when non-Christians attend its meetings but Christians live out their faith before the world daily. In both ways outsiders can begin to see that the message and lifestyle truly fit and that a Christian community actually works.

Paul relied on centrifugal evangelism (that is, by going out and speaking the gospel to non-Christians) but he did so in order to establish Christian communities.[16] Once established, the community itself was to be encouraged to grow to maturity. Centrifugal evangelism seems then to have been replaced by, centripetal evangelism; that is, by drawing non-Christians into the Christian. congregation to hear the gospel. Thus Christians lived as Christians while non-Christians observed and occasionally joined in.[17] This evangelistic style followed and developed the evangelistic duties of Israel in the Old Testament and was similar, in some respects, to that of the Jewish mission of the 1st century.[18] Throughout the early Christian centuries, the bulk of evangelism seems to have been effected through the activity of the Christian community generally rather than the labors of evangelists or missionaries.[19]

Paul seems never to have asked the churches to evangelize centrifugally and yet he was pleased when any kind of evangelism was done (Rom. 1:8; 1 Thes. 1:8; Phil. 1:14-18, *cf.* James 5:20;

Jude 1:23).[20] Furthermore, he enjoyed the support and to some extent participation of the churches in his mission.[21] But it seems that most Christians of the first few centuries did not regard evangelism as part of their God-given duties even though they might choose to speak of their faith to others on occasion.[22]

Timothy was asked to do the work of an evangelist (2 Tim. 4:5) but, in the light of the concerns of 2 Timothy, his work seems primarily concerned with the nurture of the Ephesian church rather than what we might consider to be evangelism (or mission). In the 1st century, the term *evangelists* seems sufficiently fluid to allow for both meanings.[23] If we interpret Timothy's evangelistic work in terms of mission then it might have been directed to the Jews and pagans of Ephesus who, on conversion, might have been added to the local church. This would be unusual when compared with the normal practice of an established Pauline church and could have strained to breaking point someone who seems to have been fully occupied already. Missionary activity beyond Ephesus would seem even more problematic unless it were undertaken after the resolution of the Ephesian difficulties. The grammar of the sentence reveals little.[24] On balance, it seems best, in my opinion, to interpret evangelists in terms of nurture rather than evangelism.

In the thinking and practice of Paul, the encouragement of already existing groups to maturity took precedence over the evangelization of new areas, but evangelism and nurture were really two aspects of one compound task. W.P. Bowers asserts that:

Paul has one task, a task proceeding through preaching and converting to both the founding of churches and their firm establishment. Circumstances permitting, the completion of such a task in one area takes precedence for him over beginning such a task in a new area.[25]

Similarly, as Bowers adds, when Paul sent members of his team out on tour 'they are engaged not in some new evangelistic thrust but in confirming the already existing churches'.[26] Although Paul's aides may have been involved in evangelism when away from him, as they were so involved when with him

'...Paul's team as it is visible in his letters is a church-nurturing team.'[27]

Centripetal evangelism is also encouraged in 1 Peter 2:11f, 3:15, 4:4. Thus an emphasis on centrifugal evangelism where Christian communities already exist would seem to be a distortion of New Testament methods in which the growth of the church to maturity takes precedence.[28] Many Christians in evangelical churches, where the emphasis is continually put on centrifugal evangelism, suffer the consequences of this distortion as we shall see shortly.[29] Conversely, if a Christian group is lacking in love, justice, a sense of community and richness of life, then its evangelistic programs are unlikely to succeed because either the unattractiveness of the community will dissuade potential converts from joining or, where there are conversions, these converts will be unlikely to grow to maturity. Little more will be achieved than fostering the illusion of community growth.

Only a mature church can naturally incorporate evangelism into a balanced program of growth. Such a church should make its presence felt locally without the need for orchestrated centrifugal evangelistic activity. It may give the impression of concentrating on itself but the reality will be otherwise.[30]

THE SERMON IN RELATION TO BIBLICAL KNOWLEDGE, THE DEVELOPMENT OF GIFTS AND LIVING THE CHRISTIAN LIFE

INTRODUCTION

In many churches, great hopes rest upon the regular sermon. It is used to teach the Bible and to promote the development of gifts and living the Christian life. Unfortunately, the regular sermon is an inferior teaching method. Good teaching means creating situations in which as many members of the group as possible are able to learn effectively. This inevitably involves different techniques for different gifts, interests, temperaments and abilities and requires involvement on the part of those being taught.[31] Unfortunately the regular sermon, by its very nature, cannot succeed in such a task.

Before justifying this verdict, however, it must be stressed that the failure of the sermon is not directly related to its content or the rhetorical skill of the preacher. In all the problems listed below, both content and manner of delivery are either minor considerations or are completely irrelevant. Some of the difficulties mentioned are eased by competent sermons but, in at least one case, competent sermons render the problem that much more intractable.

THE EFFECTS OF PREACHING

By using the regular sermon the preacher proclaims each week, not in words, but in the clearest manner possible, that, be the congregation ever so gifted, there is present, for that period, one who is more gifted and all must attend in silence upon him (less often her). This formidable claim is usually both unrecognized and unintended by the preacher as well as being frequently inaccurate, since many preachers are unskilled in public speaking and teaching and few have received any formal training in teaching techniques. They exercise these functions in virtue of office rather than gift. The claim is all the more significant in those churches which revere the sermon, devote a high proportion of each meeting to it and aim to produce skilled speakers.[32] This claim itself has serious consequences.

THE CREATION OF DEPENDENCE UPON THE PREACHER

Mutual dependence is a significant part of the Christian experience, but that is very different from a forced dependence upon the leader, which, in a more extreme form is characteristic of many modern cults. There is little evidence to suggest that the sermon effectively equips people for independent study. This would not matter so much were it not that many church members know little of the Christian faith and many adults—including church members—find independent study difficult. The reasons for their ignorance include, I suggest, lack of instruction within the Christian family,[33] poor educational systems in church and state and the anti-intellectualism of the age. Building on this deficiency, preachers deliver their Sermons and invite the listeners to return—and keep on returning. Thus, preachers create dependence. Sadly, competent preachers may create dependence more effectively than incompetent ones. This means, ironically, that in the long run competent Sermons may be more damaging than indifferent ones!

Teachers and preachers have different aims. Teachers aim ultimately to make themselves dispensable by being servants, stimulating their charges and lifting them up to their own level of Christian understanding and even beyond (Matt. 10:25; Luke 6:40).[34] This means that the pupil need not always be a pupil but may follow in the footsteps of the teacher or become a leader in another sphere. Sadly, only a remnant of the teaching function remains in most churches. There are several reasons for this: many clergy are not very interested in teaching, many are not competent teachers and most clergy are very busy. Institutions training clergy often fail to provide mature, effective Christian leaders and it remains to be seen whether such failings are remediable or whether the system itself needs replacement.[35]

Preachers may aim to be dispensable, at least in theory, but they frequently achieve the opposite of this intention. Preachers are usually required to undergo professional training, a requirement, which may have undesirable consequences, B.W.M. Palmer points out that:

> Churches tend to attract those whose personality predisposes them to find satisfaction in dependent relationships, that is, relationships in which individuals care and are cared for, dominate and are dominated...[36]

Failure to liberate the laity from excessive dependence upon the clergy has characterized the church throughout its history. In England the problem has been exacerbated by educational theories popular in the eighteenth and nineteenth centuries in which extensive education was seen as the prerogative of the elite. Add to this a generally poor educational system both within and without the church,[37] and the failure of the church to meet the momentous challenges of the 20th century in virtually all its aspects can hardly come as a surprise.

PROBLEMS OF DIFFERENT STARTING POINT AND GROWTH RATES AMONG THE AUDIENCE

The Sermon can occasionally stimulate, interest and inspire. It can remind, warn, exhort and encourage. Where *all* (or nearly all) the congregation has a similar need then the Sermon may be of value. But needs vary and the Sermon, as a regular item, is bound to fail because its regular use presupposes a similar starting point, learning ability, stage of faith[38] and growth rate for *all* in the congregation *all* the time.[39] An occasional Sermon may be appropriate but it is wishful thinking to imagine that most Sermons are appropriate to the majority of listeners most of the time. At best, listeners will grasp fragments and quickly forget the rest; or be distracted by one section and miss what follows. This has been a problem in the past but is especially so in our own society where congregations tend to be both large and heterogeneous. A speaker addressing an audience, which spans a variety of abilities and attainments usually aims towards the lower end of the intellectual scale in order to find some common ground. Generally, the larger the audience, the lower the level will need to be. Frank Binder laments that 'the best speaker is he who talks to the biggest fool before him'.[40]

Even where this problem is acknowledged and sermons are sometimes directed to specific sections of the congregation, success is still elusive and variations of this kind cannot be used often. The limited concentration span of most listeners (seldom more than fifteen to twenty minutes without a break), combined with the excessive strain put on the memory, help to make matters worse.[41] Concentration is possibly reduced still further because the sermon is usually placed at the end of the meeting rather than at the beginning.[42] Much of the material initially retained from a lecture—and sermons are not very different[43]—will have been lost after a week. Small wonder that many are alienated by the sermon, or simply bored.[44]

If we ignore other problems relating to the sermon and focus exclusively on those relating to concentration and memory, then it is obvious that these problems can be eased when the preacher is a virtuoso performer. But most clergy are not especially gifted speakers and, given their wide-ranging duties, it is unrealistic to expect that this aspect of their work should take precedence or that their gifts of speaking should be developed more than other gifts. Under these circumstances, the widespread use of the regular sermon is an unwise utilization of resources since the effective use of the sermon often presupposes a level of rhetorical skill, which is unavailable. In the New Testament there is a clear recognition of the limitations of the individual and the wide range of gifts available in the body.

THE SERMON FAILS TO DEVELOP POWERS OF THOUGHT AND ANALYTICAL SKILLS

As noted earlier, discussion and participation are better than lectures or sermons for critically examining ideas and stimulating thought. The point is eloquently expressed by D.A. Bligh who says that:

> ...if students are to learn to think, they must be placed in situations where they have to do so. The situations in which they are obliged to think are those in which they have to answer questions because questions demand an active response. Although it could be modified to do so, the traditional expository lecture does not demand this... The best way to learn to solve problems is to be given problems that have to be solved. The best way to 'awaken critical skills' is to practice using the canons of criticism. If this thesis seems obvious common sense, it should be remembered that some people place faith in their lectures to stimulate thought, and expect thinking skills to be absorbed, like some mystical vapors, from a college atmosphere. Psychologists are likely to wince at the impression of such a notion; and learning to think is not all absorption process.[45]

THE SERMON AS DESKILLING AGENT

Not only can the sermon fail to equip hearers, it tends to rob them of such skills as they already possess. They may become deskilled.[46] The richly gifted may overcome the problem, albeit with some frustration, but the less gifted can easily be crushed. They recognize even modest skills in the preacher and, with his or her passive encouragement, learn to despise their own, which then remain unrecognized. Being unrecognized and unacknowledged, these gifts quickly wither beyond revivification, particularly in sensitive people—'candidates for defeat' as Paul Tournier calls them.[47] Such apathy may be reinforced by ail excessive concentration by the preacher on sinfulness and failure,[48] coupled with alack of fellowship and encouragement and failure to emphasize the grace ofGod.[49] In this way, the weak and less gifted fail to mature, the blessings which they might have dispensed are lost, in part at least, and the whole church is impoverished. This is particularly the case with women, many of whom learned helplessness in childhood and found it reinforced in church.[50] In spite of this, or maybe even because of it, the church often has a greater appeal to women rather than to men.[51] The church thus apes one of the worst features of modern industrial society—the creation of a dependent, unreflective, semi-literate, relatively skill-less population, almost devoid of creativity.[52] Far from realizing that the stimulation of other minds is one of the chief duties of a teacher,[53] most preachers often do the exact opposite. And they achieve this feat in spite of the immense power of the Christian faith as an intellectual stimulus and source of human creativity. In a different context, Paul Tournier reminds us that true love is ambitious for the beloved and wants him or her to advance not retreat.[54]

The range of gifts recognized as of real value by the average church in no way corresponds with the richness of God's provision. The highly esteemed gifts are frequently inward-looking and/or designed to maintain the church as a formal organization, fashioned after a bureaucracy or machine and constituting an end in itself.[55] The biblical form of the church as a people tends to be submerged under the rapacious demands of the organization. The development of more outward-looking gifts is partial and unbalanced and tends to be orchestrated by church leaders to an extent which inhibits personal initiative. Any gift that might benefit from financial support is liable to run foul of the church's distorted financial arrangements.

Different denominations tend to favor different gifts.[56] But not all Christians have the specially favored gifts. For example, in many evangelical churches, evangelism (*i.e.* centrifugal evangelism) is seen as the duty of all believers. Those with restricted gifts in this area can be made to feel inadequate and guilty.[57] They will seldom be encouraged to explore their own talents and may suffer the unhappiness that can accompany the misdirection or non-development of gifts rather than experience the freedom and pleasure that come from taking control of elements of their own lives.[58] Sometimes their hobbies, amusements and even their artistic and literary accomplishments are denigrated by fellow Christians unless they are put to evangelistic use.[59] Even those blessed with fashionable gifts are unlikely to have them intelligently developed. On the other hand, the awkward gift:

> ... is born to blush unseen, and waste its sweetness on the desert air.[60]

It was suggested above that in the early church many gifts might initially be discovered and explored when Christians gathered together. In the bulk of English churches this does not happen during Sunday 'services'.[61] These occasions are the most significant church meetings for most Christians, attracting far greater attendance than mid-week functions. If mutual ministries and gifts are not encouraged on Sundays then, for the majority, they are unlikely to flourish at all.

In many Protestant churches, the problem is worsened by the variety and number of meetings which, taken as a whole, may involve a substantial proportion of the congregation.[62] Members are often under pressure to attend and commitment is measured by attendance. At least two difficulties arise from this attitude:

- There are *difficulties in understanding what is being measured* here. Is it commitment to God, or to the church (God's people), or to the organized church? And why is commitment to be measured primarily by easily observed outward actions? This is hardly a reliable way of assessing a person's relationship with God. The use of the term 'commitment' further clouds the issue. This word enjoys extensive currency in Christian circles but it still retains something of its existentialist background and suggests, primarily, action. The term has no precise biblical equivalent; its Christian content is subsumed under the terms 'obedience' and 'love', but these involve both doing and being. There is no way in which obedience to God and his people, or love for God and his people, can be confined to church gatherings or measured with a register.
- *Gifts are then mustered to furnish staff to run the meetings*—a very different procedure from identifying gifts and helping them to flourish. Awkward gifts are likely to be frowned upon and those who might use them to increase the richness and diversity of the church or even challenge the status quo thus

become deviants unsupported by the church and cast aside. Even so, the church does often have a beneficial effect upon the health and happiness of its members but—with more thought—the benefits could be much greater than is presently the case.[63]

The acceptance of the view that truth inevitably resides with the majority—a majority that takes little pleasure in discovery or understanding—shows how far the church as a whole has forgotten the teaching of Scripture and history that the uninformed majority is invariably wrong. In this the church follows popular non-Christian non-thinking.

ONE-WAY COMMUNICATION

In delivering a sermon, communication is primarily one-way. There is frequently no prior warning of subject matter and consequently no possibility of preparatory reading. There is no participation; there are no questions, during or afterwards, by speaker or listeners. Few take notes or do any follow-up work. There is little audience contact and judging the effects of the sermon on the individual members of the congregation is difficult.[64] Such a technique blunts curiosity and creates passivity—the opposite of responsible adulthood.[65] There is little evidence to suggest that sermons bring about change at the personal or group level in either values or behavior patterns, particularly where the congregation enjoys sparse fellowship and encouragement.[66] The sermon thus tends to reinforce beliefs and prejudices already held and supports the status quo.[67]

Passivity is heightened by the common tendency of preachers to emphasize conclusions rather than the means to achieve them—such as challenging assumptions, verifying argumentation and framing questions. This is in marked contrast to Jesus' teaching, which frequently uses these three means (particularly the first) in reaching conclusions.[68]

In spite of these deficiencies, some people like the sermon and would be sorry to see it replaced—especially by methods requiring them to be actively involved. In its present form, the sermon, like the lecture, produces few anxieties. Yet the fact that people like something does not prove that it is good for them. Some like the sermon because they enjoy watching a good performance, even though the benefits may be somewhat intangible. Some not only like the sermon, they profit from it. Such people are often of above average intelligence, knowledge and education. Given these advantages, there can be little doubt that they would profit even more from better teaching techniques and might well come to prefer them. Similarly, the competent preacher might be even more impressive were he or she to use appropriate teaching methods.[69] At the other end of the scale, the less able and ignorant frequently derive small benefit from sermons.[70]

In some churches, matters are improved in various ways. These may include announcing and discussing sermon content beforehand; working through a biblical book (which necessitates prior notice of subject matter); taking notes and discussing the sermon afterwards.[71] But these are cosmetic alterations and leave the basic inadequacy of the method untouched. The recent development of preaching as storytelling is a similarly superficial adjustment and is part of a movement that still has high hopes for the future of the sermon.[72]

Many educated Christians regard pulpit ministry as being in no small measure responsible for their own growth in understanding. But many of the better clergy encourage personal devotions, private reading, discussion and group Bible study (all likely to be more effective teaching aides than the sermon) and it is these that frequently produce growth. Christians, with clerical encouragement, often give the sermon credit where little is due. Church activities consistently lack any kind of end-product or comparative analysis (e.g. study of opportunity costs)[73] or clear goals. This helps to maintain the fiction that since our methods work (to some extent), there is no failure, no re-evaluation is necessary and Christian workers should simply continue doing what they have always done. But most methods work. The church, however, seldom asks which methods work best. It justifies traditional views by opinions resting on little more substantial than anecdote and personal experience. Such atomistic thinking needs to be replaced by holistic thinking in which a full biblical understanding can be developed by Bible study set in the widest possible context of cross-cultural, cross-historical and inter-disciplinary studies. In this way, the church can dig more gold and silver from the Scriptures and thus be delivered from the tradition of the elders.

The church can then develop adequate methods for identifying failure. Throughout its history, the church has seldom shown any enthusiasm for recognizing and acknowledging its own failure and this is certainly true of the sermon. But without such discernment and the humility required to put it into practice, progress is almost impossible. The frank recognition of failure among God's people is common in the Scriptures.[74] Furthermore, the apparently isolated problem (in this case the sermon) can then be seen as an integral part of Christian life, soluble only if examined in relation to the larger system.[75]

DOMINATION BY THE CLERGY

Equipped with inadequate notions of leadership, which owe little to biblical patterns, many clergy today preside over almost every church function within their jurisdiction. Some functions are delegated to senior members of the laity, often, but not always, as a result of a shortage of clergy. But the clergy generally perform, for example, all the baptisms, usually during the Sunday gatherings or in private baptisms, which are common in the Anglican and Roman Catholic communions.[76] The New Testament evidence, thin as it is, suggests that baptisms were usually performed by the converter or his agent[77] near the time and place of conversion—not in the house church meetings and not necessarily by elders (Acts 2:37-41, 8:12f, 27-38, 9:18, 10:44-48, 16:14f, 31-33, 18:8, 19:1-5).[78]

Generally, the clergy lead the meetings. In the New Testament, scanty though the evidence is, liturgical presidency, even for the Lord's Supper, does not necessarily reside with one person.[79] The clergy may even read the Scriptures and the notices, say the prayers, supervise the collection and announce the hymns. They also conduct marriages and funerals. By tradition, less prestigious items such as the music, flower arranging and cleaning are left to others. The clergy conduct the bulk of Christian business in church buildings, which thus enables them (intentionally or otherwise) to exert greater control over the congregation than is possible in private homes. P. Mickey, G. Gamble and P. Gilbert comment:

Churches needlessly and destructively institutionalize activities away from the living-room setting. Institutionalization allows pastors to retreat within the church's walls
where control is provided by the context. This shift in control
leaves the parishioner on the defensive.[80]

The regular sermon is an integral part of this system of control both
through its obtrusive presence in Christian gatherings and through its
failure to develop those gifts, which might empower members of the
congregation and lessen the effects of clerical domination.

In addition, many churches even practice one-minister rule.
Often the problem today is not just that of the one-man band but the
one-white-educated-middle-class-man band ministering to a congregation of unlike minds.[81] The problem is eased but not removed by
clerical assistants or even 'clergy couples' (in which both husbands
and wives are ordained).[82] When we add to the burden this system
places on one individual the further difficulties of communicating and
living the faith in a society which has largely rejected Christianity, it
is not surprising that so many of the clergy quit their ministries while
those that remain frequently suffer from severe stress.[83]

Sadly, the widespread view that the clergy should dominate
meetings may be set in the wider context of secular professions
which artificially create indispensability as a route to prestige and
job security.[84] Many of the clergy seem to be content if their flocks
accept the tenets of the faith irrespective of understanding.[85] Some
congregations contain theologically trained professional teachers but
their knowledge usually owes little to the local clergy. The fact that
so many of the clergy fail to educate or to develop the gifts of their
congregations similarly points in the direction of professionalization.
Success here would expose them to even more competition from other
competent persons in the community, although perhaps few clergy
think in these terms. The problems surrounding the professional clergy
are worsened by the uncertainty felt in many quarters concerning
their precise functions.[86] If emphasis is placed upon their professional
role and expert status this confirms the general impression that the
clergy are a professional group like any other, and that no one, no
matter how willing, can take on their work without first undergoing
professional training.[87] Once this idea takes hold, clerical domination

is difficult to resist, especially when buttressed by the view that full-time Christian service constitutes a special calling superior to secular work.[88]

Paul exhibited great trust in the Holy Spirit and in his converts—or perhaps in the Holy Spirit in his converts (2 Cor. 2:3, 7:4-16; Phil. 1:3-6; 2 Thes. 3:4; Philem. 21).[89] He saw them as his spiritual children and the immature and the wayward were frequently corrected and disciplined. This relationship was permanent and, as Robert Banks points out, was comparable with 'the parent-adult child rather than parent-infant child'.[90] As converts matured they were quickly given extensive responsibilities (including running local churches) and Paul then regarded them as fellow workers, joint servants of God, beloved brethren.[91] The actions of the bulk of the English clergy suggest a different attitude—even the titles the clergy assume emphasize distinction.

THE POVERTY OF CHRISTIAN LIFE

Jesus aimed to strengthen the bruised reed and the smoldering flax (Isa. 42:3), but it is tragically true that many in the church today suffer spiritual, intellectual and emotional impoverishment as a combined result not only of the regular and frequent use of the sermon, but also of what accompanies this—poor leadership, the absence of fellowship and inadequate preparation for service. The churches contain too many 'infant' Christians still on a milk diet, the victims of institutionalized immaturity.[92] Nobody encouraged them to grow up to maturity in Christ because the emphasis was always elsewhere.[93] In the New Testament, by contrast, maturity was expected and often achieved (Rom. 15:14; Eph. 4:11-16; 1 Thes. 4:9; 2 Pet. 1:12; 1 John 2:21,27). Where it was not, a swift rebuke was liable to follow (1 Cor. 3:1-3; Gal. 1:6; Heb. 5:12-14).

The effective development of Christians to maturity allows them to find their own place in the body of Christ; renders the group more cohesive; increases the security of group members; allows people to satisfy their need for significance by the practice of gifts; eliminates alienation and enables them to become socially more useful to the Christians and non-Christians around them.[94] This produces not only more converts but real disciples and leaders able to tackle the responsibilities presented by a community of God's people. These include being an example, serving, teaching, inspiring, managing, guiding and planning.[95] Working towards maturity develops a task force exemplifying the priesthood of all believers.[96] The regular sermon, on the other hand, is a major obstacle to a functioning priesthood of all believers.[97]

The bad consequences of clerical domination extend far beyond church meetings. They distort Christian growth in all areas of life and result in the absence of a 'Christian mind'. The churches have failed their members by not understanding how important it is for the individual in Christ to follow his or her calling, to embark upon an adventure, to develop gifts and to live for others. W.E. Chadwick, writing in 1907, said, 'If the church is to influence and guide the world she must in insight be superior to, and in foresight in advance of, the world.'[98]

Yet today, in spite of exceptions, the individual Christian is often excessively busy and unused to reflection,[99] unskilled in prayer, more concerned with doing than becoming,[100] lacking in understanding of the relevance of the faith to nearly all aspects of life,[101] ignorant of the past, anti-intellectual, materialistic, welded to the secular thought of the day, timid in the face of social and political injustice, barely capable even of recognizing the enemies of God[102] (or his friends), lacking in steady and forgiving love[103] and deficient in the skills required to detect nonsense[104]—a living monument denying the assertion of Jesus that 'I came that they may have life and may have it abundantly.' (John 10:10 RV).[105] As sociologist Jacques Ellul observes, far from being a model of freedom, most Christians are models of mediocre bondage, simultaneously the slaves of the latest fad and the ecclesiastical and humanistic traditions in which they were reared.[106] The disastrous consequence is that the non-Christian world experiences little Christian influence in any area of thought and has little, if any, understanding of the essence of biblical Christianity. Christianity is thus inexorably pushed to the margins of society.[107]

The end-product is social decay, a rise of unbelief, an increase in cults and non-Christian religions, depression and failure, among Christians, a tarnished reputation for the church as a whole and the wrath and the judgment of God.

ENDNOTES

1.   In Black preaching in the USA, participation is common, even during the Sermon. Congregations are involved in the Sermon and in a sense help to create the message (B.A. Rosenberg, 'The Psychology of the Spiritual Sermon' in I.I. Zaretsky and M.P. Leone (eds), *Religious Movements in Contemporary America*, 1974, p. 138; J.S. Tinney, 'The Miracle of Black Preaching', *Christianity Today*, 30 January 1976, 14-16)

2.   G. Lohfink, *Jesus and Community: The Social Dimension of Christian Faith*, 1985, p. 104

3.   R.J. Banks, *PIC*, pp. 84-88; J.D.G. Dunn, 'Whatever happened to the Lord's Supper?', *Epworth Review*, 19:1, 1992, 35-55

4.   'The Early Church as a Caring Community and Some Implications for Social Work Today', *Interchange*, 30, 1982, 41

5.   M. Barker, 'Models of Pastoral Care: Medical, Psychological and Biblical' in M.A.Jeeves (ed), *Behavioral Sciences: A Christian Perspective*, 1984, p. 245, *cf.* D.J. Tidball, *Skilful Shepherds*, 1986, pp. 319-321. The example of the apostle Paul in sharing and self-giving challenges this attitude (2 Cor. 1:8f, 6:11-13; 1 Thes. 2:7f)

6.   A.D. Litfin, 'In Defence of the Sermon: A Communicational Approach', *JPT*, 2,1974, 41-43; M. Barker, 'Models', pp. 243f; J. Moiser, 'The Laity on Today's Preaching', Clergy Review, 56, 1971, 786

7.   O. Guinness, *The Gravedigger File*, 1983, pp. 31-36

8.   J.M. Barnett, *The Diaconate: A Full and Equal Order*, Seabury Press, USA, 1981, p. 6

9.   On privatization see J.A. Walter, *A Long Way from Home*, 1979, pp. 47-58; A. Walker, *Enemy Territory*, 1987, pp. 121-135; O. Guinness, *The Gravedigger File*, pp. 75-92; D.A. Fraser and T. Campolo, *Sociology Through the Eyes of Faith*, 1992, pp. 34-43.

10. A. Starkey, *A Christian Social Perspective*, Leicester, Inter Varsity Press, 1979, pp. 407-410. See further, D. Lyon, *The Steeple's Shadow: On the Myths and Realities of Secularization*, 1985, pp. 50, 58-62, 148; C.E.M. Joad, *Decadence: A Philosophical Inquiry*, 1948, pp. 85-88,355f

11. R.T. Beckwith and W. Stott, *This is the Day: The Biblical Doctrine of the Christian Sunday in its Jewish and Early Church Setting*, 1978, pp. 37f; P. Ellingworth, *The Epistle to the Hebrews*, 1993, p. 223

12. Joint authors. 1 Cor. 1:1; 2 Cor. 1:1; Phil. 1:1; Col. 1:1; 1 Thes. 1:1; 2 Thes. 1:1. Secretaries: Rom. 16:22; 1 Cor. 16:21; Gal. 6:11; Col. 4:18; 2 Thes. 3:17; Philem. 19; 1 Pet. 5:12: M. Prior, *Paul the Letter-Writer and the Second Letter to Timothy*, 1989, pp. 37-50; E.R. Richards, 'The Secretary in the Letters of Paul,' *WUNT*, 2:42, 1991, pp. 153-198

13. J. Klausner, *Jesus of Nazareth*, 1925, pp. 176-178; M. Silver, *Economic Structures of the Ancient Near East*, 1985, pp. 39-41

14. M. Gibbs in J.G. Davies (ed), *A New Dictionary of Liturgy and Worship*, 1986, p. 293; D. Cartwright, 'The Nature of Group Cohesiveness' in D. Cartwright and A. Zander (eds), *Group Dynamics: Research and Theory*, [3]1968, p. 102; R.A. Baron and D. Byrne, *Social Psychology: Understanding Human Interaction*, [6]1991, pp. 534-536

15. 'Evangelism' is difficult to define. See the discussions in W J. Abraham, *The Logic

of Evangelism, 1989, pp. 1-116; J.I. Packer, Evangelism and the Sovereignty of God, 1961, pp. 37-73

16. W.P. Bowers, Studies in Paul's Understanding of His Mission, PhD Thesis (Cambridge University), 1976, p. 86; idem, 'Fulfilling the Gospel: The Scope of the Pauline Mission', JETS, 30:2,1987,185-198

17. D.W. Wead, 'The Centripetal Philosophy of Mission' in W.W. Gasque and W.S. LaSor (eds), Scripture, Tradition and Interpretation, 1978, pp. 176f; cf. M. Goodman, Mission and Conversion: Proselytizing in the Religious History of the Roman Empire, 1994, pp. 91-108

18. J. Blauw, The Missionary Nature of the Church, 1962, pp. 34f, 38-41; W.P. Bowers, 'Paul and Religious Propaganda in the 1st century', Nov T, 22, 1980, 320f; M.D. Goodman, 'Jewish Proselytizing in the 1st century' in J. Lieu et al (eds), The Jews Among Pagans and Christians in the Roman Empire, 1992, pp. 53-78; S. McKnight, A Light Among the Gentiles: Jewish Missionary Activity in the Second Temple Period, 1991, pp. 74-77, 116f

19. W.P. Bowers, Studies, pp. 184f; E.G. Hinson, The Evangelization of the Roman Empire, 1981, p. 33; A. Harnack, The Mission and Expansion of Christianity in the First Three Centuries, [2]1908, I, 387, 433f

20. W.P. Bowers, Studies, pp. 104-121. Centrifugal evangelism may be in mind at Col. 4:5 but not necessarily so (P.T. O'Brien, Colossians, Philemon, 1982, pp. 240f)

21. R.J. Banks, PIC, pp. 164.

22. K.S. Latourette, A History of the Expansion of Christianity, 1937 repr 1970, I,117

23. G. Friedrich, TDNT, II, 737; D. Guthrie, The Pastoral Epistles, [2]1990, pp. 179f; R.A. Campbell, 'Do the Work of an Evangelist', EQ, 64:2, 1992, 122-126

24. The verbal form poieson is an aorist imperative and suffers from the vagueness noted in our discussion of the aorist imperatives of 2 Timothy 4:2.

25. Acts 15:36-41, 18:23; 2 Cor. 13:1: W.P. Bowers, Studies, pp. 87-93. Similarly idem, 'Fulfilling', 188-198

26. W.P. Bowers, Studies, p. 88. He cites 1 Cor. 4:17, 16:10f; 2 Cor. 2:13, 7:6f,13-15, 8:6, 16f, 23; Eph. 6:21f; Phil. 2:19-24; Col. 4:7-9; 1 Thes. 3:1-8; 1 Tim. 1:3f; 2 Tim. 4:10,12; Titus 1:5

27. W.P. Bowers, Studies, p. 89

28. L.O. Richards, A Theology of Christian Education, 1975, pp. 55,119-122

29. For evangelism as a major emphasis, if not the major emphasis, in evangelical circles see D.W. Bebbington, Evangelicalism in Modem Britain, 1989, p. 4; G.M. Marsden, Fundamentalism and American Culture, 1980, pp. 78, 80-85, 129, 182f; idem, Reforming Fundamentalism, 1987, pp. 84-86

30. R.Y.K. Fung, 'The Nature of the Ministry According to Paul', EQ, 54,1982,144; C.L. Mitton, Ephesians, 1976, pp. 152, 201f; R.J. Banks, PIC, p. 68

31. D. Legge, 'Practical Training and Individual Tuition' in M.D. Stephens and G.W. Roderick (eds), Teaching Techniques in Adult Education, 1971, p. 66; D.A. Bligh, What's the Use of Lectures?, 1978, p. 157; R.M. Beard and J. Hartley, Teaching and Learning in Higher Education, [4]1984, pp. 80-85, 185-194

32. Many Anglican clergy consider their role as preacher less significant than that of pastor and celebrant (A. Russell, The Clerical Profession, 1984, p. 276; similarly R.C. Towler and A.P.M. Coxon, The Fate of the Anglican Clergy, 1979, pp. 37f, 109-112). Preaching is often less significant in Roman Catholic and non-evangelical Anglican churches.

33. J.G. Machen pointed out that in the USA, the family, as an educational institution, had, by 1925, 'to a very large extent ceased to do its work' (*What is Faith?*, 1925, p. 21). In England today it appears that few Christian parents give their children formal Christian instruction.

34. J.A. Grassi, *The Teacher in the Primitive Church and the Teacher Today*, 1973, p. 111; L.O. Richards, *A Theology of Christian Education*, 1975, pp. 132f, 141-144; I. Shor, *Critical Teaching and Everyday Life*, 1980, pp. 98-101

35. Several writers have begun to address this issue: L.O. Richards, *Theology*, pp. 158-163; J. Stein (ed), *Ministers for the 1980s*, 1979; E. Gibbs, *I Believe in Church Growth*, [3]1990, pp. 249-252; E.R. Dayton and D.A. Fraser, *Planning Strategies for World Evangelization*, 1980, pp. 399f; R.J. Banks, *All the Business of Life*, [2]1989, pp. 119-147

36. B.W.M. Palmer, 'Work and Fellowship in Groups and Organizations' in C.L. Mitton (ed), *The Social Sciences and the Churches*, Edinburgh, T.T. Clark, 1972, p. 22 (cf. p. 25); similarly M.J. Meadow and R.D. Kahoe, *Psychology of Religion: Religion in Individual Lives*, 1984, pp. 353-355; P. Mickey, G. Gamble and P. Gilbert, *Pastoral Assertiveness: A New Model for Pastoral Care*, 1978, pp. 44-46, 69,159

37. D.S. Landes, *The Unbound Prometheus: Technological Change and Industrial Development in Western Europe from 1750 to the Present*, 1969, pp. 340-348; J. McLeish, *Evangelical Religion and Popular Education*, 1969, pp. 20-22, 30f, 42-66; T.W. Laqueur, *Religion and Respectability: Sunday Schools and Working Class Culture 1780-1850*, 1979, pp. 124-146, 190f

38. J.W. Fowler, *Faith Development and Pastoral Care*, 1987, pp. 53-98; S. Shaw, *No Splits*, 1989, pp. 61-71. On the extent to which our understanding of God is dependent upon emotional and social influences see D.G. Myers, 'Social Psychology and Christian Faith' in M.A. Jeeves (ed), *Behavioral Sciences: A Christian Perspective*, 1984, pp. 112f; M.J. Meadow and R.D. Kahoe, *Psychology of Religion*, pp. 78f; H.N. Wright, *Always Daddy's Girl*, 1989, pp. 193f; D.M. Wulff, *Psychology of Religion: Classic and Contemporary Views*, 1991, pp. 54f, 106, 312f, 364-367, 585, 633, 635

39. J. Rogers, *Adults Learning*, [3]1989, pp. 45, 119

40. F. Binder, *Dialetic or the Tactics of Thinking*, London, Partridge, 1932, p. 242. 41 D.G. Myers and M.A. Jeeves, *Psychology Through the Eyes of Faith*, 1991, pp. 75f;

41. G. Reid, *The Gagging of God*, 1969, pp. 99f; R. Baxter, *The Reformed Pastor*, 1656 (edited and abridged by W. Brown, preface dated 1862), pp. 228f; similarly Martin Luther (H. Robinson-Hammerstein, 'Luther and the Laity' in idem (ed), *The Transmission of Ideas in the Lutheran Reformation*, 1989, pp. 30f)

42. G.K. Morlan, 'An Experiment on the Recall of Religious Material', *Religion in Life*, 19, 1950 repr in L.B. Brown (ed), *Psychology and Religion*, 1973, p. 250

43. B.A. Miiller, 'The Role of the Sermon in Intergroup Relationships' in J.P. Louw (ed), *Sociolinguistics and Communication*, 1986, pp. 96-98

44. J. McLeish, *The Lecture Method*, 1968, pp. 5-12, 16 (cf. 43t); J. Moiser, 'The Laity on Today's Preaching', *Clergy Review*, 56, 1971, 783, 790; H. Levinson, 'The Trouble with Sermons', *Journal of Pastoral Care*, 22, 1968, 65-69; J. Stacey, *Preaching Reassessed*, 1980, pp. 39-44; J.M. Hull, *What Prevents Christian Adults From Learning?*, 1985, pp. 137-143; D.A. Bligh, *What's the Use of Lectures?*, 1978, pp.

29-35, 48-50

45. D.A. Bligh, *What's the Use of Lectures?*, Exeter University, pp. 13, 16

46. On the danger of deskilling in groups see P.M. Turquet, 'Leadership: The Individual and the Group' in G.S. Gibbard, J.J. Hartman and R.D. Mann (eds), *Analysis of Groups*, 1974, pp. 360f; B.W.M. Palmer, 'Dependence' and R.W. Herrick, 'Dependence and Worship' in C.L. Mitton (ed), *The Social Sciences and the Churches*, pp. 28f, 31-33, 62f

47. P. Tournier, *The Strong and the Weak*, London, SCM 1963, p. 45, *cf.* pp. 162-169, 218

48. Jesus often referred directly to the sinfullness of his hearers (Matt. 7:11, 12:34f, 39, 16:4, 23; Mark 10:18: G. Harder, *TDNT*, VI, 554t). Paul also pointed out the sins of those in the churches for which he was responsible (1 Cor. 5; Gal. 1:6-8, 3:1; 2 Thes. 3:6-15) and, in his theological analyses, the sinfulness of all human beings is frequently mentioned (Rom. 3:23, 5:12; Gal 3:22 and similarly in 1 John 1:8-10). But generally, in the New Testament, the regenerate have specific faults pointed out and, after repentance and restoration, these faults are forgotten (2 Cor. 2:5-11; Gal. 6:1; *cf.* Heb 10:17). God's people are not then subject to continual non-specific accusations of sinfullness for they are seen, not so much as sinners, but as forgiven sinners (John 13:10, 15:3; Rom. 4:1-8; Col. 2:13; 1 John 2:12; Rev 1:5). In the New Testament, the motivation of Christians is seldom achieved by the evocation of guilt (*cf.* S.B. Narramore, *No Condemnation*, 1984, pp. 309f). The contemporary overemphasis upon sin in some churches may have its roots in the Puritan approach to the doctrine of sin (A. Carden, *Puritan Christianity in America: Religion and Life in Seventeenth-Century Massachusetts*, 1990, pp. 48f, 61, 127f; D.W. Bebbington, 'Evangelical Christianity and the Enlightenment' in M. Eden and D.F. Wells (eds), *The Gospel in the Modern World*, 1991, p. 71)

49. L.J. Crabb and D. Allender, *Encouragement*, 1986, pp. 85-91; S.B. Narramore, *No Condemnation*, pp. 304--311; A. McGrath, *Evangelicalism and the Future of Christianity*, 1994, pp.148-151

50. H.N. Wright, *Always Daddy's Girl*, 1989, pp. 122-126; G.C. Davison and J.M. Neale, *Abnormal Psychology*, [5]1990, p. 230; E. Storkey, *What's Right with Feminism*, 1985, pp.46-55.

51. Reasons for the preponderance of women in the churches are analyzed in W. Neuer, *Man and Woman in Christian Perspective*, 1990, pp. 169f; Shirley Dex, 'Why are there so many women in churches?' (*Ilkley Group Paper*).

52. J. Holt, *Teach Your Own*, 1981, pp. 72-74; D. Ehrenfeld, *The Arrogance of Humanism*, [2]1981, pp. 256f, 269; N. Postman, *Conscientious Objections: Stirring Up Trouble About Language, Technology and Education*, 1989, pp. 63f, 110~115, 162-174; J.A. Walter, *All You Love is Need*, 1985, pp. 31-33

53. C.G. Seerveld, *Rainbows for the Fallen World*, 1988, pp. 104f, 114-121; J. Rogers, *Adults Learning*, [3]1989, pp. 27-38

54. *The Meaning of Persons*, 1957, p. 205

55. R. McCluskey, 'Formal Organizations' in S.A. Gruulan and M. Reimer (eds), *Christian Perspectives on Sociology*, 1982, pp. 275-288; W.E. Diehl, *Christianity and Real Life*, 1976, pp. 1-40

56. For a brief list of some of the creative gifts favored in the main streams of Christianity see A.F. Homes, *Contours of a World View*, 1983, pp. 205f; E. Brunner, *Christianity*

and Civilization, 1948, I, 146f

57. G.M. Marsden, *Reforming Fundamentalism*, 1987, p. 86; J.R.W. Stott, *Our Guilty Silence*, 1967, pp. 18f, 61-65; E.M.B. Green, *Evangelism Through the Local Church*, 1990, pp. ix, 17f, 19f, 399; S.B. Narramore, *No Condemnation*, 1984, pp. 307f; *cf.* J.M. Frame, *The Doctrine of the Knowledge of God*, 1987, pp. 138f

58. C.M. Narramore, *Encyclopedia of Psychological Problems*, 1966, p. 100; D.G. Myers and M.A. Jeeves, *Psychology Through the Eyes of Faith*, 1991, pp. 138-140

59. S. Shaw, *No Splits*, 1989, pp. 53-57; H.R. Rookmaaker, *Art Needs No Justification*, 1978, pp. 33-35; C.G. Seerveld, *Rainbows for the Fallen World*, 1988, pp. 207f

60. Thomas Gray, *Elegy Written in a Country Churchyard*, v. 14

61. 'Service' is an inappropriate term for the meeting (I.H. Marshall, 'How Far Did the Early Christians *Worship* God?', *Churchman*, 99, 1985, 218, 226f)

62. In Roman Catholic churches, the proportion is often much lower (B. Hargrove, *The Sociology of Religion*, [2]1989, p. 173)

63. M. Argyle, 'New Directions in the Psychology of Religion' in L.B. Brown (ed), *Advances in the Psychology of Religion*, 1985, p. 12; D. G. Myers and M.A. J eeves, *Psychology Through the Eyes of Faith*, 1991, pp. 145-150; H.W. Darling, *Man in His Right Mind*, 1969, pp.129-147

64. D. Legge, 'The Use of the Talk in Adult Classes' in M.D. Stephens and G.W. Roderick (eds), *Teaching Techniques in Adult Education*, 1971, p. 58; R. Baxter, *The Reformed Pastor*, 1656 (edited and abridged by W. Brown, preface dated 1862), pp. 227f, 285f. Augustine and other Fathers managed to observe the changing moods of their congregations during the sermon but they were dealing with volatile, emotional people who gave clear indication of their thoughts throughout the sermon (F. van der Meer, *Augustine the Bishop*, 1961, pp. 140f; G.W. Doyle, 'Augustine's Sermonic Method', *WTJ*, 39, 1977, 219, 222; A. Olivar, *La Predicación Cristiana Antigua*, 1991, pp. 770-812, 850).

65. J. Zens, 'Why is the Order of Our Church Service Set in Concrete?', *ST*, Autumn 1982, 47

66. L.J. Crabb and D. Allender, *Encouragement*, 1986, pp. 85-91

67. B.A. Milller, 'The Role of the Sermon in Intergroup Relationships' in J.P. Louw (ed), *Sociolinguistics and Communication*, 1986, pp. 99-102; S.S. Boocock, 'Toward a Sociology of Learning: A Selective Review of Existing Research', *Sociology of Education*, 39:1, 1966, 12; *cf.* K.I. Pargament and D.V. DeRosa, 'What Was That Sermon About? Predicting Memory for Religious Messages from Cognitive Psychology Theory', *JSc SR*, 24, 1985, 180-193

68. Assumptions: Matt. 5:1-12, 23f; Luke 10:30-37; John 3:1-9, 4:20-24; 9:1-3. Argumentation: Matt. 12:22-29, 22:23-46; Mark 7:6-13, 12:13-17; John 8:1-9. Questions: Matt. 16:13-16, 19:17, 21:23-27. On Jesus' use of logic and questions see W.A. Curtis, *Jesus Christ the Teacher*, 1943, pp. 78-82; M.E. Manton, *The Teaching Methods of Christ*, London Bible College Annual Lecture, 1966, pp. 4-10; R.H. Stein, *The Method and Message of Jesus' Teachings*, 1978, pp. 20f, 23-25

69. These issues are common to sermons and lectures G. Rogers, *Adults Learning*, [3]1989, pp. 80-82, 187; J. McLeish, *The Lecture Method*, 1968, pp. 23, 37; D.A. Bligh, *What's the Use of Lectures?*, 1978, p. 22)

70. D. Legge, 'The Use of the Talk', pp. 58f; B.A. Milller, 'The Role of the Sermon', p. 98, *cf.* J. McLeish, *Evangelical Religion and Popular Education*, 1969, p. 19; idem,

The Lecture Method, 1968, p. 37; K.I. Pargament and D. V. DeRosa, 'What Was That Sermon About?', 180-193

71. L.O. Richards, *A New Face for the Church*, 1970, pp. 148-152

72. On this technique see M.J. Townsend, 'Preaching: Twenty-Five Years of Ups and Downs', *Exp T*, 95, 1984, 135; S. Greidanus, *The Modem Preacher and the Ancient Text*, 1988, pp. 148-154; M. Willshaw, 'The Decline and Rise of Preaching?' in R. Davies (ed), *The Testing of the Churches 1932-1982*, 1982, pp. 175-187; R.L. Eslinger, 'Narrative and Imagery' in idem (ed), *Intersections: Post-Critical Studies in Preaching*, 1994, pp. 69f

73. On end-product analysis see D. Ehrenfeld, *The Arrogance of Humanism*, [2]1981, pp. 59-64. C. West Churchman defines opportunity costs as 'the loss one incurs in not doing x because one has done y, x and y being mutually exclusive' (*Thought and Wisdom*, 1982, p. 97. See also pp. 13-15, 97f)

74. Exod. 18:13-27; 1 Sam. 2:22-36, 8:1-9; 1 Kings 19:1-8; Jer. 4:10; Matt. 17:14-20; Mark 6:35-37; Luke 7:20; Acts 10:9-15; 1 Cor. 1:11-17; Gal. 2:1-21; Phil. 4:2f; 2 Thes. 3:1-15. Sin may be involved in some of these examples, but the main emphasis is on failure.

75. C. West Churchman, *Thought and Wisdom*, pp. 8-15; D. Ehrenfeld, *Humanism*, pp. 57-129

76. R.T. Beckwith, C.O. Buchanan and K.F.W. Prior (eds), *Services of Baptism and Communion*, 1967, pp. 18f

77. The apostles occasionally delegated the task of baptism to others (Acts 10:44-48; *cf.* 1 Cor. 1 :14-17), possibly in a desire to imitate the practice of Jesus (John 4:1f: R.T. Beckwith, *Priesthood and Sacraments: A Study in the Anglican-Methodist Report*, 1964, pp. 25, 27)

78. Most of these cases occur in missionary situations where there was no existing Christian community, but that is not the case at Acts 9:18 and 16:31-33. The general procedure here seems quite fluid as it is in the *Didache* (7:1-4). Ignatius, on the other hand, required the presence of the bishop, or at least his permission, before baptism might take place (*Ad Smyrn* 8:2), and this thinking, combined with a desire to locate baptism precisely as regards time and place, came to take precedence in the early church (W.B. Marriott and A. Nesbitt, *DCA*, I, 166, 173f; K. Lake, *ERE*, II, 384; G. Delling, *Worship in the New Testament*, 1962, pp. 132f). The reason for the New Testament practice of baptism by the converter or his agent is unspecified, but I suspect that one purpose is to allow the relationship of 'spiritual father' to 'spiritual child' to be seen as significant and to grow in order that the newly converted might have a variety of counsellors at their disposal without being dominated by the elders. It would also promote the maturity of the 'spiritual father' (1 Cor. 4:14f, 9:1; 2 Cor.12:14; 1 Thes. 2:11; 1 Tim. 1:2; Philem. 10). Note that the kind of 'spiritual fatherhood', which Paul has in mind is not directly related to the act of baptism (*cf.* 1 Cor. 4:14f with 1:14-16). See further H. von Campenhausen, *Ecclesiastical Authority and Spiritual Power in the Church of the First Three Centuries*, 1969, pp. 44-48; E. Best, *Paul and His Converts*, 1988, pp. 35-39

79. P. Bradshaw, *Liturgical Presidency in the Early Church*, 1983, pp. 6-8; H.N. Ridderbos, *Paul: An Outline of His Theology*, 1975, pp. 482-484; C.F.D. Moule, *Worship in the New Testament*, 1977, pp. 24f

80. P. Mickey, G. Gamble and P. Gilbert, *Pastoral Assertiveness: A New Model for*

Pastoral Care, Abingdon Press, Nashville, 1978, p. 60

81. J. Benthanl, *Worship in the City*, 1986, pp. 12f; A. Russell, *The Clerical Profession*, 1984, pp. 283f, 292

82. B. Hargrove, *The Sociology of Religion*, [2]1989, pp. 218f Team leadership is a feature of some charismatic churches (J. Noble, *House Churches: Will They Survive?*, 1988, pp. 68-76)

83. R.E. Towler, 'The Role of the Clergy Today—A Sociological View' in E.L. Mitton (ed), *The Social Sciences and the Churches*, 1972, pp. 155f; P. Beasley-Murray, *Pastors Under Pressure*, 1989, pp. 10-13; P.D. Meier et al, *Introduction to Psychology and Counseling*, [2]1991 , pp. 288f. On the stress caused to clergy by having to preach see M.A. Coate, *Clergy Stress*, 1989, pp. 124-130.

84. A. Storkey, *Transforming Economics*, 1986, pp. 118f; idem, *A Christian Social Perspective*, 1979, pp. 391f; J. Freytag, 'The Ministry as a Profession: A Sociological Critique' in D.M. Paton (ed), *New Forms of Ministry*, 1965, pp. 62-69; D.F. Wells, *No Place for Truth*, 1993, pp. 112f, 218-257

85. L.B. Brown, *The Psychology of Religion: An Introduction*, 1988, pp. 78f; cf. B. Mitchell, *The Justification of Religious Belief*, 1973, pp. 132f

86. D. Lyon, *The Steeple's Shadow*, 1985, pp. 128-131; A. Russell, *The Clerical Profession*, 1984, pp. 261-306; R.C. Towler and A.P.M. Coxon, *The Fate of the Anglican Clergy*, 1979, pp. 34-40; *cf.* P.D.L. Avis, *Authority, Leadership and Conflict in the Church*, 1992, pp. l03f

87. J. Freytage, 'The Ministry', pp. 73-76; A. Russell, *Clerical Profession*, pp. 294f. That some do not regard the clergy as a professional group hardly affects the argument (R. C. Towler and A.P.M. Coxon, *Anglican Clergy*, pp. 45-49)

88. This idea is criticized in P. Helm, *The Callings: The Gospel in the World*, 1987, pp. ix-xiii, 44-69; L. Ryken, *Work and Leisure in Christian Perspective*, 1989, pp. 136-152; J.W. Fowler, *Faith Development and Pastoral Care*, 1987, pp. 27-32

89. R. Allen, *Missionary Methods: St Paul's or Ours?*, 1912 repr 1962, pp. 149f; A.B. MacDonald, *Christian Worship in the Primitive Church*, 1934, pp. 23, 53-56. This attitude was not restricted to Paul (2 Cor. 8:22).

90. R.J. Banks, *Paul's Idea of Community*, Carlisle, Paternoster Press, 1980, p. 176

91. N.R. Petersen, *Rediscovering Paul: Philemon and the Sociology of Paul's Narrative World*, 1985, pp. 128-131

92. T.F. O'Dea and J. O'Dea Aviad, *The Sociology of Religion*, 1983, pp. 112f

93. R.E. Coleman, *The Master Plan of Evangelism*, [2]1964, pp. 33-35, 43-49; W.E. Diehl, *Christianity and Real Life*, 1976, pp. 1-40

94. L.J. Crabb, *Basic Principles of Biblical Counseling*, 1975 repr 1989, pp. 59-66

95. R. Pointer, *How Do Churches Grow?*, 1984, pp. 120-122

96. The main emphasis of the Great Commission (Mattt. 28:18-20) is precisely on making real disciples (P. O'Brien, 'The Great Commission of Matthew 28:18-20', *RTR*, 35, 1976, 73; D.W. Wead, 'The Centripetal Philosophy of Mission' in W.W. Gasque and W.S. LaSor (eds), *Scripture, Tradition and Interpretation*, 1978, p. 185; D.A. Carson, *Matthew*, EBC, 1984, VIII, 595f)

97. K. Craig, 'Is the "Sermon" Concept Biblical? A Study in Greek Origins', *ST*, 15:1-2, 1986, 22, 24; similarly G. Reid, *The Gagging of God*, 1969, p. 102; H. Kraemer, *A Theology of the Laity*, 1958, pp. 65f

98. *Pastoral Teaching of Paul*, 1907 repr 1984, p. 197

99. R.J. Banks, *The Tyranny of Time*, 1983, pp. 57-73

100. R.J. Banks, *Time*, pp. 204-212

101. R.J. Banks, *All the Business of Life*, [2]1989, pp. 42-61

102. J. Bright, *The Authority of the Old Testament*, 1967, p. 248; H. Schlossberg, *A Fragrance of Oppression: The Church and Its Persecutors*, 1991

103. H.R. Mackintosh, *The Christian Experience of Forgiveness*, [2]1934, pp. 279f; D.J. Drew, *Images of Man: A Critique of the Contemporary Cinema*, 1974, p. 70

104. N. Postman and C. Weingartner, *Teaching as a Subversive Activity*, 1969 repr 1976, pp.15-27

105. These defects reflect many of the characteristics of Anglo-North American society, particularly its cultural and spiritual immaturity (M.F. Sciacca, *Philosophical Trends in the Contemporary World*, 1964, pp. 106f, 388-397; H. Schlossberg, *Idols for Destruction*, 1983; E. Rosenstock-Huessy, *The Christian Future or the Modem Mind Outrun*, 1947, pp. 3-91)

106. J. Ellul, *The Ethics of Freedom*, 1976, pp. 291f; similarly H. Schlossberg, *Idols*, pp. 235-239; S.A. Kierkegaard, *Attack Upon 'Christendom'*, 1854-1855 (ET 1946), pp. 33-47 et passim

107. D. Lyon, *The Steeple's Shadow*, 1985, pp. 58-62; V.A. Harvey, 'On the Intellectual Marginality of American Theology' in MJ. Lacey (ed), *Religion and Twentieth-Century American Intellectual Life*, 1989, pp. 172-192

Objections to Retiring the Sermon

6

Some readers may argue that, in spite of the evidence and arguments presented so far, there still remain good reasons for continuing to use the regular sermon. This chapter considers some of these reasons.

'GOD HAS BLESSED THE SERMON THROUGHOUT CHURCH HISTORY'

BENEFITS—AND THEIR PRICE

Christians know from experience that God blesses that which is in some way defective. But the defective is not necessarily tolerated forever. There are biblical examples, where God was directly responsible for creating, or at least tolerating, an institution, which might seem to have a permanent blessing, but which might be removed because of failure or inadequacy. We might mention the Law and the cultus, the national pre-eminence of Israel, the monarchy and the bronze serpent of Moses (Num. 21:6-9; 2 Kings 18:1-4).[1] It would be wrong to argue back from failure and conclude that God was not the originator of the failed or replaced institution just as it would also be wrong to argue back from blessing to the essential correctness of that which is blessed. Rather, any blessing should be seen as an example of the graciousness of God.[2] Since all beliefs and actions are swathed in ignorance and error,[3] it follows that if blessing were dependent on the complete absence of either, then there would be no blessing at all. Nonetheless, error and disobedience restrict the work of God.

As we have seen, the sermon fails at many points. Yet it does sometimes produce good results. All teaching methods, no matter how inadequate, can succeed occasionally, but this hardly amounts to proof that all teaching methods are equally effective. For example, N.M. Watson argues from the occasional effectiveness of the sermon to its general effectiveness as a method. A better way would have been to consider the effectiveness of the sermon in relation to other methods.[4]

The benefits that derive from the sermon are for the most part secondary and include:

- teaching and communication from God
- benefit to the preacher through preparation
- inspiration
- enjoyment
- the preservation of order

The first has been dealt with above; the second requires no comment. As for inspiration, the sermon has no unique power in this respect and the inspirational sermon is in any case a rarity besides being inadequate as a regular diet.[5]

Many church-goers enjoy sermons and may become connoisseurs of sermons wedded to one particular form. Others, through lengthy exposure and internalization of ecclesiastical dogma,[6] accept the sermon as the only valid form. Yet others enjoy the passivity and anonymity of merely listening and would find more active methods threatening. These groups could oppose reform, especially where the sermons are competent. God's people frequently misunderstand deliverance when it is offered and prefer the familiarity of bondage to the uncertainties of liberation; the emotional security of institutionalized immaturity to the rigors of responsible adulthood (Exod. 5:20f; Judg. 15:10-13; Jer. 5:31f; Acts 7:25).[7]

The sermon eliminates disorder but does so at the cost of individual freedom. Paul's response to the disorder at Corinth shows that his answer to the abuse of freedom was its correct use, not the exercise of a control eliminating, not just the problems associated with free expression, but the free expression itself. The attempt to eliminate even the risk of ever allowing one problem to surface, unwittingly creates a host of attendant problems.[8] All the gifts of God come without guarantees and can be abused, but this is no excuse for eliminating any of those gifts.

Paul trusted in the Holy Spirit to guide and mature his converts—even to the point of putting them at risk (Acts 20:29; Gal 1:6).[9] He also trusted his converts and generally expected the best from them in spite of being let down occasionally (Acts 15:37-39; 1 Tim 1:19f; 2 Tim. 1:15, 4:10f). But the sermon, and the controlling apparatus of which it is a part, suggests little trust or confidence in God or the congregation and frequently results in little growth and lack of peace.[10] Thus the preservation of order is illusory.

THE PURITANS AND THE SERMON

INTRODUCTION

Our concern is with the effectiveness of the sermon in England today and this can hardly be determined by its effectiveness in any earlier period; which, in any case, is difficult to assess. To illustrate the point it may be helpful to examine the matter in the context of Puritanism. This is a particularly appropriate example as many Christians believe the Puritan period to be a golden age of preaching.

Throughout much of Europe from the 15th to the 17th century, the sermon was highly regarded and widely popular in an age when the pulpit was the primary means of communicating news and clergymen were of some authority in their own communities.[11] Many of the Puritans considered preaching to be the primary duty of the clergy and held the sermon in such uncritical admiration that one might attribute conversions to pulpit activity irrespective of attendant circumstances.[12] Many Puritan congregations truly enjoyed sermons and were happy to listen regularly to expositions lasting an hour or more. Two-hour sermons were not rare and some were even longer.[13] For some, on the margins of Christianity, preaching was frequently little more than 'bibble babble' or a time for sleeping but many Puritans saw Sunday sermons as the most significant events of the week and of inestimable importance to the Christian life.[14]

PURITAN SUPPLEMENTS TO THE SERMON

Listening to sermons was, however, not the only means available for acquiring information and spiritual riches. Other means included private reading of the Bible and other literature including letters,[15] domestic religion, catechetical instruction, singing psalms, hymns and ballads, reciting poetry,[16] attending schools and public lectures,[17] individual and family discussions with the clergy[18] and meetings of Christian groups—often led by laymen. At a different level, traditional lore was given by various wandering bards[19] and, in the early days of Puritanism, mystery plays, which, however, had died out by the beginning of the 17th century.[20]

Three of the more significant Puritan supplements to the sermon merit closer examination.

READING

Many Puritans respected and loved learning and their interest was not necessarily confined to matters theological. Believing in the unity of all knowledge, they had an active interest in all the major branches of learning and were active in many areas of social reform (including education) although they were not original social thinkers.[21] As Perry Miller observes, the Puritans did not

> renounce all learning save theology or lose interest in other inquiries besides the religious. They did indeed subordinate all concerns to salvation, and they did force their social and philosophical thinking into conformity with religious conclusions, but they were incapable of confining themselves solely to dogma or giving over the arts and sciences into the keeping of the unregenerate.[22]

The Puritans encouraged public and private reading and produced a considerable range of literature, particularly religious literature, and in their hands the printing press became the pulpit's greatest rival.[23] Books of all sorts were available from a wide variety of sources, from stationers and printers to peddlars, ballad-singers and mariners and could be obtained even in the remotest areas.[24] But of all the literature available, it was the Bible itself which stimulated the most excitement and all, including children, were encouraged to devote considerable time to mastering and memorizing it.

The Christian who wished to master the elements of the faith might have been illiterate but, as Thomas Kelly points out, 'the desire to read the words of Holy Scripture became for centuries one of the greatest incentives to literacy among humble people.[25] Some illiterate adults were fortunate in finding those (including Puritan clergy) who were prepared to teach them to read and illiterate live in servants may have been helped to read by various aspects of the life and religion of their employers. Those who remained illiterate had to content themselves with listening to the reading of others either at home, the homes of literate neighbours, the workshop, the inn (a meeting place of the godly) or in church.[26] Those who could write as well as read might take notes as they studied the Scriptures.[27] The precise extent to which the population was literate in this period is difficult to estimate but recent studies suggest that many could read even if they could not write; that literacy was more common in the towns than the countryside; that more men were literate than women; that literacy was most widespread among professional people; that literacy increased with social standing; and that regional variations were considerable.[28]

With the advent of printing, relatively cheap books were produced in large numbers, on a wide variety of subjects and for all sections of society including women and children.[29] Bound books might be expensive. For example, the works of Shakespeare could be purchased for 18/6d or 22s—92-1/2p . or £1.10p (1623 and 1632) and Richard Sibbes' *Saints Cordialls* sold for 8s—40p (1637). The price of Bibles in the 17th century varied considerably and might be as much as £2 or as little as 1/8d (8p). Unbound items might cost as little as a few pence: in 1632 a single Shakespeare play might cost 6d (2-1/2p) and numerous godly chapbooks were available at 2d (1p) each.[30] Second-hand items could be even cheaper.[31] The occasional purchase of such items was, therefore, possible for all but the poorest.[32] The Puritan divine Richard Baxter (1615-1691) referred to the reading habits of the relatively affluent weavers of Kidderminster: 'as they stand in their loom they can set a book before them or edify one another...'[33]

Baxter also noted that many workers lower down the social scale never read the Bible at all.[34] Furthermore, not even all the clergy could afford to keep their personal libraries adequately stocked. This is not surprising as many curates earned less than £10 per year and some lived on the verge of starvation.[35]

To encourage reading, some Christians lent or gave Christian books to the poor or arranged for books to be sold at reduced rates.[36] Speaking of the effects of the widespread dissemination of the devotional literature produced by the Puritans, J.I. Packer maintains that:

> England had had no devotional literature worth speaking of until this flow started; hence, writing at layman's level, the same level at which they preached, the pastors were soon able to capture a very large readership, and the influence of their published works in the first half of the 17th century was far-reaching and profound.[37]

There were also small libraries attached to some grammar schools and churches as well as separate town libraries (the first of which appeared at Norwich in 1608) although not all of these were truly 'public' as lending was often restricted. The first mention of a free lending library in Great Britain refers to one in Repton, Derbyshire in 1622—it had only 15 volumes.[38] A number of 'public' libraries were established under Puritan influence in the 17th century, but by 1700 lending libraries were still rare and their influence small.[39] In 17th century New England, the poor tended to borrow books from large private collections. The subscription or circulating library appeared in America in 1731 and public libraries followed in the 19th century.[40] Where opportunities for adult learning were few, the printed word was supremely important.

DOMESTIC RELIGION

Inspired by the Reformers, Puritanism flourished in the life of the family with each household seen as a religious community. In the words of William Gouge 'a family is a little church'.[41] The father usually acted as 'priest' to his family and, where present, the extended household. He would instruct the children, read the Bible or some other godly book and lead the prayers. Private and family devotions were to be performed daily or even twice daily.[42] On Sundays these might occupy a substantial proportion of the day and often included, after the midday meal, a careful examination of the morning sermon. This must have acted as an extra incentive to concentrate during the sermon, particularly when praise was given for prodigious feats of memory.[43]

To be effective in all his priestly duties, the father of the household needed to spend time mastering his faith. For some Puritans, self-examination, the keeping of a spiritual diary and fasting were aides to growth. Some of the poorest in society, such as small tenant farmers, could hardly afford books, spare the time to read the Bible or instruct their own families even where they had the ability to do so.[44] But, in spite of such difficulties, Puritanism helped to create a more godly home life than had existed in Elizabethan England, particularly in the realm of sexual morality and at least something of this ethos has remained to the present day.[45]

INFORMAL GROUP MEETINGS

The numerous Puritan informal meetings often led to an extensive exchange of ideas and experiences along with discussion of biblical matters and practice of mutual ministries. Some took notes during sermons (or immediately afterwards) perhaps using shorthand. In subsequent group meetings, often led by laymen, the sermon might be recapitulated and discussed sometimes with further questions set for homework.[46] The effects of these meetings are estimated by William Haller as follows:

Of the effect of such teaching upon the popular mind, aside from any specific religious results, there can also be little doubt. The people were brought together. They learned to read, to use a book, to exchange ideas and experiences, to confer intellectually after their own fashion upon common problems, to partake of the exhilaration of discussion and self-expression. The perplexities of the individual were the focus of attention, but the individual got the relief, which came from bringing perplexities into the light and so discovering that they are but the common lot, for which, peradventure, there might be a common remedy. That the authorities should have come to regard such activities as dangerous to the status quo is not surprising. But their influence upon popular taste, imagination and modes of thought was in the long run to be no less important than the immediate disturbance they caused in the matter of government.[47]

THE PLACE OF THE SERMON IN PURITANISM

We are now in a position to evaluate the place of the sermon in its Puritan context and see how this may affect our evaluation of the sermon today.

First, Puritanism made an impact on England's history, possibly greater than that of any other religious movement.[48] It emphasized the presence of God in human affairs; it fostered a certain independence of mind and character and, within limits, helped to develop Christian maturity among its followers[49] in spite of tendencies to concentrate power in clerical hands and to overemphasize specific doctrines.[50] Like any other human embodiment of Christianity, Puritanism had defects[51] but these do not altogether nullify its achievements. Even so, Puritan influence did not spread uniformly throughout society; the countryside was probably less affected than the towns, and magic and superstition continued to be rife in both England and New England.[52]

Second, it is important to recognize that some (perhaps many) Puritans as well as non-Puritans were in no doubt that all the major means outlined above contributed significantly to Christian life and that sermons on their own were likely to prove inadequate.[53] Richard Baxter, who had a positive view of the sermon, said of conversations with his parishioners:

> I profess again, it is to me the most comfortable work, except public preaching—for there I speak to more, though yet with less advantage to each individual—that ever I yet did set my hand to.[54]

Elsewhere Baxter even says, 'It is but the least part of a Ministers work, which is done in the Pulpit.'[55] In the same vein, N.H. Keeble has assembled a catena of Baxter quotations on the value of books in comparison with sermons:

> ... it was his (Baxter's) confident belief that the printed word

offered the most effective means by which teachers and learners could pursue their related duties. By publication a teacher might reach a much greater number of people; as an author he was not subject to the time-limit imposed on the preacher; and he could in writing address himself at large to any particular subject. As learners, we do not have to rely upon our own memories, for 'a Book we may read over and over till we remember it', and it is always there for consultation; we may select a work suited to our particular case and in a style appropriate to our abilities; we may have the benefit of a good book at any time, so that we 'may read an able Preacher when (we) have but a mean one to hear'; and 'Books may be kept at a smaller charge than Preachers'. Furthermore, 'The eye taketh in sentiments more effectually than the ears, since the reader can take his own time to digest the matter, 'And with very many it doth more than *Hearing* also to move the *Heart*, though *Hearing of it self* in this hath the advantage: Because lively Books may be easilier had, than lively Preachers'. He concludes, therefore, that '*Reading* with most doth more conduce to Knowledge than *Hearing* doth, and that a course of reading will 'above all other ways increase your knowledge.' In short, 'If other Books (than the Bible) were not needful, Teachers were not needful; for Writing is but the most advantageous way of Teaching.'[56]

While Baxter is in no way denigrating the sermon, he shows a keen awareness of its limitations and the relative superiority of alternative ways of learning. It should be added that in the writings of Baxter and the Puritans generally there is often no sharp distinction between evangelistic and non-evangelistic sermons.[57] At times, Puritan writers seem to use the term 'preaching' to cover more than what we might call the 'sermon' although the latter is chiefly in mind.

Attempts to advance further in our understanding of the relative effectiveness of the Puritan sermon when compared with other forms of instruction would bring us up against the old problem of too many variables, none of which can be examined in complete isolation. Baxter's analysis is useful, but I know of no precise studies of the individual effectiveness of each of the above means as applied in the Puritan context; consequently, the effectiveness of the Puritan sermon cannot be assessed accurately. All we can say with any confidence is that the sermon, in conjunction with numerous other means, achieved a certain result but the precise effectiveness of the individual means remains in doubt.

An examination of the role played by the sermon in other past periods of reformation or revival, particularly those in which Christian literature was widely available, would probably yield a similar null result. For example, preaching was greatly revered in Germany during the 16th century but, along with the sermon, all the other means of growth outlined above were also used, to some extent, and the precise effects of the sermon are, again, difficult to assess.[58] The idea of preaching with the pen goes back to Cassiodorus (485-580 AD) and, ultimately, to the Bible so it should come as no surprise to find that the sermon is frequently merely one of several means available for the communication of the Word of God.[59]

Third, it does not follow that if the sermon proved effective in Puritan times, then it must be or ought to be effective today. Our circumstances are different. Today lengthy speeches do not inspire respect and many people are unused to concentrating for lengthy periods on information presented in that form. The average listener today would be hard pressed to cope with regular, serious, reasoned one-hour expositions because, as Neil Postman argues, techniques of communication are dominated by visual images inspired primarily by television and this affects not just the form of what is communicated but the substance as well.[60]

Preachers today should be aware of the cultural limitations of their audience; there is no compelling reason to try to re-educate hearers to appreciate a popular method of yesterday.[61] There can be little doubt that many Puritans profited from the sermons they heard and it may well be the case that 1st century Christians would have pro-fited similarly. Even so, God, in his wisdom, did not prescribe for them a diet of sermons; through Paul and others he offered a different and better form of learning and it so happens (to put it no higher) that this form can be effective today. The sermonic exploits of past worthies provide no reason for the use of regular sermons in the present and no reason for idolizing a method, which should be reckoned among things indifferent.

Fourth, it is frequently assumed that regular sermons are characteristic of periods of spiritual awakening and their absence is characteristic of periods of spiritual impoverishment. There is truth here but mixed with misunderstanding. In revivals, sermons are used initially for evangelistic purposes or on occasions when the Christian community *as a whole* stands in the *same* need of encouragement, rebuke, exhortation and instruction—as for example at the start of the Reformation. These usages parallel those of the New Testament. As we have already seen, the regular sermon became common early in the life of the church and then, for the most part, was not sharply distinguished from the evangelistic sermon. It is, therefore, hardly surprising that when the sermon is legitimately resuscitated in revivals, the traditions of the church guarantee that the regular sermon also gains a new lease of life. That this happened in the Puritan period indicates the extent to which the Puritans had but a slight grasp of the relevant New Testament data.

But the fault was not theirs alone. Many of the great Reformation preachers who paved the way for Puritanism had studied rhetoric and men such as John Calvin, Ulrich Zwingli and John Oecolampadius had been deeply influenced by the sermons of Augustine, John Chrysostom, Origen, Gregory of Nazianzus and Gregory the Great.[62] Thus the flaws in the preaching of the Fathers were duplicated by the Reformers and again by the Puritans. That the Puritans should fall foul of this tradition is strange, in a way, because, following Erasmus, they were aware of the dangers of custom, which he so eloquently described as 'the fiercest tyrant of them all', and were happy to experiment with new methods.[63] In some respects the position has deteriorated since then; a lack of originality, a non-intellectual approach, narrow emphases and a failure to challenge traditional methods are characteristic of many later evangelical movements. In one form or another, these problems have always plagued the church.[64]

Finally, however desirable an understanding of the Puritan period may be for Christians today, an understanding of the early period of the Christian church is surely more important. There are at least two reasons for this. First, for at least part of the early period we are in close contact with Jesus and the apostles and have a biblical commentary on some of the material. Second, the present state of the church—weak, without the powerful support of nation states and in a world alien to Christian life and forms—arguably has more in common with the Christian life of the first few centuries than that of the middle ages, the days of the Reformers or the Puritan period. As Sir Herbert Butterfield observes:

> In these days, therefore, we have much to learn from the Christianity of the very earliest centuries; and it would be wiser for us to keep that early period of Church history in our minds as our basis of reference rather than be hankering after the middle ages or attempting to hold on to an order of things which is now disintegrated.[65]

THE APPEAL TO PROVIDENCE

'GOD WOULD NOT ALLOW THE CHURCH TO USE A DESTRUCTIVE METHOD FOR SO LONG.'

The Bible contains numerous examples of injustice and error extended over lengthy periods. In these circumstances, God's people have prayed for deliverance, which was often slow to arrive (Job 19; Ps. 13:1, 44:23-26, 74:10; Isa. 64:1; Hab. 1:2). The Bible shows that God's ways are not our ways; any apparent slowness on his part is for the ultimate good of his people (Isa. 55:8f; Rom. 3:25; Gal. 4:4; 2 Pet. 3:8f).[66] Here are a few examples of long-term error and injustice from the Bible and church history:

1. After the death of Joshua and the elders who survived him, the Israelites were, in a sense, left to themselves in order to grow up and be tested. They forsook the Lord and there followed a lengthy period of spiritual darkness.[67]

2. For centuries, the church persecuted witches. It generally failed to notice that those whom it designated witches had almost nothing in common with the witches of the Bible.[68] It failed to notice that most of the punishments dispensed were cruel and

had no biblical sanction. It failed to notice that its own corrupt and pagan procedures helped to magnify rather than diminish the problem.[69] It failed to notice that its view of the activities of spirits in the world owed more to a modified Aristotelian cosmology combined with mediaeval superstition than to the Bible. It failed to notice that its treatment of witches (usually women and often old women)[70] derived largely from its low opinion and unbiblical view of women and was a response to the changing social and economic status of women.[71] It failed to notice that although the activity of Satan was most assuredly manifest in the witchcraft saga it appeared principally in the superstitious ignorance and corrupt behavior of clergy, lawyers and scholars and the anonymous masses supporting them. The persecution of witches by the church was sporadic for many centuries but took on a more systematic character from the 15th century and continued until the 18th.[72] A few Christians at least did see the issues clearly and helped to bring an end to the witch craze. But those who spoke out were usually ignored or badly treated until the folly had finally run its course.[73]

3. The response of the church to the issue of slavery reveals further long-term error.[74]

It is thus entirely consistent with God's ways and purposes that the world in general, and the church in particular, should have been in costly error for a lengthy period; and there is no inherent difficulty in the idea that the church could have used a destructive method for a long period.

But more needs to be said. The question, as stated, wrongly implies that the church is an innocent victim. We have already seen that the sermon arose in the context of the neglect of Scripture and the unintelligent embracing of pagan ideas. The church continued in its unquestioning path until the problems of the sermon were tackled afresh in the 19th century but to no avail. More insistent voices in the present century have fared little better. Responsibility for failing to apply biblical teaching rests not only with the individual but with the ecclesiastical structures through which the church operates. These structures are always liable to fall prey to the powers of evil and those responsible for church organization have an awesome duty and one, which can easily be exercised badly.

'PRESUMABLY THE SERMON HAS ENDURED FOR SOME GOOD REASON—HERE WE MAY SEE THE PROVIDENCE OF GOD.'

It is difficult, if not impossible, to point out examples of the special providence of God in particular circumstances; nor is it obvious that we should attempt to discern the providence of God in specific events beyond acknowledging his hand in all things.[75] Christians have frequently attributed precise events and practices to the hand of God at work in contemporary events. Such theological interpretations of history are usually little more than wild guesses.[76] G.C. Berkouwer comments:

> The interpretation of an historical event as a special revelation of Providence too easily becomes a piously disguised form of self-justification... It may be said that no event speaks so clearly that we may conclude from it a certain disposition of God—as long as God Himself does not reveal that His disposition comes to expression in the given event... A subjective invocation of 'special providence' in connection with very extraordinary events is actually worthless. This is particularly evident when men, as they often do, call upon the idea of 'special providence' in order to involve God in the realization of their own dubious plans. It is relatively simple in this way to conclude the leading of God from historical facts... It is often forgotten that we have not been given a norm for explaining the facts of history, and that in the absence of a norm only an untrustworthy plausibility remains... Where fragments of history are not interpreted by God Himself, we are not permitted to explain them out of their entire context as though their meaning were intuitively and, hence, irrationally perspicuous to us.[77]

The existence of a particular practice in the church may indicate the providential guidance of God but it does not follow that the practice itself must inevitably be good. Nor does it follow that an extant practice must be that which God desires[78] for there are many examples in Scripture of the frustration of God's desires.[79] Nor does it follow that, in the exercise of his providence, God has eliminated human stupidity and sin, although they may be overruled in the attainment of God's ultimate purposes.[80]

Furthermore, there is no known direct connection between the truth of a doctrine or practice and the length of time that human beings have believed or practiced it. Readers may care to compile their own list of abhorred doctrines and practices and then reflect upon the frightening possibility that these could be legitimized by merely pleading their antiquity. The pathway to truth lies along a different route and the long reign of the regular sermon is no guarantee of its legitimacy or effectiveness. No human activity can be justified merely by its' antiquity or by vague reference to the providence of God.

'THE SERMON HAS BEEN VALUABLE IN EVANGELISM.'

NEW TESTAMENT PRACTICE

The sermons in the New Testament were usually directed to people outside the Christian community, on an irregular basis as need arose, rather than at regular intervals. Even when outsiders came to Christian meetings, there is nothing to suggest that they heard or were converted through sermons (1 Cor. 14:23-25). We have already seen that, in the New Testament, mission strategy was both centrifugal and centripetal, but in the latter case potential converts were attracted by the Christian community (Acts 2:42-47, 5:13f; 1 Cor. 14:23). Once the Christian community had been formed, there would be little need of narrow evangelistic sermons. Evangelists might then train others with the gift of evangelism or even move out to previously unevangelized towns and cities but little information is available on their activities.

Support for the regular evangelistic sermon in a church context is sometimes sought from Paul's work in the hall or lecture room of Tyrannus at Ephesus (Acts 19:9). Precise detail on both Tyrannus and his establishment is lacking[81] but it appears that Paul was able to use the place regularly over an extended period for the purpose of Christian instruction. Just who attended and for what purpose is also unclear. The establishment of house churches was Paul's normal practice in the centers where he preached. (Possible exceptions occurred at Beroea and Athens but since both were visited while escaping from persecution by Jews from Thessalonica and were very brief visits, the omission is understandable—Acts 17:10 - 18:1).[82] At Ephesus, as elsewhere, Christians required somewhere to celebrate the Lord's Supper and this could hardly have been the synagogue. It seems fair to assume that since Paul had been in Ephesus some time before the break with the synagogue, house churches were already in operation when the move came. This suggests that the hall of Tyrannus may have served an essentially evangelistic function.[83]

Until about the 4th century, Christian meetings were open to outsiders by invitation only.[84] This was to maintain the purity of the congregation in all respects but was, in any case, almost inevitable when meetings were held in private homes. Paul's evangelistic meetings may have been exceptional, with non-Christians attending at will, but evidence is lacking.

The school approach was particularly fitting at Ephesus since regular lectures by philosophers and rhetoricians were common throughout the empire but especially in Asia Minor.[85] It may be, as T.G. Soares suggests, that Paul's fame in Ephesus was such that a visit to hear this preacher of foreign divinities was customary for a visitor to Ephesus.[86] Alternatively, Christians may have widely advertised these lectures and invited others along by card or word of mouth as did the sophists.[87] Those who attended may have been following the common practice of searching around for the best philosophy of life on the market.

The use of *dialegomai* (Acts 20:8f) suggests discussion and debate. A lecture may have been involved but there is the suggestion here of audience participation.[88] Judging from Paul's suggestions on conducting conversations, we may assume that he concentrated on a positive presentation of the gospel as well as dealing with questions raised—with the emphasis on understanding rather than argument for its own sake (Eph. 4:29; Col. 4:6; 2 Tim. 2:24-26).[89]

After conversion, new Christians would probably attend house churches although some, along with older Christians, might remain to help Paul and use the opportunity to develop their gifts. They would not have remained passive observers of a virtuoso performer for long because Paul was a fine teacher. Those with evangelistic gifts would soon have found work to do in the numerous towns in the province of asia. It was particularly fitting that Christians at such a strategic missionary center should have had high caliber instruction available to them. Its fruits were to be seen in the numerous churches established in the region, probably including most of the 'Seven Churches of Asia' (Acts 19:10; Col. 1:6f, 4:12f).[90]

We conclude that Paul's work in the hall of Tyrannus provides no support for regular evangelistic Sermon s in a church context because:

- If Paul used Sermons at all in this work, they involved a great deal more discussion and audience participation than is common in an English setting.
- Paul's evangelistic work seems to have been separate from the nurture of the Christian community, which took place in the house churches.
- Paul's work was perfectly suited to the prevailing cultural conditions and appropriate to a center of missionary activity.

THE MODEM PERIOD

Sermons have been prominent in revivals.[91] But here, the New Testament method of preaching to the unconverted has generally been followed although many church members have been converted in revivals.[92] For growth following conversion, small scale meetings were often established such as those of Howell Harris (1714-1773) in South Wales from 1736 and the bands and class meetings of early Methodism.[93] Just as the Sermon can be a channel for the work of the Spirit in conversion, so it can be an aid to fossilization if continued as the principal method of teaching and growth. Such fossilization has often occurred in the aftermath of revivals (for a variety of reasons) and the results can be seen today in many British churches, which experienced revival in the 19th century.

'THE GIFT OF PREACHING IS PREFIGURED IN THE NEW TESTAMENT.'

In the New Testament, there is mention of the gift of prophecy but not the gift of preaching. Preaching, as we know it, is different from prophecy and although both may involve learning and spiritual growth (*cf.* 1 Cor. 14:31), the emphasis and form are different in each case.[94] Preaching is a form of teaching and requires reflection, interpretation and explanation, with the focus on Scripture. In fact, preaching is just one method of teaching and hence does not merit a separate mention in a list of spiritual gifts.[95] Prophecy, on the other hand, centers on the report of a direct revelation from God. In the early church, there may well have been some overlapping. Prophets may have joined with teachers in warning, correcting and teaching traditional material (*cf.* Acts 15:32) as did Old Testament prophets.[96] Some prophets may have been teachers. One with the prophetic gift, like Paul, may have prophesied when instructing others, as in his own letters, but this would be teaching with prophetic elements added. The essential differences between preaching (or teaching) and prophesying remain.

The gifts of prophecy, wisdom and knowledge, whatever we are to understand by them, did not result in preaching after our pattern. If any traces of these gifts remain today, they do not necessarily have any greater connection with the sermon than with any other form of Christian communication.

'THE HOLY SPIRIT WORKS THROUGH THE SERMON.'

'THE SERMON IS GOD'S CHOSEN METHOD, HOWEVER INADEQUATE IT MAY SEEM.'

This argument sees the effectiveness of the sermon as depending on the power of the Holy Spirit operating through the chosen instrument of God—the preacher. At the human level, the effects of the sermon can hardly be defined or analysed.[97] This implies a sharp distinction between the sacred and the secular. Secular learning is seen as shedding little light on spiritual matters. Consequently, the criticisms of the sermon outlined above are of little or no value, even though such criticism may be seen as legitimate when applied in the secular sphere.

In effect, this view denies that God is the Lord of creation; it denies that all truth is God's truth;[98] and it insists that God behaves as a stranger in the world of his creation since he constantly needs to operate apart from or in opposition to natural processes in order to achieve his aims. Christian growth is attained by processes that verge on the magical. Edward Schillebeeckx describes this schizophrenic attitude to secular learning as a form of 'theological reductionism'.[99]

This deficient doctrine of creation owes a debt to both Greek dualism[100] and to an inflated view of the extent of Satan's power over the world. The latter derives, not so much from biblical data,[101] as from pagan and Jewish views of demonology.[102] Both dualism and an exaggerated demonology entered the church swiftly and to some extent remain to this day, not least in a distorted understanding of worldliness.[103]

It is worth noting that although methods are important, they are not primary; God may bless well-motivated bad methods more than badly motivated good methods. Even so, this would be a poor excuse for retaining bad method—especially after their defects had become known. Some Christians object to applying techniques in any area of the Christian life but, in Scripture, technique or skills frequently commended, the only stipulation being that it should be used under the guidance of the Spirit of God.[104] Similarly, there is no justification for endorsing the Aristotelian dichotomy between theory and practice. In the Bible, life is not so divided, so that Christians should neither exalt reason as opposed to anti-intellectualism nor right doctrine as opposed to wise living.[105]

The view set forth in the objection tends to ignore the existence of other teaching methods; thus the relative effectiveness of the sermon cannot be assessed. The sermon is, in practice, beyond criticism. It has become an end in itself, sacred—the product of a distorted reverence for the tradition of the elders. In this area theological progress has come to an end.[106]

As to 'God's chosen method which he can utilize and bless', the sparkling brilliance of the communication techniques of Jesus and Paul shows us just what God desires to utilize and bless for his own purposes.

'IN THE SERMON, THE PREACHER SPEAKS THE VERY WORD OF GOD.'

The idea that the preaching of the word of God is the very Word of God appears in the Confession Helvetica Posterior of 1566.[107] Although it has been widely influential, particularly among those of the Reformed tradition,[108] it is devoid of biblical support and, in its strong form as stated, is virtually impossible to defend from any standpoint.

It is not my intention to denigrate language or discourse in any way[109] but rather to expose a false emphasis. The Bible contains no clear assertion that any single means used by God to communicate with his servants is superior to any other.[110] Nor is it suggested that one kind of discourse is superior to another. In particular, there is nothing to suggest that, other things being equal, a sermon conveys the word of God more faithfully than, say, a conversation—in both Old and New Testaments, a great deal of truth is conveyed through conversation. Furthermore, the argument, as stated, confuses biblical truth with a method of delivering that truth. The danger of confusing means with ends is ever present in the Christian life, particularly during Christian gatherings when the worship of God can so easily be displaced by the forms of idolatry.[111]

The contemporary Christian emphasis on means rather than ends is characteristic of western society as a whole in which instrumental values take precedence over ultimate values and in which ends are seldom considered.[112]

'THE SERMON IS BETTER SUITED TO OUR TIME THAN NEW TESTAMENT METHODS.'

This argument emphasizes the cultural differences between the 1st century and our own. The Holy Spirit is seen as providing us, not with better means, but with means better suited to our time.

Inasmuch as they relate to the matters in hand, cultural differences are not as great as is often claimed.[113] The principles and practice of communication revealed in the work of Jesus and Paul are superb and timeless.[114] New Testament methods offer more consistent and more effective patterns of communication and growth, and more intelligent ways of producing mature individuals and communities than those commonly used today. It would be wishful thinking indeed to maintain that the sermon is used today because of its methodological superiority or specific relevance to 20th century culture. The prevailing culture, far from supporting the use of the sermon, points to its abandonment. Furthermore, present-day methods are usually not newly minted but are often the product of late antiquity or even earlier. When the church does utilize new methods, they are frequently pressed into an already existing mould and suffer accordingly. The problems are compounded by the extent to which contemporary aims are ill-defined, rendering both success and failure almost impossible to recognize, except perhaps on an attendance basis—and even that is difficult to assess accurately.

In every age some disharmony has existed between God and his people. It is extremely unlikely that the church in our own day (or at least a substantial proportion of it) has finally achieved such a degree of conformity with God's will that only the most minor of adjustments is required in order to fulfill his purposes totally. Such an attitude is characteristic of the church at its most decadent.

It seems strangely inconsistent that those who are most disposed to claim that the Bible is the Word of God, the 'supreme guide in all matters of faith and practice'[115] are among the first to reject biblical methods in favor of the 'broken cisterns' of their fathers (Jer. 2:13).

'HOUSE CHURCHES ARE DIVISIVE AND THEREFORE TRADITIONAL PATTERNS ARE TO BE PREFERRED.'

House churches may well be divisive and throw up dictatorial leaders. This is not a recent tendency. But there is no obvious reason for regarding these difficulties as so significant that they override all other considerations. The small group, in which members meet face-to-face and actively participate, seems to represent most nearly the form of early Christian meetings and, in spite of difficulties, offers the most effective way forward.[116] Robert Banks believes that 'if churches developed house churches rather than house groups they would find more cohesiveness and less drifts.'[117]

It may be worth adding that even the most intimate of contemporary church buildings is hard pressed to develop Christian community life as efficiently as can be done in the home.

'THE NEW TESTAMENT PROBABLY ASSUMES REGULAR SERMONS.'

This objection takes up the argument that the New Testament contains no evidence for the use of the regular sermon. It points out that absence of evidence is not the same as evidence of absence and urges that regular sermons will have been used in the primitive church and that their existence was taken for granted by the New Testament writers.

However the thesis of this book is not based exclusively upon the silence of the New Testament concerning a method, which today is taken for granted throughout Christendom; it also shows that the primitive church used a variety of means to achieve the growth in knowledge and maturity, which are allegedly secured today by the regular sermon. In addition, it describes how the church came under the influence of a variety of non-Christian influences of a kind, which would encourage the development of the regular sermon.

Those who defend the regular sermon have no choice but to acknowledge the silence of the New Testament, to which they nevertheless appeal as supposed evidence of what they suggest, might have been 'taken for granted'. What they build on this fragile foundation, however, is a habitual use of the sermon of which the New Testament knows nothing. In support of their present practice they cite a less than unanimous scholarly consensus, popular church opinion, and the 'tradition of the elders'. These are formidable allies and might be worthy of respect, provided only that one remembers one's church history. For it is precisely these forces that have always been mustered to oppose any new thought or (which has often amounted to the same thing) any return to the New Testament. Tertullian recognized the danger when he warned that 'Christ is truth, not custom' (*De Virg Vel* 1:1).[118]

For this objection to carry any weight at all it would be necessary to show that the regular sermon was a likely candidate for inclusion in the activities of the primitive church. This could be achieved by demonstrating that:

- The sermon was necessary in order to accomplish that which either could not be done by other means or could be done no better by other means.
- The sermon was required, not just occasionally, but on most of the occasions when the local community of Christians gathered together.
- The regular sermon was consistent with other church

activities and would not militate against the practice of mutual ministries or distort church structures. (In short, the material assembled above, relating to these matters, must be shown to be substantially in error.)

- The regular sermon did not achieve dominance primarily as a result of the ecclesiastical borrowing of pagan forms.
- There was good reason for the silence of the Bible and Apostolic Fathers on such an important issue.

Such evidence has not been forthcoming, nor is it likely to be, in view of the analysis presented above.

ENDNOTES

1. G.E. Wright, *The Biblical Doctrine of Man in Society*, 1954, pp. 84f; H.N. Schneidau, *Sacred Discontent: The Bible and Western Tradition*, 1976, pp. 4, 11-14; T.R. Hobbs, *2 Kings*, 1985, p. 252

2. J. Calvin, *Institutes of the Christian Religion*, 3:2:31 (ed: J.T. McNeill, 1960, I, 578); G.C. Berkouwer, *The Providence of God*, 1952, pp. 172-175; K. Barth, *Church Dogmatics*, 1969, IV:4, 190, 194; N. Wright, *The Radical Kingdom*, 1986, pp. 133f

3. H. Wheeler Robinson, 'The Ministry of Error' in idem, *Redemption and Revelation*, 1942, pp. 21-38;]. Calvin, *Institutes*, 3:2:4 (pp. 546f).

4. N.M. Watson, *Striking Home: Interpreting and Proclaiming the New Testament*, 1987, pp. 122f

5. G. Reid, *The Gagging of God*, 1969, p. 101. Many students find seminars more inspiring than lectures (D.A. Bligh, *What's the Use if Lectures?*, 1978, pp. 18-22)

6. Institutionalized attitudes are discussed in S.I. Hayakawa, *Language in Thought and Action*, [4]1978, pp. 289-291

7. J. Ellul, *The Subversion of Christianity*, 1986, pp. 166-170; T.F. O'Dea and J. O'Dea Aviad, *The Sociology if Religion*, [2]1983, pp. 112f

8. See further J. Zens, 'Why is the Order of Our Church Service Set in Concrete?', *ST*, Autumn 1982, 46-48

9. R. Allen, *Missionary Methods: St Paul's or Ours?*, 1912 repr 1960, pp. 90f; J.A. Grassi, *A World to Win: The Missionary Methods of Paul the Apostle*, 1965, pp. 35f, 152f

10. Under Old Testament influence, Paul sees peace as the opposite of disorder in 1 Cor. 14:33: G.D. Fee, *The First Epistle to the Corinthians*, 1987, p. 697; H. Beck and C. Brown, *NIDNTT*, II, 780; W. Foerster, *TDNT*, II, 412

11. H. Davies, *Worship and Theology in England*, I (From Cranmer to Hooker, 1534-1603), 1970, pp. 294-301; P. Collinson, *The Religion of Protestants: The Church in English Society 1559-1625* 1982, pp. 143, 154-158, 170

12. N.H. Keeble, *Richard Baxter: Puritan Man of Letters*, 1982, pp. 80f; P.E. Hughes, *Theology of the English Reformers*, 1965, pp. 123-127

13. W. Haller, *The Rise of Puritanism*, 1938, pp. 54f, 59; H. Davies, *Worship and Theology in England*, 1970, I, 315; 1975, II, 139f

14. K. Wrightson, *English Society 1580-1680*, 1982, pp. 218f; J.I. Packer, *A Quest for Godliness: The Puritan Vision of the Christian Life*, 1990, pp. 281f; H. Davies, *The Worship of the American Puritans, 1629-1730*, 1990, pp. 77-79,105, 247

15. On the widespread use of letter-writing by Christians in the 17th and 18th centuries see W.R. Ward, *The Protestant Evangelical Awakening*, 1992, pp. 1-3.

16. E.G. Rupp, 'The Age of the Reformation 1500-1648' in S.C. Neill and H.-R. Weber (eds), *The Layman in Christian History*, 1963, pp. 144f; *The Westminster Confession of Faith*, 1646, section xxi:5; M. Spufford, *Small Books and Pleasant Histories: Popular Fiction and Its Readership in Seventeenth-Century England*, 1981, pp. 10f; G.H. Jenkins, *Literature, Religion and Society in Wales 1660-1730*, 1978, pp. 53, 146-164

17. J. Morgan, *Godly Learning: Puritan Attitudes Towards Reason, Learning and Education, 1560-1640*, 1986, pp. 184-190, 197-200; T. Kelly, *A History of Adult Education in Great Britain*, [2]1970, pp. 41f; J. Lawson and H. Silver, *A Social History if Education in England*, 1973, pp. 103-107, 112, 117, 139-141, 153

18. R. Baxter, *The Reformed Pastor*, 1656 (edited and abridged by W. Brown, preface dated 1862), pp. 7-10; N.H. Keeble (ed), *The Autobiography of Richard Baxter*, 1974, pp. 77f

19. P. Collinson, *The Birthpangs of Protestant England*, 1988, pp. 70, 106-112

20. G. Wickham, *Early English Stages 1300-1660*, 1963, I (*1300-1576*), 112, 133; P. Collinson, *Birthpangs*, pp. 101-106, 112

21. R. Hooykaas, *Religion and the Rise of Modem Science*, 1973, pp. 94-96, 135-149; P.A. Scholes, *The Puritans and Music in England and New England*, 1934; M. Todd, *Christian Humanism and the Puritan Social Order*, 1987; A. Carden, *Puritan Christianity in America: Religion and Life in Seventeenth-Century Massachusetts*, 1990, pp. 153, 185-193

22. P. Miller, *The New England Mind: The 17th century*, Harvard University Press, ²1954, pp. 65f

23. D.D. Hall, *Worlds of Wonder, Days of Judgment: Popular Religious Belief in Early New England*, 1990, p. 265 n56; N.H. Keeble, *The Literary Culture of Nonconformity in Later Seventeenth-Century England*, 1987, pp. 127-135; G.H. Jenkins, *Literature*, pp. 198-229

24. M. Spufford, *Small Books*, pp. 111-128; A. Carden, *Puritan Christianity*, pp. 43f, 187, 215

25. T. Kelly, *A History of Adult Education in Great Britain*, University of Liverpool Press, p. 9. Other reasons for wishing to became literate are listed in K. Wrightson, *English Society*, pp. 195f.

26. T. Kelly, *Adult Education*, pp. 15f, 21, 42; M. Spufford, *Small Books*, p. 66

27. J. Morgan, *Godly Learning*, p. 165

28. J. Lawson and H. Silver, *Social History*, pp. 141-143; D. Cressy, 'Levels ofLiteracy in England, 1530-1730' in H.J. Graff (ed), *Literacy and Social Development in the West: A Reader*, 1981, pp. 105-124; M. Spufford, *Small Books*, pp. 19-44; R.A. Houston, *Scottish Literacy and the Scottish Identity: Literacy and Society in Scotland and Northern England 1600-1800*, 1985, passim

29. M. Spufford, *Small Books*, pp. 45-110; C. Hill, *A Tinker and a Poor Man: John Bunyan and His Church, 1628-1688*, 1989, pp. 28-38; P. Clark, 'The Ownership of Books in England, 1560-1640: The Example of Some Kentish Townsfolk' in L. Stone (ed), *Schooling and Society: Studies in the History of Education*, 1976, pp. 95-111. For details of books in New England in the 17th century see D.D. Hall, *Worlds of Wonder*, pp. 43-61; J.D. Hart, *The Popular Book: A History of America's Literary Taste*, 1950 repr 1961, pp. 3-21

30. F.R. Johnson, 'Notes on English Retail Book Prices, 1550-1640', *The Library*, 5th series, 5:2, 1950,83-112; M. Spufford, *Small Books*, pp. 92f, 134-138, 194-213,258, 262f; C. Hill, *The English Bible and the Seventeenth-Century Revolution*, 1993, pp. 18, 66; G.H. Jenkins, *Literature*, pp. 244-246.

31. P. Clark, 'The Ownership of Books', pp. 107f

32. G.H. Jenkins, *Literature*, p. 299

33. N.H., Keeble (ed), *The Autobiography pf Richard Baxter*, 1974, p. 80. Weavers were by no means the most literate section of the working community (D. Cressy, 'Levels of Literacy in England', pp. 109, 124).

34. C. Hill, *The English Bible*, p. 11

35. A. Tindal Hart, *The Curate's Lot: The Story of the Unbeneficed English Clergy*,

1971, pp. 55f, 67-72, 112

36. N.H. Keeble, Richard Baxter: *Puritan Man of Letters*, p. 45; M. Todd, *Christian Humanism*, pp. 256f; R. Baxter, *The Reformed Pastor*, pp. 38, 92, 283f; G.H. Jenkins, *Literature*, pp. 66, 253f, 265, 269, 273, 278, 303f

37. J.I. Packer, *A Quest for Godliness*, p. 59

38. T. Kelly, *Early Public Libraries: A History of Public Libraries in Great Britain Before 1850*, Nottingham, Crossway Books, 1966, pp. 49-85

39. T. Kelly, *Early Public Libraries*, pp. 70-76, 94-99, 104

40. J.D. Hart, *The Popular Book*, pp. 5, 9, 25, 67, 85

41. R.L. Greaves, *Society and Religion in Elizabethan England*, 1981, pp. 291-301

42. R. Baxter, *The Reformed Pastor*, pp. 91-93, 214, 307; J. Morgan, *Godly Learning*, pp. 150-156

43. A. Tindal Hart, *The Man in the Pew 1558-1660*, 1966, pp. 200f; C.F. Richardson, *English Preachers and Preaching 1640-1670*, 1928, p. 76

44. R. Baxter, *The Reformed Pastor*, p. 93; N.H. Keeble, Richard Baxter: *Puritan Man of Letters*, 1982, pp. 44f

45. J.I. Packer, *A Quest for Godliness*, pp. 25f, 259-273. For other views on the extent of Puritan influence on the development of English family life see P. Collinson, *Birthpangs*, pp.60-93.

46. P. Collinson, *The Religion of Protestants*, pp. 264-268; J. Morgan, *Godly Learning*, pp. 152, 165,170,189,198,214; H.S. Bennett, *English Books and Readers 1558 to 1603*, 1965, pp. 152-154; idem, *English Books and Readers 1603 to 1640*, 1970, pp. 116f

47. W. Haller, *The Rise of Puritanism*, Columbia University Press, USA., 1938, p. 63.

48. H.G. Wood, *ERE*, X, 507a

49. N.H. Keeble, *Richard Baxter: Puritan Man of Letters*, 1982, pp. 46f; J.I. Packer, *A Quest for Godliness*, pp. 11f, 22, 25f, 46; A.G. Dickens, *The English Reformation*, 1967, pp. 329, 430, 435. The extent to which Puritanism engendered maturity in women has been variously assessed. See the discussions in J. Morgan, *Godly Learning*, pp. 165-168, 176f; A. Porterfield, 'Women's Attraction to Puritanism', *CH*, 60, 1991, 196-209; M. Todd, *Christian Humanism*, pp. 105-108, 113-117; D. Willen, 'Godly Women in Early Modern England: Puritanism and Gender', *JEH*, 43:4,1992, 561-580

50. J. Morgan, *Godly Learning*, p. 83; A. Carden, *Puritan Christianity*, pp. l00f, 111-119, 127-130; E.B. Holifield, *Era of Persuasion: American Thought and Culture, 1521-1680*, 1989, pp. 93f; P. Miller, *The New England Mind*, pp. 295-299

51. A.G. Dickens, *Reformation*, pp. 433-437; J.I. Packer, *A Quest for Godliness*, 1990, pp. 26, 247; A. Carden, *Puritan Christianity*, pp. 84, 96f, 100f, 109-114, 217-219

52. D.D. Hall, *Worlds of Wonder*, pp. 71-94; K. Wrightson, *English Society*, pp. 199-201; R. Godbeer, *The Devil's Dominion: Magic and Religion in Early New England*, 1992

53. S. Patrick, *The Parable of the Pilgrim: Written to a Friend, 1663*, corrected 1687, p. 156; Jenkins, *Literature*, pp. 33f, 74; H.S. Bennett, *English Books and Readers 1603-1640*, 114

54. *The Reformed Pastor*, p. 14, *cf.* pp. 28, 36, 197f, 227-229, 250f, 285f

55. This is discussed briefly in N.H. Keeble, Richard Baxter: *Puritan Man of Letters*, pp. 81f; Nuttall, *Richard Baxter*, 1965, pp. 48, 57

56. N.H. Keeble, *Richard Baxter: Puritan Man of Letters*, Oxford University Press, pp. 33f

57. J.I. Packer, *A Quest for Godliness*, pp. 165f, 169

58. R.W. Scribner, 'Oral Culture and the Transmission of Reformation Ideas' in Robinson-Hammerstein (ed), *The Transmission of Ideas in the Lutheran Reformation*, 1989, pp. 83-104; R.W. Scribner, *For the Sake of Simple Folk: Popular Propaganda for the German Reformation*, 1981, pp. 1-8; M.A. Noll, 'The Earliest Protestants and the Reformation of Education', *WTJ*, 43, 1980, 97-131; M.H. Black, 'The Printed Bible', *CHB*, 1963, III, 429-432; A.E. McGrath, *A Life of John Calvin*, 1990, pp. 4-6

59. B.M. Metzger, *The Text of the New Testament*, [3]1992, p. 18; E.L. Eisenstein, *The Printing Press as an Agent of Change*, 1979, I, 373f; John 20:31.

60. N. Postman, *Amusing Ourselves to Death*, 1986; similarly J. Ellul, *The Humiliation of the Word*, 1985, pp. 46, 114-154; G. Reid, *The Gagging of God*, 1969, pp. 27-38

61. The Reformed community appears to have been at least partially successful in recapturing this ability.

62. H.O. Old, *The Patristic Roots of Reformed Worship*, 1975, pp. 187-193; T.H.L. Parker, *Calvin's Preaching*, 1992, pp. 79f

63. M. Todd, *Christian Humanism*, pp. 170-172, 182, 192, 202

64. A.S. Wood, *The Inextinguishable Blaze: Spiritual Renewal and Advance in the Eighteenth Century*, 1960, pp. 223-226

65. C.T. McIntire (ed), *Herbert Butterfield: Writings on Christianity and History*, Oxford University Press, 1979, p. 249

66. R.J. Bauckham, 'The Delay of the Parousia', *Tyn B*, 31, 1980, pp. 26-28, 36

67. Judg 2: C.J. Goslinga, *Joshua, Judges, Ruth*, 1986, pp. 238-244

68. M.F. Unger, *Biblical Demonology*, 1952, pp. 148-155; E.G. Parrinder, *Witchcraft: European and African*, [2]1963, pp. 117-125; R. Scot, *The Discoverie of Witchcraft*, 1584 repr 1930, pp. 62-66

69. H.R. Trevor-Roper, *The European Witch-Craze of the 16th and 17th Centuries*, 1969, pp. 18f, 42-52, 85f; B.P. Levack, *The Witch-Hunt in Early Modern Europe*, 1987, pp. 13-15, 65-67, 70-77; G.R. Quaife, *Godly Zeal and Furious Rage: The Witch in Early Modern Europe*, 1987, pp. 136-138; R. Godbeer, *The Devil's Dominion: Magic and Religion in Early New England*, 1992, pp. 206-211

70. N. Ben-Yehuda, 'The European Witch Craze of the 14th to 17th Centuries: A Sociologist's Perspective', *American Journal of Sociology*, 86, 1980, 6-8; R.R. Ruether, 'The Persecution of Witches: A Case of Sexism and Agism?', *Christianity and Crisis*, 23 December 1974, 291-295; B.P. Levack, *The Witch-Hunt*, pp. 124-128

71. B.P. Levack, *The Witch-Hunt*, pp. 134-136; N. Ben-Yehuda, 'The European Witch Craze', 16-22

72. J.B. Russell, *Witchcraft in the Middle Ages*, 1972, pp. 71-73, 86-88, 227f, 244f

73. E.G. Parrinder, *Witchcraft*, pp. 29, 33[, 105, 115f; H.R. Trevor-Roper, *The European Witch-Craze*, pp.101-103, 110f, 121; E. Peel and P. Southern, *The Trials of the Lancashire Witches: A Study of Seventeenth-Century Witchcraft*, [2]1972, pp. 129-138

74. See W.M. Swartley, *Slavery, Sabbath, War and Women: Case Issues in Biblical Interpretation*, 1983, pp. 31-64; J. Murray, *Principles of Conduct*, 1957, pp. 93-103, 259-262; G.E.M. de Ste Croix, *The Class Struggle in the Ancient Greek World*,

1981, pp. 418-425; A.A. Rupprecht, 'Attitudes on Slavery Among the Church Fathers' in R.N. Longenecker and M.C Tenney (eds), *New Dimensions in New Testament Study*, 1974, pp. 261-277

75. G.C Berkouwer, *The Providence of God*, 1952, pp. 161-187
76. G.C Berkouwer, *Providence*, pp. 161-166; G.M. Marsden and F.C. Roberts (eds), *A Christian View of History?*, 1975, pp. 10-12, 38-40
77. G.C. Berkouwer, *Providence*, pp. 166, 170, 171, 172. Similarly P. Helm, *The Providence of God*, Eerdmans Publishing Co., USA., 1993, pp. 121-130
78. See the discussion in P. Helm, *Providence*, pp. 136f, 232
79. H.H. Fanner, *The World and God*, [2]1936, pp. 247f; H.D. McDonald, *The God Who Responds*, 1986, p. 68
80. C. Hodge, *Systematic Theology*, repr 1960, I, 589f; G.C Berkouwer, *Providence*, pp. 90f; P. Helm, *Providence*, pp. 230-232
81. See the discussions in G.F. Hawthorne, *ISBE*, IV, 932; A.J. Malherbe, *Social Aspects of Early Christianity*, [2]1983, pp. 89f; F.F. Bruce, *The Acts of the Apostles*, [3]1990, p. 408; C.J. Herner, *The Book of Acts in the Setting of Hellenistic History*, WUNT, 49, 1989, pp. 120, 234
82. There are no letters extant from Paul to the Beroeans or Athenians and we know of no Athenian converts who subsequently joined Paul's mission. Sopater of Beroea did join Paul later (Acts 20:4 and possibly Rom. 16:21)
83. I.H. Marshall, *The Acts of the Apostles*, 1980, p. 310
84. W. Elert, *Eucharist and Church Fellowship in the First Four Centuries*, 1966, pp. 75-83; G. Dix, *The Shape of the Liturgy*, [2]1945, pp. 16-18, 304-306; A. Chupungco, 'Diaconate', *EEC*, I, 232
85. Th Mommsen, *The Provinces of the Roman Empire from Caesar to Diocletian*, 1909, I, 363-366; C.A. Forbes, 'Expanded Uses of the Greek Gymnasium', *Class Phil*, 40,1945, 33-35
86. 'Paul's Missionary Methods', *Biblical World*, 34, 1909, 333
87. E. Hatch, *The Influence of Greek Ideas and Usages Upon the Christian Church*, 1897, p. 92
88. *BAGD*, p. 185b; M. Zerwick and M.D. Grosvenor, *A Grammatical Analysis of the Greek New Testament*, [3]1988, p. 415
89. Sir Norman Anderson, *Christianity and World Religions*, 1984, pp. 183-192; M.B. Green, *Evangelism in the Early Church*, 1970, pp. 205f
90. C.J. Herner, *The Letters to the Seven Churches of Asia in Their Local Setting*, 1986, pp. 66, 110, 181; P.T. O'Brien, *Colossians, Philemon*, 1982, pp. xxviif; F.F. Bruce, *The Epistles to the Colossians, to Philemon and to the Ephesians*, 1984, pp. 13-15
91. A.S. Wood, *The Inextinguishable Blaze*, 1960; J.E. Orr, *The Light of the Nations: Progress and Achievement in the Nineteenth Century*, 1966; D.E. Meek, 'Revivals', *DSCHT*, pp. 713-715
92. J.E. Orr, *The Second Evangelical Awakening in Britain*, 1949, pp. 78f, 201; T.C. Smout, 'Born Again at Cambuslang: New Evidence on Popular Religion and Literacy in Eighteenth-Century Scotland', *P&P*, 97, 1982, 119f
93. R. Bennett, *The Early Life of Howell Harris*, 1962, pp. 78-81, 146; E. Evans, *Revivals: Their Rise, Progress and Achievements*, 1986, p. 23; L.F. Church, *The Early Methodist People*, 1949, pp. 149-181; D.L. Watson, *The Early Methodist*

Class Meeting, 1985, pp. 93-152

94. G. Friedrich, *TDNT*, VI, 854; W.A Grudem, *The Gift of Prophecy in the New Testament and Today*, 1988, pp. 142-144; M.M.B. Turner, 'Spiritual Gifts Then and Now', *VE*, 15, 1985, 13f, 54f

95. I owe this point to Peter Cousins.

96. D. Hill, *New Testament Prophecy*, 1979, pp. 129f; E.E. Ellis, 'The Role of the Christian Prophet in Acts' in W. W. Gasque and R.P. Martin (eds), *Apostolic History and the Gospel*, 1970, pp. 58f, 62-64, 66; K.N. Giles, *Patterns of Ministry Among the First Christians*, 1989, pp. 132, 146

97. B.A. Miiller, 'The Role of the Sermon in Intergroup Relationships' in J.P. Louw (ed), *Sociolinguistics and Communication*, 1986, pp. 96f

98. The idea that God is the ultimate source of all truth, no matter how tainted its immediate source, goes back to John Calvin, Thomas Aquinas, the Fathers and in germ, the Bible (J. Calvin, *Institutes of the Christian Religion* 2:2:15 with n58 [ed J.T. McNeill] 1960, I, 273-275); J. Calvin, *Commentaries on the Epistles to Timothy, Titus and Philemon*, 1856, pp. 300f [on Titus 1:12]; C. Brown, *Christianity and Western Thought*, 1990, I, 120f, 151-154; R. Hooykaas, *Religion and the Rise of Modern Science*, 1973, pp. 117-121; A.D. Sertillanges, *Saint Thomas Aquinas and His Work*, 1957, pp. 58-72). Not surprisingly, the notion that all truth is God's truth has been pushed to extreme limits by some Christians in order to justify the use of ideas which may conflict with the biblical revelation. See the discussion in M. and D. Bobgan, *Psychoheresy: The Psychological Seduction of Christianity*, 1987, pp. 31-35

99. E. Schillebeeckx, *The Church with a Human Face*, 1985, London, S.C.M. Press Ltd., pp. 4f

100. Although multi-faceted, Greek dualism is essentially cosmological or metaphysical, whereas biblical dualism is primarily ethical and religious (G .E. Ladd, *The Pattern of New Testament Truth*, 1968, pp. 13-43,71; idem, *A Theology of the New Testament*, [2]1994, pp. 259-272)

101. Based on John 12:31; 2 Cor. 4:4; 1 Pet. 5:8; 1 John 5:19. Note that the 'world' in 1 John 5:19 excludes orthodox believers (S.S. Smalley, *1, 2, 3 John*, 1984, pp. 81, 304)

102. E. Langton, *Satan, A Portrait*, nd (preface dated 1945), pp. 44-95; idem, *Essentials of Demonology*, 1949, PP: 37-144; W. Foerster, *TDNT*, II, 1-16; R.A Stewart, *Rabbinic Theology*, 1961, pp. 59-61; S. Dill, *Roman Society from Nero to Marcus Aurelius*, [2]1905, pp. 425-434

103. J. Danielou, *A History of Early Christian Doctrine Before the Council of Nicaea*, 1964-1977, I, 187-192, II, 427-441, III, 405-418; E. Langton, *Satan*, pp. 44-95. The essence of worldliness is analysed in J.B. Mayor, *The Epistle of St. James*, [3]1913 repr 1977, pp. 224-226

104. J.E. Adams, *The Christian Counselor's Manual*, 1973, pp. 98f

105. A.M. Wolters, *Ideas Have Legs*, 1987, pp. 8f; A.F. Holmes, *Contours of a World View*, 1983, pp.142-145

106. On the importance of progress in theology see J.M. Frame, *The Doctrine of the Knowledge of God*, 1987, pp. 307f; A. McGrath, *Evangelicalism and the Future of Christianity*, 1994, pp. 111-122.

107. This is stated and briefly discussed in H. Pietersma, 'The Place of Preaching in the

Christian Life', *Calvin Theological Journal*, 8, 1973, 66f, *cf.* J. Calvin, *Institutes of the Christian Religion*, 4:1:5 with n11 (ed: J.T. McNeill, 1960, II, 1018)

108. Views of the Reformers are given in R.S. Wallace, *Calvin's Doctrine of the Word and Sacrament*, 1953, pp. 82-95, 115-122; T.H.L. Parker, *John Calvin: A Biography*, 1975, pp. 89f; T. George, *Theology of the Reformers*, 1988, pp. 91, 187f, 243

109. On this see J. Ellul, *The Humiliation of the Word*, 1985

110. B.B. Warfield, *The Inspiration and Authority of the Bible*, 1948, pp. 83-86; G. Vos, *Biblical Theology: Old and New Testaments*, 1948 repr 1985, pp. 71f

111. L.O. Richards, *A New Face for the Church*, 1970, pp. 49-51; J. Macquarrie, *Principles of Christian Theology*, [2]1977, p. 489

112. B.R. Wilson, *Religion in Sociological Perspective*, 1982, p. 48; S. Bruce, *A House Divided: Protestantism, Schism and Secularization*, 1990, p. 21

113. D .E. Nineham claimed that the cultural and historical distance between our time and that of the New Testament is so great that its interpretation is made extremely difficult thereby, and the application of biblical material to our own situation even more so. This and other similar relativistic views are criticized in A.C. Thiselton, *The Two Horizons*, 1980, pp. 52-60, 70-74; J. Barton, 'Reflections on Cultural Relativism', *Theology*, 82, 1979, 103-109, 191-199; L. Morris, *I Believe in Revelation*, 1976, pp. 142-147; P. Helm, *The Divine Revelation*, 1982, pp. 47-54; P. Helm, E. Fudge, J. Houston and S. Dex in P. Helm (ed), *Objective Knowledge*, 1987, pp. 31-33,111-127, 149-165, 185f; R.H. Trigg, *Reason and Commitment*, 1973, pp. 1-26; P. Roubiczek, *Existentialism For and Against*, 1964, pp. 73-98

114. On the extent to which biblical methods have proved effective on the mission field see R. Allen, *Missionary Methods: St Paul's or Ours?*, 1912 repr 1962; J.L. Nevius, *Planting and Development of Missionary Churches*, [3]1899 repr 1958, p. 9; D.J. Hesselgrave, *Communicating Christ Cross-Culturally*, 1978, p. 340; D. Birkey, *The House Church*, 1988, pp. 71-76

115. C. Hodge, *Systematic Theology*, repr 1960, I, 151f

116. The strengths and weaknesses of house groups are discussed in L.O. Richards, *A New Face for the Church*, 1970, pp. 152-162; H.A. Snyder, *The Problem of Wineskins*, 1977, pp. 129-138; E. Gibbs, *I Believe in Church Growth*, [3]1990, pp. 155-181; R.J. and J. Banks, *The Home Church*, 1986; P. Cotterell, *All About House Groups*, 1985; G.W. Icenogle, *Biblical Foundations for Small Group Ministry*, 1994.

117. Private communication dated July 1991

118. This is cited in E.H. Blakeney, *The Epistle to Diognetus*, 1943, p. 36 and is a loose translation of the original Latin.

7

The Way Ahead

DOES THE NEW TESTAMENT ADVOCATE ONE PARTICULAR CHURCH STRUCTURE?

There is widespread agreement that patterns of church structure and ministry in the various strands of the New Testament are so divergent that no single pattern can be discerned which might be regarded as the New Testament pattern.[1] This diversity may suggest that the church is justified in opting for whatever structures it chooses, confident in the belief that they too will be the work of the Holy Spirit, no less than the structures of the primitive church. But the diversity of New Testament patterns of structure and ministry has been exaggerated—a point recently argued by R.A. Campbell.[2] In the areas examined, we have seen that the New Testament displays practices and principles which, when taken together, provide a consistent and moderately comprehensive guide to ministry and structure, even though precise detail is lacking. Do Christians have any obligations to operate within these guidelines? The extent to which biblical patterns are prescriptive is difficult to say and will not be discussed here. My aim is the more limited one of arguing that New Testament methods are both applicable to the church in the West and also superior to methods currently in use. In particular, as has been shown above, New Testament methods are directly related to the aims sought. Robert Banks expresses it well when he says, speaking of Paul's methods, 'All these things I have mentioned are simply the gospel itself expressed in corporate form. They are the shape it takes when translated into community terms.'[3]

If the primary aim of the church is to build mature Christian communities, then the New Testament offers means to that end, which are both loving and efficient—in short, godly. To my knowledge, no one has produced anything better. Utilizing New Testament patterns does not necessarily mean slavish reproduction but, rather, intelligent interpretation. In this way, a close study of the New Testament enables us to see how a Christian community can be developed and nurtured. It is then possible to see, for example, that although the regular sermon might be thought of as nothing more than the extension of a New Testament practice, it does in fact cut across biblical patterns of growth and is consequently an illegitimate deformation. (An examination of many, it not most, of our ecclesiastical activities is similarly revealing in that they can frequently be shown to be inefficient and to have little basis in New Testament practice.)

THE PROBLEM OF CHANGE

Any church considering the introduction of change along these lines will need to proceed carefully. Three years or more are often required for a new idea to be accepted in a community or organization. G.E. Wright points out that 'forms of worship are the most conservative elements in any culture.'[4] There is thus little reason to suppose that an issue as contentious as abandoning the regular sermon could be resolved quickly, especially as this would involve restructuring much else besides with, inevitably, numerous unanticipated consequences. There is at least one consolation here. If God is the inspiration for the biblical methods outlined above and if these methods are intended for our guidance and emulation, then any unexpected consequences ought to be beneficial, just as the unexpected consequences of extensive sermonizing have been harmful.

Precipitate action is risky. There are many contemporary illustrations of New Testament ideas being applied to the church without adequate preparation, resulting in acrimony and division.[5] Moreover, Satanic activity, in all its forms, should not be ignored. In the light of the problems which so frequently attend any projected reform of the church, it is appropriate, and a Christian duty, to begin with prayer and Bible study for it seems frequently the case that whenever God has a work to accomplish, he marshals his people long before any outward signs of the battle appear (Jer. 1:4-10; Amos 3:7; Luke 1:26-38, 2:25-38).[6] But, for many church members, the idea of serious study is unattractive, especially if it fails to deliver instant practical dividends. In contrast, John Goldingay, in the preface to his recent commentary on Daniel, says:

> It has been my experience with Daniel as with other books that an appreciation of its inherent significance and its particular meaningfulness for us emerges from close working with the text in all its detailed 'irrelevance', and I cannot promise that one hears the Scriptures speak without that close and prosaic work.[7]

Study might, I suggest, center on the biblical data and on Christian cultural analysis. Unfortunately, few Christians understand their own culture or see such an understanding as significant in living the Christian life. There are exceptions. Some Reformed thinkers, particularly those following in the footsteps of Guillaume Groen van Prinsterer (1801-1876), Abraham Kuyper (1837-1920) and Herman Dooyeweerd (1894-1977), have written penetrating analyses of contemporary culture from a Calvinistic perspective, but this work has been confined, for the most part, to the Netherlands, Canada and the USA.[8] In Europe and North America numerous Christian sociologists have done similar work (see Appendix II). But in England, the impact has been slight and ignorance is still widespread. Frequently this ignorance is compounded by suspicion of those disciplines, such as anthropology, psychology and sociology, which might offer insight and assistance. This suspicion is frequently cast in the form of disdain, but this often conceals ignorance and fear, which are not banished by posturing out by disciplined study. Only then can that which is of benefit in these disciplines be discerned from that which is hostile to Christianity or in other ways inadequate.[9] Using these means and others it is then possible to build up a rich cultural picture. The Old and New Testaments both contain instances of a number of God's people making an effort to understand the cultures around them. The church today is not called to do less in this respect, even though such study will not be the province of all Christians.

Difficult though cultural analysis may be, the effort is nonetheless worthwhile. Depending on the results obtained, this might be followed by enlisting the support of as many members as possible for any projected changes. The co-operation of the group should be sought at all stages because, in general, a group tends to retain the methods it knows irrespective of their effectiveness or the quality of what replaces them. Insensitivity here can produce antagonism and more failure. On the other hand, careful handling should create a sound platform for the implementation of further gradual changes. Changes should be introduced to the group as a whole as it is usually easier to change the behavior of groups than to change the behavior of group members as individuals,[10] although allies from the group may emerge early on and may even be sought out at the start.

Many people fear the introduction of fresh forms. The church throughout the ages has generally chosen not to recreate church structures after biblical patterns.[11] Many today would argue that the church in England has nevertheless survived and in some respects is healthy. Surely it would be wiser to maintain the present structures, albeit with minor adjustments, rather than to undertake extensive reorganization and put our trust in methods, which for most of us, are untried? This fear is justified to some extent. The early days of experimentation might bring a feeling of loss, bewilderment and a sense of even greater alienation and failure than before—a feeling common to the people of God whenever he introduced change (Exod. 16:3; Hag. 2:3; John 6:60-66). This sense of failure might take the tangible form of a decline in attendance—or threats of non-attendance.[12] In view of this, the organized churches may feel unable to respond. As has happened so often before in the history of the church, advance will then come from individuals who are no longer prepared to be shackled by tradition and who feel that division is the lesser evil. Ideally division should be avoided, yet it has often been beneficial in the history of the church.[13]

If Christians had done all things well and yet reaped the failure we see all around, then what to do in the future would be a frightening problem. Much failure, however, is self-inflicted. To speak frankly, it can be attributed directly to Christian arrogance, willful ignorance, stupidity and refusal to think. All of these can be forgiven and indeed need to be forgiven. Failure, or more precisely an awareness of failure, often brings one inestimable blessing—the recognition of the need for change. Sadly, however, this may prove to be worthless unless given concrete expression. The first step can be achieved by a purposeful reassessment of church involvement and activities.[14]

ENDNOTES

1. C.F. Evans, 'Is the New Testament Church a Model?' in idem, *Is 'Holy Scripture' Christian?*, 1971, pp. 86f; E. Schweizer, *Church Order in the New Testament*, 1961, pp. 13f (section 1a); W.D. Davies, *A Normative Pattern of Church Life in the New Testament: Fact or Fancy?*, nd (about 1949), pp. 22

2. *The Elders: Seniority within Earliest Christianity*, 1994, pp. 252-254

3. R.J. Banks, 'Small is Beautiful': The Relevance of Paul's Idea of Community for the Local Church Today', *Theological Review*, 22, November 1982, 10

4. G.E. Wright, *The Old Testament Against its Environment*, London, SCM Press Ltd., 1950, p.77

5. Liturgical disputes can be a contributory factor in division and schism (S.L. Greenslade, *Schism in the Early Church*, [2]1964, pp. 92f)

6. J.I. Packer, *A Quest for Godliness*, 1990, pp. 325-327; A.S. Wood, *The Inextinguishable Blaze*, 1960, pp. 27-32, 57, 117f, 120, 123; J.E. Orr, *The Second Evangelical Awakening in Britain*, 1949, passim; idem, *The Light of the Nations: Progress and Achievement in the Nineteenth Century*, 1966, passim; D.E. Meek, 'Revivals', *DSCHT*, p. 715

7. J. Goldingay, *Daniel*, Word Publishing, USA., 1989, p. x

8. This movement is discussed in H. Dooyeweerd, *Roots of Western Culture: Pagan, Secular and Christian Options*, 1979

9. Help on this point can be fotmd in J.A. Walter, *A Long Way from Home: A Sociological Exploration of Contemporary Idolatry*, 1979; D. Lyon, *Sociology and the Human Image*, 1983; A. Storkey, *A Christian Social Perspective*, 1979; M.A. Jeeves, *Psychology and Christianity: The View Both Ways*, 1976; R.H. Trigg, *Understanding Social Science: A Philosophical Introduction to the Social Sciences*, 1985; P. Helm (ed), *Objective Knowledge: A Christian Perspective*, 1987

10. J.A.C. Brown, *The Social Psychology of Industry*, 1954 repr 1986, pp. 67, 178-180; D.A. Bligh, *What's the Use of Lectures?*, 1978, p. 22

11. E. Kasernann, *Essays on New Testament Themes*, 1964, p. 93

12. G. Reid, *The Gagging of God*, 1969, p. 102

13. S.L. Greenslade, *Schism in the Early Church*, [2]1964, pp. 204-207; D. McGavran and C.P. Wagner, *Understanding Church Growth*, [3]1990, p. 4

14. E.R. Dayton and D.A. Fraser, *Planning Strategies*, pp. 421f; S. Bruce, *A House Divided: Protestantism, Schism and Secularization*, 1990, p. 28

Conclusion

This book has worked with a definition of the sermon, which corresponds quite closely with the general practice of churches today and for many centuries. In general, the 'sermon' is a speech, concerned with biblical, ethical and related material, designed to increase understanding and to promote godly living among the listening congregation, delivered by someone in good standing with the local Christian community and addressed primarily to the faithful in the context of their own gatherings. We have seen that in both Old and New Testament times, and in the sub-apostolic period, such sermons were delivered on special occasions or in order to deal with specific problems. The evidence suggests that they were not a common occurrence, as they are in almost all churches today.

We have also seen that the altered status of the sermon can be explained as resulting from the influence upon the church of the non-Christian culture surrounding it, which led to the establishment of the regular sermon by the 3rd century and to its becoming the norm by the fourth. At the same time the church adopted a number of other ecclesiastical practices, which owed little to the practice, teaching or principles found in the New Testament and many of which remain to this day, with consequences which are often harmful.

We have seen that in the New Testament churches the growth into spiritual maturity of both individuals and communities was achieved by a variety of means, which did not include the regular sermon. Indeed, the experience of the churches and current knowledge about the learning process suggest that regular use of the sermon tends to have harmful consequences. It frequently fails to instruct;

it deskills; it fosters an unhealthy dependence on the clergy. In these ways the regular sermon not only fails to promote spiritual growth but also· intensifies the impoverishment of Christian life, which characterizes large areas of the church to clay.

The regular sermon does not, of course, stand alone as the one great corrupter of Christian faith and life. It is embedded in a complex organizational structure which is far removed from biblical patterns and which also inhibits Christian growth to maturity. The sad irony is that many preachers want to see their congregations grow in knowledge and love. Many take a great deal of trouble over preparing their sermons. Yet the teaching method they have chosen to use is, in practice, working with other factors to frustrate their hopes.

It may be too much to expect the reshaping of the whole structure. But to re-evaluate and to replace the sermon would be a comparatively modest first step. Although the enterprise would prove more difficult in some churches than in others, the benefits resulting would surely be immense.

Appendix I
The Length of Speeches in Antiquity

JUDAISM

In the Old Testament, the time taken for specific addresses is not given but lengthy speeches seem unusual. On rare occasions, the people could cope with a six or seven hour reading (Neh. 8:3) and a three hour reading—perhaps with running commentary—followed by three hours of worship (Neh 9:3).[1]

4 Maccabees may have been a sermon. The text is appreciably longer than that of the Sermon on the Mount and is generally dated between 63BC and 70AD.[2] The writings of Josephus contain numerous speeches. Some are expansions of biblical material (*Ant* II:56f, III:40-46; *cf.* Gen. 39:17f; Exod. 17:8) and others are fairly free rhetorical creations related to more recent events.[3] It is, therefore; hardly possible to assess the length of the speeches as originally delivered. *The Talmud* also mentions lengthy sermons.[4]

CHRISTIANITY

Many of the speeches in the Gospels and Acts appear to be summaries rather than verbatim reports and so the duration of the original speeches cannot be established.[5]

2 Clement may be the oldest extant post-New Testament sermon in Greek (*2 Clem.* 17:3, 19:1)—perhaps a baptismal sermon. In length, it slightly exceeds the Sermon on the Mount and may be as early as 100AD although many would date it later.[6] The status of *2 Clement* as a sermon or homily has been questioned on the grounds that it was read to the people (*2 Clem.* 19:1).[7]

Long sermons were common from the third to the 5th century. Origen preached often and long—Charles Bigg estimates that 'many of Origen's homilies must have taken an hour and a half in the delivery'.[8] In spite of his attempts to communicate with his audience, this was often not appreciated. Origen himself tells us that, on occasion, his preaching received a mixed reception. Hilary of Arles (403-449AD) may have preached for four hours on fast-days. Arguing from the length of Augustine's surviving sermons, Alexandre Olivar estimates that many of Augustine's sermons lasted for less' than 30 minutes and some lasted for over two hours. Such lengthy sermons were often well received but whatever the length of the sermons, some in the audience wanted more—or less.[9]

References to brevity in numerous early Christian writings (some of which may have been homilies) appear to be simply a polite literary convention and, consequently, give no indication of the expected length of such material (Heb. 13:22; 1 Pet. 5:12; Ign *Rom* 8:2; *Mag* 14).[10]

GREECE AND ROME

A Greek audience at the City Dionysia in Athens might listen to literary recitals from dawn to evening for three or four consecutive days. So great was their enthusiasm that many visitors travelled considerable distances in poor weather in order to be there.[11] Later on, sophists such as Polemo (88-144AD) delivered frequent, lengthy discourses, again sometimes over a period of several days (Philostratus *Vit Soph* 533, 537f)—great stamina indeed on the part of speakers and audiences.

Many Romans found public readings something of a bore and preferred shows of various kinds. But some could endure readings of an hour or more on two or three successive days without too much difficulty (Pliny *Ep* 3:18:4; 8:21:4).[12] Many found forensic oratory more entertaining. Forensic speeches were often brief or lasted less than one hour, but some were so long as to be spread over several days and frequently speeches lasted for several hours. Pliny seems to have regarded a forensic speech as brief if it lasted less than half a Roman hour.[13] On one occasion, he spoke for seven hours and still managed to hold at least a part of his audience (Pliny *Ep* 1:20:8; 2:11:14; 4:9:9;

4:16:2f).[14] Declaimers in the schools were subject to no time limits and could speak as long as they wished.[15]

The length of speeches, as delivered, cannot be gauged accurately by the length of speeches written since they might have been abbreviated, enlarged or in various ways adjusted for publication.[16] And in ancient texts, references to 'hours' may be very imprecise. 'Not only was time-measurement itself imprecise but an hour was taken as one twelfth of the day or night and consequently varied in length with the season and the latitude—in Rome, the hour varied between 75 and 44 minutes.[17] Furthermore, as F. van der Meer suggests, speakers in the ancient world may have tended to speak more slowly than we do which would make the length of a speech that much more difficult to determine from written records.[18]

ENDNOTES

1.   H.G.M. Williamson, *Ezra, Nehemiah*, 1985, p. 288; F.D. Kidner, *Ezra and Nehemiah*, 1979, p. 110

2.   G.W.E. Nickelsburg, *Jewish Literature Between the Bible and the Mishnah*, 1981, pp. 226f; B.M. Metzer and R.E. Murphy (eds), *The New Oxford Annotated Apocrypha*, (NRSV), 1991, p. 341

3.   S. Mason, *Josephus and the New Testament*, 1992, pp. 59, 62,71, 192-194; T. Rajak, *Josephus: The Historian and his Society*, 1983, pp. 80-83, 89

4.   J. Heinemann, 'The Proem in the Aggadic Midrashim: A Form Critical Study' in J. Heinemann and D. Noy (eds), *Studies in Aggadah and Folk-Literature*, 1971, pp. 105f

5.   C.J. Herner, *The Book of Acts in the Setting of Hellenistic History*, WUNT, 49, 1989, pp. 418-427

6.   F.L. Cross, *The Early Christian Fathers*, 1960, pp. 13f; *cf.* K.P. Donfried, *The Setting of Second Clement in Early Christianity*, 1974, pp. 25-36

7.   S. Tugwell, *The Apostolic Fathers*, 1989, p. 136

8.   C. Bigg, *The Christian Platonists of Alexandria*, Oxford University Press, [2]1913, p. 166 n3

9.   B.J. Kidd, *A History of the Church to AD461*, 1922, III, 355; A. Olivar, *La Predicación Cristiana Antigua La Predicación Cristiana Antigua La Predicación Cristiana Antigua*, 1991, pp. 682f, 699-712

10. W.L. Lane, *Hebrews 9-13*, 1991, pp. 568f; J.N.D. Kelly, *The Epistles of Peter and of Jude*, 1976, p. 216

11. A.W. Pickard-Cambridge, *The Dramatic Festivals of Athens*, [2]1988, pp. 64-66, 272, 361; L. Casson, *Travel in the Ancient World*, 1974, p. 81

12. A.N. Sherwin-White, *The Letters of Pliny*, 1968, pp. 251f; L. Friedländer, *Roman Life and Manners Under the Early Empire*, 1909, III, 39-42; M. Bieber, *The History of the Greek and Roman Theater*, [2]1961, p. 222

13. A.N. Sherwin-White, *Pliny*, p. 132

14. A.N. Sherwin-White, *Pliny*, p. 293

15. M.L. Clarke, *Rhetoric at Rome: A Historical Survey*, 1968, p. 92

16. G.A. Kennedy, *The Art of Rhetoric in the Roman World*, 1972, pp. 177, 186, 203, 276f, 531-533, 544f; A.N. Sherwin-White, *Pliny*, p. 133; L.P. Wilkinson, 'Cicero and the Relationship of Oratory to Literature' in E.J. Kenney (ed), *The Cambridge History of Classical Literature*, 1982, II, 250; G.W. Doyle, 'Augustine's Sermonic Method', *WTJ*, 39,1977, 219; A Olivar, *La Predicación*, pp. 696f

17. J. Carcopino, *Daily Life in Ancient Rome*, 1956, pp. 151-154

18. *Augustine the Bishop*, 1961, p. 416

Appendix II
Absence of a Christian Mind

We have seen that the problems generated by the regular sermon have contributed to a wider failure affecting the church as a whole. This failure may, at least in part, be attributed to an unthinking acceptance of the 'traditions of the elders' and a refusal to think through the wide-ranging implications of Christian faith.

The following works document the way in which Christians have, for many years, refused to think in a Christian way about their faith and its application in the church and the world. Consequently, what passes for Christianity today is often a counterfeit.[1]

- R.J. Banks, *The Tyranny of Time*, 1983, idem, *All the Business of Life: Bringing Theology Down to Earth*, [2]1989
- J. Drane, *Evangelism for a New Age: Creating Churches for the Next Century*, 1994
- D. Ehrenfeld, *The Arrogance of Humanism*, [2]1981
- G. Graham, *The Idea of Christian Charity: A Critique of Some Contemporary Conceptions*, 1990
- O. Guinness, *The Gravedigger File*, 1983
- C.E.M. Joad, *Decadence: A Philosophical Inquiry*, 1948
- D. Lyon, *The Steeple's Shadow: On the Myths and Realities of Secularization*, 1985
- M.A. Noll, *The Scandal of the Evangelical Mind*, 1994
- E.R. Norman, *Christianity and the World Order*, 1979
- N. Postman, *Amusing Ourselves to Death: Public Discourse in the Age of Show Business*, 1986
- G. Reid, *The Gagging of God*, 1969

- L.O. Richards, *A New Face for the Church*, 1970
- H. Schlossberg, *Idols for Destruction: Christian Faith and its Confrontation with American Society*, 1983 idem, *A Fragrance of Oppression: The Church and Its Persecutors*, 1991
- C.G. Seerveld, *Rainbows for the Fallen World*, 1988
- H.A. Snyder, *The Proble of Wineskins*, 1977
- M. Starkey, *Born to Shop*, 1989; idem, *Fashion and Style*, 1995
- A. Storkey, *A Christian Social Perspective*, 1979
- E. Storkey, *What's Right with Feminism*, 1985
- D.J. Tidball, *A World Without Windows: Living as a Christian in a Secular World*, 1987
- A. Walker, *Enemy Territory: The Christian Struggle for the Modern World*, 1987
- D. Walsh, *After Ideology: Recovering the Spiritual Foundations of Freedom*, 1990
- J.A. (Tony) Walter, *A Long Way from Home: A Sociological Exploration of Contemporary Idolatry*, 1979; idem, *The Human Home: The Myth of the Sacred Environment*, 1982; idem, *All You Love is Need*, 1985
- D.F. Wells, *No Place for Truth or Whatever Happened to Evangelical Theology?*, 1993

ENDNOTES

1. The idea of modem Christianity as essentially a counterfeit is a major theme in S.A. Kierkegaard, *Attack Upon 'Christendom'*, 1854-1855 (ET 1946), pp. 59f, 117, 150f, 209f et passim.

Appendix III
Norrington Responds to Critics

(This material originally appeared in Searching Together, 36:1-2, 2009, pp. 2-22)

For those who may not be familiar with my book, *To Preach or Not To Preach? The Church's Urgent Question*, let me begin by providing a summary of its four main points:

1. Today's custom of making the sermon the "main attraction" of weekly gatherings has no clear New Testament support nor was it the norm for church gatherings of the first two centuries.

2. The regular weekly sermon did not become such a featured part of church life until about the 3rd century—along with other non-biblical practices including the acquisition of elaborate buildings and the adoption of hierarchical forms of leadership. Sadly, it was also about this time that many true New Testament patterns based on "one another" ministry were abandoned.

3. The New Testament paradigm was community oriented with a *mutual* effort to develop and exercise everyone's gifts and skills—most of such group life taking place in homes without the benefit (or distraction) of a professional clergy.

4. The traditional "sermon" is actually a poor teaching method and does little to foster spiritual growth among God's people.

The basic arguments supporting these four premises were contained in a manuscript first circulated to interested parties to invite reaction and feedback. Paternoster Press then published it under the title *To Preach or Not To Preach* in 1996. Since its initial release, there have been at least fifteen published reviews. At first, I simply ignored them. But with the subsequent release of a related book by Ian Stackhouse,[1] I am all the more convinced of the truths of *To Preach* and have decided to respond to my critics with special attention to reviews by Stackhouse in *The Evangelical Quarterly* and by Andrew Davies in *Foundations*.

Before I begin, let me comment briefly on what should characterize a good review—of any book. Unfortunately, the tendency is to ignore the author's strong points and focus instead on the weakest arguments. A good reviewer, however, will also give a fair summary of the author's *strongest* arguments. There is certainly nothing wrong with exposing the weaknesses of a "good" book, but it is also a mark of a fair review to point to whatever strengths can be found in a "bad" book—especially in discussions of matters of faith and practice. Should not a spirit of meekness and fair play be the hallmark of any exchange of ideas by those who profess to be followers of Jesus Christ?

For a reviewer to conclude that, taken as a whole, *To Preach* is based on false premises, he or she should convincingly disprove at least two, if not three of my four basic propositions. So far, most have conceded—albeit reluctantly—that the first proposition is true, yet somehow dismissed it as irrelevant. To date, there has been no serious interaction with the second and third propositions and at most a rather flippant dismissal of the fourth. How can such published responses to *To Preach* be fairly called "reviews"? With that necessary caveat, let me turn to my reviewers.

I am aware of fifteen published reviews. Nine are by members of the "clergy"[2] and six unidentified, as such.[3] The article by Ian Stackhouse will be examined first and in the most detail, since it is by far the longest critique—though not strictly a review. Next, we will consider the article by Andrew Davies. Most of the comments by the remaining reviewers will be considered as they touch on themes that parallel Stackhouse's comments. One other review will be examined in a bit more detail at the end of this section. I will end this article with a discussion of general issues related to the main theme of *To Preach*.

REVIEWING THE REVIEWS

Ian Stackhouse's article in *Evangelical Quarterly*, "Negative Preaching and the Modern Mind: a Crisis in Evangelical Preaching" appears to have two aims: to refute the principal arguments of *To Preach* (and similar works) and to establish what he considers to be the correct view of preaching—the sacramental view.

On the very first page, with no previous quotations or efforts to summarize any content from *To Preach*, Stackhouse concludes, "... Norrington derides sermons as mere rhetoric..." (p. 247). On the next page, both *To Preach* and *We Must Stop Meeting Like This* by M. Pearse and C. Matthews[4] are vilified as "...vitriol against the grand manner..." (p. 248) and later as "a kind of slander against the text" (p. 255). Ignoring the vindictive tone, I will respond to the essence of these charges in the order of my four-point summary provided above.

ABSENCE OF REGULAR SERMONS IN NT AND EARLY CHURCH

This point is made in *To Preach* chapter 1 (pp. 1-19 *in the original,* pp. 17-42 in new version). My concern is to demonstrate the absence of a *particular form,* not to critique sermon content (pp. 1, 69, 75 *in the original,* pp. 17, 111, 121 in new version).[5] I do not deny that the sermon was used as an evangelistic tool to "preach the gospel." But there is no evidence that sermons were an essential component, much less the "main attraction" of regular Sunday-by-Sunday gatherings of believers. Yet Stackhouse writes:

> What Norrington may regard as fragmentary evidence of sermonic material in the New Testament actually amounts to quite an impressive array of texts in which kerygmatic discourse is prominent. But clearly, for Norrington, this is not a significant factor (p. 255).

IIis "impressive array" is examined in *To Preach,* (pp. 5-12 *in the original,* pp. 22/23, 32/33 in new version). But the fact remains that none of these texts provides support for today's customary, if not sacrosanct, Sunday after Sunday sermon. Stackhouse could easily have confirmed this point, had he examined the texts more carefully. I would also point out that "kerygmatic discourse" normally refers to content rather than form and therefore has no relevance in proving either the presence or absence of regular sermons in church meetings. But Stackhouse continues:

Traces of a preaching ministry in the church are discernible elsewhere in the New Testament, and even Norrington admits as much in the case of 1 Timothy 4:13 and 2 Timothy 4:2— the command to Timothy to preach the word. Norrington adds a disclaimer of his own at this point, namely that such a command in no way justifies a regular pattern of preaching in the church, both then and now (p. 251).

Here is what I actually wrote about 2 Timothy 4:2:

The reference may be to a sermon, or even a series of sermons, but it need not be... The sermon, if such it was, was an aid in the battle but there is nothing here to suggest that it was already a regular feature of church life or that it should ever become such, although it might be repeated if needed to counter other errors in the future (p. 11 *in the original*, p. 32 in new version).

Is my observation right or wrong? Stackhouse offers no valid counter-argument but simply dismisses my point as "...a personal disclaimer of his own..." On the previous page, Stackhouse writes:

In his denunciation of this form of communication Norrington singularly fails to convince that this proclamatory manner was not a feature of early church practice... Because precise details about homiletic style are beyond recovery, he argues, we cannot deduce from such texts, or project back on to them our own sermonic forms. But others may equally well assert that if precise details have conveniently been lost to us, there is nothing to suggest either that sermonizing or regular preaching in the church was not an early church practice. Indeed it may have been more widespread than even we are suggesting here (pp. 250-251).

My "denunciation of this form of communication"? That seems a bit strong. Actually, what I concluded at the end of the first section of *To Preach* was that:

There is nothing here to indicate regular sermons in the context of Christian gatherings although this does not amount to a proof that they were not delivered (p. 12 *in the original*, p. 33 in new version).

Stackhouse is apparently willing to acknowledge that there is no provable pattern of regular sermons in the New Testament. With the caveat I added to the conclusion, therefore, there should be nothing in the first point in *To Preach*, if considered fairly, that he could not accept.

THE REGULAR SERMON APPEARS LATE ON THE SCENE ALONG WITH THE ABANDONMENT OF BIBLICAL PATTERNS AND THE RISE OF NON-BIBLICAL PRACTICES

This material is covered in *To Preach*, chapter 2 (pp. 20-41 *in the original*, pp. 43-72 in new version). As the regular sermon is not found in the New Testament it is necessary to study the history of the church in order to discover its origins. Ignoring church history strengthens the naïve tendency to look at the ecclesiastical structures of our own day and assume that they must be an accurate reflection of New Testament practice. Otto Pfleiderer reinforces this point:

> The history of the past can never be properly understood when a series of historical facts is interpreted by its modern form and meaning; we have to begin at the beginning, and trace the new elements step by step through succeeding centuries.[6]

Stackhouse, however, quotes P.T. Forsyth to make his point that the roots of the "sermon" need not be traced back to Greek rhetoric because they already existed in the Hebrew prophet, the "herald" of good tidings (p. 251).

But one cannot substantiate the validity of a personal opinion simply by quoting someone else who shares that opinion.[7] In *To Preach*, I provided clear historical evidence that the regular sermon *did not* arise with the prophets (pp. 1-4 *in the original*, pp. 17-21 in new version), but rather with the increasing influence of Greek-style rhetoric upon church dialogue (pp. 20-24 *in the original*, pp. 43-

48/49 in new version). The resulting change in teaching forms (pp. 24-25 *in the original*, pp. 43-72 in new version) was also precipitated by increasing church numbers (pp. 25-26) and by the acquisition of special church buildings with architecture specifically designed to accommodate the growing focus on a single "preacher" and regular Sunday after Sunday sermons (pp. 26-33).[8] Fifteen negative reviews notwithstanding, all of these arguments still await convincing refutation.

It is worth emphasizing the extent to which New Testament practice had been distorted in virtually all aspects by the 4th century. Attempts to defend so many of these later practices as *biblical* while at the same time denouncing numerous Roman Catholic practices as without biblical foundation rightly provokes derision by Roman Catholic apologists.[9] (See: F. Viola/Barna, *Pagan Christianity*, Tyndale, 2007)

WHAT TOOK PLACE IN EARLY CHRISTIAN MEETINGS IF THERE WERE NO SERMONS?

This material is covered in *To Preach*, chapter 3 (pp. 42-68 *in the original*, pp. 73-110 in new version). In New Testament gatherings, we have one-another activities aimed at mutual growth. Paul expresses concern in all his epistles that Christians should continually grow in grace and spiritual maturity. Part of this process involves the development—in the widest corporate sense—of *every* member's gifts and skills. Leaders are not to dominate, but rather to ensure that everyone's gifts and abilities are used effectively.

In the early church meetings, we see a practical outworking of the priesthood of *all* believers in which every member contributes freely, maturing and developing gifts and skills to be used for the benefit of all both within and without the meeting (1 Cor. 14:23-40). This paradigm is evident everywhere in the New Testament (*cf.* Heb. 3:13, 10:24, 25; 1 Pet. 4: 7-11). Indeed, the New Testament provides no other pattern. The notion that these gatherings regularly featured just one speaker and a passive audience is, as E. Schweitzer observes, "completely foreign to the New Testament" (*To Preach*, p. 52 *in the original*, p. 73 in new version).

The sermon—even when (or if) occasionally delivered in early church gatherings, was probably quite different from today's pulpit monologue and, as I stated in *To Preach*, contrary to:

> ...the passive occasions so frequently experienced in churches today... [1st century] Christian sermons were often punctuated by interruptions such as applause, footstamping, restlessness, suggestions to the preacher, discussion among a group in the audience, joining in the reciting of biblical passages, tears, laughter and dialog between preacher and congregation (p. 14 *in the original*, p. 35 in new version).

While New Testament and extra-biblical records of these early meetings are sketchy, it is quite clear that 1st century believers were expected to be fully involved in all of the activities of the church. The practice of small-scale meetings in homes was ideally suited for such one-another ministry. One simply cannot find any support, either in the New Testament or in early church history for today's professional clergy and specialized church buildings (*To Preach*, pp. 24-33 *in the original*, pp. 49-62 in new version). These were clearly later departures from the New Testament paradigm as shown in detail in pp. 24-33/49-62. Such developments certainly aided and reinforced the practice of regular sermons. But they also created an increasingly hostile environment in which to exercise the kind of one-another ministry that the New Testament so clearly mandates. The sad result of this paradigm shift was the exchange of architectural grandeur for the fellowship-conducive setting of the home and hierarchical leadership structures for the "you are all one in Christ" (Gal. 3:28) model of the early church. Yet Mr. Stackhouse confidently declares that:

> ...there is nothing to suggest either that sermonizing or regular preaching in the church was not an early church practice. Indeed it may have been more widespread than even we are suggesting here (p. 251).

The system he offers cannot be forced upon New Testament practice without distorting the record. If a house church—the only kind of gathering documented in the New Testament—had been dominated by modern style monologue sermons, the mutual ministries actually taught and exemplified in the New Testament would have been virtually unworkable. Furthermore, Stackhouse's suggestion that the regular sermon may have been common in the early church is guesswork at best, unsupported by any convincing historical evidence. This argument from silence is analyzed in *To Preach* (pp. 104-105 *in the original*, pp. 161-163 in new version).[10]

It is perhaps telling that reviewers who are clergy themselves show so little interest in the many pages I devoted to this subject. Perhaps it betrays their reluctant awareness of the extent to which current practices are at variance with the New Testament, or that simply ignoring potentially embarrassing material is the safest policy.

Some reviewers claim that my treatment is "highly selective." That may be true, but are not all treatments of historical and theological issues necessarily selective? The question is, "Have I deliberately omitted anything essential?" Without a demonstration of how such selectivity distorts my conclusions, such allegations are meaningless.

THE REGULAR SERMON IS A POOR MEANS OF TEACHING AND COUNTER-PRODUCTIVE TO REAL GROWTH AMONG GOD'S PEOPLE

This material is covered in *To Preach* chapter 4 (pp. 70-89 *in the original*, pp. 113-140 in new version). Interestingly, Stackhouse himself admits that:

> ...it is undoubtedly true that preaching, as I am advocating it here, is not the most efficient method for learning (p. 249).

Since the first part of proposition four has been conceded,[11] it only remains for Mr. Stackhouse and other reviewers to prove that the second part of my fourth proposition is unaffected by the so called sacramental view of preaching. But first, I will answer a final set of charges against the convictions expressed in *To Preach* including that of being obsessed with relevance. Mr. Stackhouse complains,

> ...preaching will continue to receive a bad press precisely because it falls foul of the relevancy criteria. One suspects that Norrington's own criticisms of preaching are driven by this agenda, more than by the actual biblical evidence

against preaching which, as we have seen, is tenuous to say the least. What he may regard as fragmentary evidence... is not a significant factor. More important is the need to be culturally relevant in our communication and for Norrington "the prevailing culture, far from supporting the use of the sermon, points to its abandonment." Such a comment betrays the underlying antipathy he has against preaching and the weakness of his overall methodology (p. 255).

The "relevancy" charge is a straw man. The only reason he can allege that the biblical evidence against sermons is "tenuous" is because he so carefully avoids providing the readers of *Evangelical Quarterly* with any of the actual biblical evidence presented in *To Preach*. And when he does quote me, it is so taken out of context as to totally obscure my original intent.

THE REVIEW OF ANDREW DAVIES

Mr. Davies begins by showing a clear understanding that my concern is with "the regular sermon within the weekly life of the early churches" (*Foundations*, p. 41). Unfortunately, this clarity is short-lived. Under the heading "The Sermon is Actually Injurious to the Life of the Christian Community," Davies begins:

> Norrington delivers a breathtaking onslaught on the sermon, which he regards as being largely responsible for the following evils: [Davies then lists a wide range of issues relating to the fourth proposition in *To Preach* and concludes] In short, almost every evil in modern church life is due to the sermon! It is a great pity that Norrington over states his argument in this way because he gives the impression that he is grinding an axe rather than reasoning a case.

On page 42 (p. 73 in new version) Davies reacts to another list of five points where I dealt with historical and biblical issues. Two he simply quotes or summarizes out of context and dismisses with a derisive exclamation mark. His reaction to the other three totally distorts what was actually said. He responds,

Thus, restive congregations in the early church prove the

inadequacy of the sermon, not the preacher! (*Foundations*, p. 42).

Note the derisive exclamation point again. I assume he is referring to my allusion to Origen, which reads as follows:

Origen regularly preached for an hour or more, usually in a simple, Attic [Greek] style with imperatives and rhetorical questions but his congregations often grew restive, talked throughout, left before the sermon started or attended irregularly. The audiences probably did not appreciate subject matter or speaker... (*To Preach*, p. 13 *in the original*, p. 34 in new version).

This was simply one observation from early church history germane to the overall subject of preaching, but hardly sufficient by itself to "prove" anything. Davies then misrepresents another out-of-context quotation and once again adds the dismissive exclamation point:

Sermons may have been useful in evangelism, but believers must break free from the "familiarity of bondage to the uncertainties of liberation"! (*Foundations*, p. 42).

Actually, I made no mention of evangelism in this section. The phrase he misappropriated followed a discussion of the regular sermon after which I concluded:

God's people frequently misunderstand deliverance when it is offered and prefer the familiarity of bondage to the uncertainties of liberation; the emotional security of in-stitutionalized immaturity to the rigors of responsible adulthood (Exod. 5:20ff.; Judg. 15:10-13; Jer. 5:31ff.; Acts 7:25) [*To Preach*, p. 91 *in the original*, pp. 142-143 in new version].

There are more distortions in Mr. Davies' review. The view attributed to me that the sermon alone is largely responsible for "almost every evil in modern church life" is actually contrary to clear statements that I made in *To Preach*. For example, in a summary of the many ills in church life I not only identified the "regular and frequent use of the sermon" as a cause, but also attributed the problems to:

> ...poor leadership, the absence of fellowship and inadequate preparation for service (*To Preach*, p. 82 *in the original*, p. 131 in new version).

And again, even more clearly:

> The regular sermon does not, of course, stand alone as the one great corrupter of Christian faith and life. It is embedded in a complex organizational structure which is far removed from biblical patterns and which also inhibits Christian growth to maturity (*To Preach*, p. 115 and *cf.* x *in the original*, pp. 177-178 in new version).

Mr. Davies also makes no mention of my analysis of the impact of the sermon in Puritan England where I argued that the relative effectiveness of the sermon compared to other forms of instruction cannot be ascertained accurately because there are so many variables (*To Preach*, pp. 95-96).

Towards the end of his review, Mr. Davies says:

> ...he [Norrington] argued that the NT's comparative silence about what happened in church gatherings means that there were no regular edificatory sermons. Absence of evidence constitutes evidence of absence. But arguments from silence can work both ways, and the other (overwhelming) New Testament evidence for the sermon—the sermons of Jesus, the sermons in Acts, the speeches referred to in the Letters, the Pastoral Letters, Hebrews ("my word of exhortation")—cannot be simply explained away as *ad hoc* or evangelistic or occasional matters (p. 42 *in the original*, pp. 73 in new version).

Again, the first sentence is simply wrong. Here's what I actually wrote:

> There is nothing here to indicate regular sermons in the context of Christian gatherings although this does not

amount to a proof that they were not delivered (p. 12 *in the original*, pp. 32 in new version).

My objection to the regular sermon is based on the substance of the following chapters relating to origins and New Testament practices (*To Preach*, pp. 20-68 *in the original*, pp. 43-110 in new version) therefore, and not on arguments from silence. I will leave that methodology to supporters of the regular sermon—who, sadly, have no other choice to defend their cause. The New Testament evidence concerning sermons is carefully examined in *To Preach* (pp. 5-12 *in the original*, pp. 22-34 in new version) and no reviewer to date has critically examined this material.

GENERAL ISSUES ARISING FROM THE REVIEWS

THE USE OF LITERATURE
Mr. Stackhouse cites literature but to little purpose. Aside from him, only four other reviewers use literature to bolster their case. Dr. Michael Quicke says:

> His [Norrington's] historical analysis was faulty with no reference, for example, to Brilioth's brilliant history of Christian preaching, which goes back to Luke 4 (*Christianity*, p. 41).

Dr. Leslie Griffiths makes a similar argument:

> Many of Norrington's pages are devoted to footnotes (692 in all) and an index. But there is not one single reference to C. H. Dodd's masterly little book *The Apostolic Preaching and Its Developments*, which would certainly have demolished most of the claims put forward in this book (*Church Times*, p. 17).

I am quite familiar with both of these two books, and neither refutes anything I wrote in *To Preach*. Brilioth[12] does not discuss any kind of re-evaluation of the regular sermon along the lines I have followed. Dodd, as we have already seen from Stackhouse's treatment, is not concerned with the actual justification for the regular sermon, but only with its content.[13] On the dust cover of my own copy, it reads, "The purpose of this book is to discover the actual content of the Gospel preached or proclaimed by the Apostles." Furthermore, apart from the appendix "Eschatology and History"[14] this work concentrates on the New Testament.

Pastor Denis Campbell complains that I made sparing use of the "New Homiletic" (*cf. To Preach* pp. 80, 87 *in the original*, pp. 127/128, 137/138 in new version)[15] though it is not obvious from his comments that this is relevant to my four propositions (*Irish Biblical Studies*, p. 129). Similarly, Rev. J. F. Dunn would have liked me to interact more with others who have written on preaching (*English Churchman*, p. 8). The truth is that I have diligently studied most of the significant books on the subject—both pro and con—and did cite other authors who made significant arguments in favor of preaching, although I may not have always mentioned the books from which those citations were taken. To his credit, Mr. Campbell's review is written in a friendly and engaging spirit. And the analysis of *To Preach* by Mr. Dunn is probably the most gracious of all—particularly bearing in mind that he does not accept my conclusions.

ERRORS IN *TO PREACH OR NOT TO PREACH*

Unfortunately, some reviewers were so keen to discredit *To Preach* that they ignored the humbler task of identifying specific errors. Dr. Quicke objects that, "... his definition of preaching as speech biased the entire book." But I never defined "preaching" in *To Preach*, so I assume he is referring to my definition of "sermon." Given the importance of such a statement it is curious that he never elaborates on that point and leaves the reader to wonder what he means. It is a criticism he repeats in his recent book:

> There are glaring weaknesses in Norrington's argument. He seems to define preaching narrowly as speech and pays little attention to the significance of Jesus' preaching in Luke 4 as the origin of Christian preaching. While the Greek homily and Latin rhetoric certainly had a later influence on preach-ing, as noted in Origen's and Augustine's contributions,

Christian preaching has deeper roots than Norrington allows. He omits any discussion about preaching's theology and its relationship with Scripture and the Holy Spirit—all of which we will consider later. He makes little room for anointed preaching, for which the first apostles were set aside (Acts 6:4, 7). Indeed, he seems to take the positive aspects of the Holy Spirit's work in developing Christian maturity and place them uncritically within the model of small groups.[16]

Once again, Quicke fails to notice that there is no definition of preaching in *To Preach*. Jesus' preaching in Luke 4 has no relevance to the origins of the regular sermon in later church life. The roots of Christian preaching and the origins of the regular sermon are not the same thing. My concern is with the latter. The theology of preaching and its relationship with scripture and the Holy Spirit are, again, irrelevant to the use of one particular method of preaching. The apostles and their preaching ministry would be relevant if it could be shown that they preached to Christian congregations on a Sunday-by-Sunday basis. There is not a shred of evidence that they did. There is nothing of substance in Professor Quicke's remarks so we will move on to other comments on my definition of "sermon."

Dr. Young comments that, "...I feel that the definition used by Norrington devalues the sacramental aspect of preaching."[17] Mr. Townsend disliked my definition so much that he chopped it in half and passed off just the first half as my definition.[18] Even if my definition were in some way erroneous, it would not necessarily follow that the conclusions to the four propositions would be substantially affected, much less refuted.

Some disliked my criticism of church structures—particularly the post 1st century acquisition of dedicated buildings,[19] but that is not my primary concern and will not be defended here.

Not all of the criticism received, however, can be as easily dismissed. A few errors have been brought to my attention that need to be corrected—some perhaps necessitating further research. In the original release of *To Preach* I wrote:

But to re-evaluate and to replace the sermon would be a comparatively modest first step.

An editor who is also a clergyman noticed that I should have written "regular sermon," and I thank him for his keen eye. At this point, I think I should have ended the sentence differently as well. Instead of "a comparatively modest first step," perhaps I should have written "a giant leap in the right direction."

In private correspondence, a friend suggested that my treatment of the Temple (*To Preach*, p. 27 *in the original*, pp. 53 in new version) may need rethinking. I agree. Also, my statement concerning the presence of non-teaching elders in 1 Timothy 5:17 (*To Preach*, p. 53 *in the original*, pp. 89/90 in new version) is perhaps questionable. It is indeed possible that only one group of elders is in mind in this verse, but there are other opinions.[20]

It is clear that I made a mistake concerning Dr. J. I. Packer's de-finition of the sermon. I alleged that he maintained that sermons[21] were the only form of discourse inspired by God (*To Preach*, p. 1 *in the original*, p. 17 in new version). I now realize that this is not the case and Packer clearly teaches that other forms of communication may be just as inspired of God. I apologize to him and to my readers for such a careless misreading of his text.

My comments on mutual ministry (*To Preach*, p. 51 in the original, pp. 86/87 in new version) should have at least mentioned the concerns some have about the ministry of women in Corinthians 14:34-36 and 1 Timothy 2:11-12. These concerns were not part of my main thrust and would have required much further discussion.

A FALSE STARTING POINT

For many reviewers—and Christians in general—the standard of reference for judging truth is the ecclesiastical structure of the day, often defended as the very litmus test of orthodoxy.[22] Whatever biblical support may be provided is often out of context and incidental to the approved status quo.

The reviews by clergy demonstrate their inability to look at the New Testament evidence in any way except through the myopic lens of their own traditional presuppositions. To re-examine the New

Testament validity of the centrality of preaching to church life would be a threat to their chosen vocation. This stubborn obstacle to needed change may be an even more serious problem than originally stated in *To Preach*.

POOR EDITING

The fault for publishing such poorly researched reviews of *To Preach* does not lie with the reviewers alone. The various media editors who permitted such biased analysis are also partly to blame. The editor of any journal is ultimately responsible for all the content in that journal. When it comes to reviews, they should expect—and demand—rigorous, well-researched and disinterested analysis. Sadly, such was not the case. Except for Young, Dunn and Campbell, all of the other reviews by members of the clergy were less than honest in their argumentation and presentation of evidence. The editors should have challenged them before running their reviews or, at a minimum, added a disclaimer. Perhaps even more disappointing is the fact that to my knowledge none of the readers of these distorted reviews wrote in to complain. That may be the saddest commentary of all on the current assumptions and convictions of today's professing believers.

Perhaps some editors (and readers) are willing to excuse unsubstantiated accusations in published reviews as the inevitable consequence of the brevity of available space. If so, it is a poor defense of careless editing—and reading. The secular world is much more careful about unsubstantiated accusations, if only to avoid law suits.

If a reviewer cannot be fair and thorough in the space available he should ask the editor for more space. Mr. Dunn was conscious of the limited space at his disposal (*English Churchman*, p. 8) as was Dr. Smith (*Evangelicals Now*, p. 21). Dr. Quicke's review could have been easily increased by about 20 lines by simply removing the reproduction of the *To Preach* cover (*Christianity*, p. 41). The same is true of Dr. Smith's review (*Evangelicals Now*, p. 21). If an editor requests a review but will not provide enough space, it would be more honorable if the potential reviewer simply returned the book to the editor. Surely this would be better than providing an unfair review as the result of forced brevity.

NON-CLERGY REVIEWS AND OTHER REACTIONS

Reviews by Roberts (*Banner of Truth*) and Wilson (*Reformed Theological Review*) were quite hostile, but added no new arguments to the debate apart from guilt by association. Four others were actually quite positive in their assessment of *To Preach*, even if their argumentation was not the best.

So far, while negative reviews outweigh positive reactions, the basic premises in *To Preach* have not been refuted. Admittedly, unless there are other serious efforts to examine the evidence, ideas that must appear to most Christians as a novelty are not likely to be widely accepted. Thankfully, there are other such contributions being made. The writings of Frank Viola, Jon Zens and others are having an increasing impact on the debate.[23] Many aspects of current church practice are being re-evaluated. This is an exciting, if not uncomfortable development.

THE SACRAMENTAL VIEW OF PREACHING

In his book, *Negative Preaching*, Ian Stackhouse asserts that "Preaching is not just a word *about* Christ; it is a word *of* Christ" (p. 249). He quotes Bonheoffer who wrote, "The preacher should be assured that Christ enters the congregation through those words he proclaims from the Scripture." He then alleges that:

> It is nothing that the scripture does not claim for itself. Paul talks about faith that comes by hearing and hearing through the word of Christ [Rom. 10:17], by which he understands preaching as effective speech; the word itself being the deed, achieving that for which God has purposed it [Isa. 55:10-11]...it is the presence of the Risen Christ, and a celebration of his gospel that is the goal of good preaching, more than a lesson about Christ (p. 250).

After quoting Hansen, "The point of preaching is not so much to teach the incarnation as it is for Jesus to become present through our stammering words," Stackhouse continues, "But what many fail to understand is the dynamic whereby in the preaching event, and it is an event that is being advocated here, a word of Christ impacts the church" (p. 253).

How do we answer such an ardently expressed view? The first problem concerns the claim that the presence of Christ with the congregation is dependent upon the preacher. There is nothing in Scripture to suggest that the presence of Christ is in any way dependent on the presence of any one individual or on a particular method of delivering his word. Furthermore, we are assured by Christ himself that he is present whenever two or three gather in his name (Matt. 18:20).

Most of Stackhouse's observations could apply equally well to other types of communication but are presented as though they provide unassailable support for the sacramental view. John Stott makes a similar mistake.[24] In his defense of regular preaching, Stackhouse also demonstrates his disdain for small groups who are not similarly devoted to the sermon. It is, according to him:

> ...a kind of slander against the text, and, one might add, against the grace-filled world it heralds the arrival of. It is this grace which must be performed Sunday by Sunday, not for nostalgia's sake, but because it actually has the power to transform (p. 255).

On what authority is such a charge made? Those accused of high crimes against the text, the church, and heaven itself, have a right to know the source of such a charge. Mr. Stackhouse would have us believe it derives from Scripture and cites Rom. 10:17. But this reference is to the communication of the gospel—with no reference to method. And his citation of Isa. 55:10-11 (p. 250, note 13) is especially infelicitous. The implication is that pulpit preaching—and *only pulpit preaching*—is on the same level as the words of the prophet, the same level as divine revelation.[25]

Later we are told that "...the Spirit does not transfigure our words to the status of canon" (p. 253). But isn't that exactly what he seems to be claiming for regular preaching by citing the Isaiah verses? In fact, whatever promises Scripture contains concerning the efficacy of the "word," they are by no means tied to one specific mode of communicating that word.

Consider the inherent contradictions in his views. We are

asked to believe that when the clergyman (our modern professional replacement for the plurality of elders in the New Testament church) in the dedicated church building (as opposed to in homes as was the practice in New Testament times) mounts the pulpit (that elevated fixture introduced in the 3rd century) and addresses a passive audience (who were not passive in the New Testament) or "laity" (a designation added long after New Testament times) in the pews (13th century addition) via the regular sermon (which did not exist in New Testament practice) then and only then is the event especially pleasing to God, who responds with a special, if not unique channel of his grace.[26] How can it be that such a radical departure is more pleasing to God than emulating clear New Testament patterns and practices? Does this mean that those first acts of obedience are now offensive to God?

In short, there is simply no biblical evidence for the sacramental view of preaching. This is further confirmed by the observation of F. C. Senn:

> Luther was articulating a new understanding of the word. The word is as much a means of grace as the sacraments, but grace no longer understood in terms of substance but in terms of communication: address and response.[27]

Mr. Stackhouse seeks to confirm the truth of what he advocates by citing theologians who agree with him. As he moves from one to another, he appears to be seeking an *imprimatur*, which the Scriptures refuse to supply. Unless the charges directed against those of us who question the propriety of the regular sermon can be related to New Testament truth, however, they are without substance.

> To crave for relevancy at all costs, and to prize the democratic speech of the small group, in the way that Pearse and others do, is a "kind of slander against the text" (p. 255).

Just what he means by "democratic speech" is not clear in his objection, but I will make two observations. *First*, his issue is not, in the final analysis, with Pearse, Matthews, Viola, Zens, or me. It is with the very character and structure of the NT church since. It cannot be denied that the open participation and mutual ministry we advocate were very much a part of early church life (*To Preach*, pp. 50-52 *in the original*, pp. 86-89 in new version). And there is no reason to think that women were prevented from contributing.[28] *Second*, the assumed authority of the preacher in his lofty pulpit may seem obvious to many, whereas authority in a house church seems problematic if not totally lacking. That may be the popular perception, but it is nothing more than cultural conditioning. From a true New Testament perspective, special schooling, ordination rituals, prestigious titles, skilled oratory, lofty pulpits, or special dress has nothing to do with true "authority." In God's redemptive plan, Christ alone is invested with such authority. And it is his words, not the messenger or method of delivery that must be revered and obeyed.

Assigning one function (or person) in a corporate system a dominant role inevitably diminishes the importance of all other functions (or persons) in that system. In the sacramental view, as defended by Ian Stackhouse, non-pulpit teaching, mutual encouragement and correction and all of the other New Testament forms of shared, one-another ministry fall short of the hallowed place assigned to the week-after-week sermon (and preacher).

So when two believers, or a believer and a non-believer, have a conversation about the things of Christ—on a bus, in a café, at a ball game—is it a word of Christ? Is Jesus present in their conversation? Do their words have a role in fulfilling Jesus' promise to "build my church"? Or is the primary means and power to accomplish that goal reserved for the pulpit? Must we believe that a simple conversation on a bus cannot achieve what a sermon in a church does? If so, what about the conversation in a chariot between Philip and the Ethiopian Eunuch (Acts. 8:26-29)? Would it have been more effective if Philip had instead invited him to come to and hear him preach a sermon? It probably would have been in someone's home or the city court or a hillside, of course, since church buildings and elevated pulpits hadn't been invented yet.

J. I. Packer defines Christian preaching as "the event of God bringing to an audience a Bible-based, Christ-related, life-impacting message of instruction and direction from himself through the words of a spokesperson." He then argues that various forms of communication such as a conversation—he cites Acts 8:35—ought also to be categorized as preaching. He adds, "This is not our usual modern way of looking at the matter, but it is the biblical way, and it is always best to follow the Bible." By his definition, a discussion in a Bible class or any other edifying conversation between believers would qualify for what he regards as "preaching."[29]

This would be a good place to take a closer look at the word "preaching." For Stackhouse, it may be narrowly defined as the delivery of a sermon to a passive audience. In practice, of course, he means the regular Sunday-by-Sunday monologue from the pulpit. But it's not that simple. As I wrote in *To Preach*:

> About thirty different words are used in the Greek New Testament for proclaiming the word of God, but in the Authorized or King James Version (AV) they are usually rendered "preach." ...the tacit assumption is often made that the activity under consideration is similar to that undertaken by Christian Clergy in their pulpits. This assumption often results in a serious misunderstanding of the text... no word for verbal communication in the New Testament can give much of a clue concerning context, length, place of delivery, regularity or audience; and, as A. C. Thiselton reminds us, "It is a mistake to insist on a greater degree of precision than suggested by the text" (*To Preach*, pp. 7-8 *in the original*, pp. 26/28 in new version).

The various Greek terms translated as "preach" or "preaching" in the AV or KJV, together with their many nuances can be examined quite easily in Young's Concordance. Unfortunately, most of these differences in meaning have been obscured by contemporary assumptions attached to the presence of the word "preach." It may also come as a surprise to some that most, if not all of the contexts where "preaching" occurred in the New Testament involved speaking to unbelievers, not to fellow believers in their regular gatherings.

Mr. Stackhouse seems to have some familiarity with the Greek language. It would have helped his readers if he would have admitted to his readers that the various words translated "preach" simply cannot refer exclusively to pulpit oratory. By using the word "preaching" more than 60 times in his article (not counting its appearance in titles) and "preach" or "preacher(s)" more than a dozen times without such an explanation adds to the confusion by associating those terms exclusively with regular pulpit activity.

Also, whereas preaching in the New Testament is predominantly an activity taking place *outside* of church gatherings, generally in a context of evangelism, Stackhouse asserts that:

> The word of the church is the word of Christ because its body is his also. From this we deduce a very practical point: preaching not only takes place in the sermon but also via pastoral care and, as we shall see, through the sacraments. Preaching can only find its proper context within the overall pastoral care of the church... (*Gospel-Driven*, p. 109).

Contrary to Packer's wider definition, Stackhouse refuses to admit that edifying conversations by ordinary believers qualify as "preaching," yet boldly asserts that "pastoral care" does. It is clear, therefore, that in his sacramental view, it is not the word itself that is exalted but a particular method of delivering that word. Similarly, it is not ordinary believers who are divinely qualified to communicate the "mind of Christ," but only the clergy and the establishment structures of which they are a part. It is a view, therefore, that ultimately denigrates the New Testament concept of the priesthood of all believers, substituting instead the hierarchical priest-craft of the "ordained" elite.[30]

CONCLUSION

I have endeavored to carefully consider the published reviews of *To Preach*, and do not believe any major errors in argumentation or in the handling of the biblical and historical evidence have been proven. This, in itself, is not proof that every premise in my book is correct. But it does mean that readers should carefully consider the points I have made, compare them with biblical truth, and not be deterred in doing so by the mere existence of negative reviews.

In addition to responding to the reviews of *To Preach*, I have briefly examined the sacramental view of preaching defended by Stackhouse and others. It is a view that cannot be sustained with any sound biblical evidence. I also remain convinced that it has had a negative impact on true spiritual growth by suppressing a true one-another ministry in favor of entrenched ecclesiastical establishments.

I will freely confess that in spite of the overwhelming evidence from both Scripture and church history, it is not easy to convince believers to abandon errant convictions and practices that are so deeply rooted in centuries of church history. The natural tendency is to assume the soundness of one's own presuppositions and to bristle at the suggestion that they may be in error. Simply going with the flow is much more comfortable and less disconcerting than honestly considering challenges to the system and diligently searching the Scriptures to see "whether such things are so." Thus, for most of today's Christian church, meaningful contributions to the welfare of the body by other than the elite few remains stifled by non-biblical traditions and hierarchical structures. I can only pray that God himself will mercifully jar his people loose from such a debilitating bondage to the status quo.

—David C. Norrington

ENDNOTES

1. *The Gospel-Driven Church: Retrieving Classical Ministry for Contemporary Revivalism* (Milton Keynes, 2004)

2. D. Campbell, *Irish Biblical Studies* 20 (June, 1998), 127-130; A. Davies, *Foundations* 40 (Spring 1998), 41-42; J. F. Dunn, *English Churchman*, no. 7451 (28 March and 4 April, 1997), 8; L. Griffiths, *Church Times*, no. 7003 (2 May, 1997), 17; M. Quicke, *Christianity* (June, 1997), 41; D. Smith, *Evangelicals Now* (March, 1997), 21; I. Stackhouse, "Negative Preaching and the Modern Mind: a Crisis in Evangelical Preaching," *Evangelical Quarterly* 73:3 (2001), 247-256; M. J. Townsend, *Expository Times* 108:9 (1997), 285; E. Young, *The Fellowship Paper,* 103

3. J. Baigent, *Partnership Perspectives* no. 5 (April, 1997), 26; T. Gray, *Themelios* 22:3 (April, 1997), 69-70; H. Roberts, *The Banner of Truth*, Issue 403 (April, 1997), 30-31; M. Scott, *Anabaptism Today* (June, 1997), 23-24; J. P. Wilson, *Reformed Theological Review* 56:2 (May-August, 1997), 103-4; C. Wright, *Christianity and Society* 8:2 (April, 1998), 28-29

4. Eastbourne, 1999

5. The accusation of following C. H. Dodd in his distinction between *kerygma* and *didache* is not only false but also irrelevant (Stackhouse, "Negative Preaching," pp. 250-251). The claim that Romans 1:15 is "crucial" here (p. 251, note 17) has already been answered (*To Preach*, p. 9). Mr. Stackhouse might have started his discussion of Romans 1:15 by accepting or refuting my treatment of this verse. But he prefers to pretend that my analysis does not exist. He is at least consistent and has no intention of engaging seriously with any argument from *To Preach*.

6. O. Pfleiderer, *The Development of Theology in Germany since Kant, and its Progress in Great Britain since 1825* (London, 1890), 399

7. Does P. T. Forsyth agree with Stackhouse here? The problem arises from Stackhouse's careless use of the term "preaching" which suggests both form and content. My concern is primarily with form, but P. T. Forsyth seems primarily concerned—at least in the section, which Stackhouse cites—with content. Forsyth seems to be taking the pulpit-form for granted. See *Positive Preaching and the Modern Mind* (London, 1960), 1-3

8. Financial issues may also be relevant here and are examined in my: "Fund-raising: The Methods used in the Early Church compared with those used in English Churches Today," *Evangelical Quarterly* 70:2 (1998), 115-134 esp. 128-9

9. K. Keating, *Catholicism and Fundamentalism* (San Francisco, CA, 1988), 38-39

10. See also R. P. Feynman, *The Character of Physical Law* (London, 1965; reprint, 1992), 165, 166

11. For a critical discussion of the view that the sermon is not intended to be a teaching method see T. Halewood, "The Foolishness of Preaching: A Critical Examination of the Sermon and a Consideration of Alternative Teaching Methods in Church Services" (M. Ed. Thesis, University of Liverpool, 1991), 25-27

12. Y. Brilioth, *A Brief History of Preaching* (Philadelphia, PA, 1965). I assume this is the volume Dr. Quicke is referring to. He gives no detail.

13. C. H. Dodd, *The Apostolic Preaching and its Developments* (London, 1936; reprint, 1956)

14. C. H. Dodd, *Apostolic Preaching*, 79-96

15. There is a misprint on page 80 of *To Preach*. The endnote number 70 occurs twice. The second (following "future of the sermon") should be 72

16. M. J. Quicke, *360 Degree Preaching: Hearing, Speaking, and Living the Word* (Grand Rapids, MI/Carlisle, 2003), 37

17. Young, *Fellowship Paper*, 103

18. Townsend, 1997, 285

19. Quicke, 1997, 41; Wright, 1998, 29

20. See the discussions in R. A. Campbell, *The Elders: Seniority within Earliest Christianity* (Edinburgh, 1994), 200-201; W. D. Mounce, *Pastoral Epistles* (Nashville, TN, 2000). 307-308; I.H. Marshall, *The Pastoral Epistles* (London, 2004), 610-612

21. J. I. Packer, "Authority in Preaching," in M. Eden and D. F. Wells (eds), *The Gospel in the Modern World: A Tribute to John Stott* (Leicester, 1991), 199-200

22. See, for example, Stackhouse, "Negative Preaching," 254; Roberts, *The Banner of Truth*, 403, (April, 1997), 29.

23. See the following: Frank Viola, *Rethinking the Wineskin: The Practice of the New Testament Church* (Brandon, FL, 1998); F. Viola, *Pagan Christianity: The Origins of*

our Modern Church Practices (Brandon, FL, 2002); Jon Zens, "Building Up the Body: One Man or One Another?" *Baptist Reformation Review*, 10:2, 1981, 10-29; Jon Zens, "Four Tragic Shifts in the Visible Church," *Searching Together*, 21:1-4, 1993, 1-10; M. Burkhill, *The Parish Systems: The same yesterday, today and forever?* Latimer Studies, 59 (London, 2005); S. Murray, *Beyond Tithing* (Carlisle, 2000); S. Murray, *Post-Christendom* (Carlisle, 2004); S. Murray, *Church After Christendom* (Milton Keynes, 2004); R. P. Stevens, *The Abolition of the Laity: Vocation, Work and Ministry in a Biblical Perspective* (Carlisle, 1999); D. Hilborn (ed), *Picking Up the Pieces: Can Evangelicals Adapt to Contemporary Culture?* (London, 1997); R. Chester, "How are we to learn?" *Evangelicals Now* (May, 1998), 18; M. Pearse and C. Matthews, *We Must Stop*; A. Atherstone, *"I Absolve You": Private Confession and the Church of England*, Latimer Studies 60 (London, 2005); T. Halewood, "*The Foolishness of Preaching*"; D. C. Norrington, "Fundraising," and the items cited in Note 1

24. The sacramental view of preaching held by J. R. W. Stott in *I Believe in Preaching* (London, 1982), 80-83, is discussed critically in T. Halewood, "The Foolishness of Preaching" (26-28). See also G. H. Clark, *Today's Evangelism: Counterfeit or Genuine?* (Jefferson, MD, 1990), 41

25. These ideas may be compared with the teaching of the second Helvetic Confession of 1566 (P. Schaff, *The Creeds of Christendom*, revised by D. S. Schaff (Grand Rapids, MI, 1931; reprint 1990), III, 237-238, 832, 889); P. Adam. *Speaking God's Words: A Practical Theology of Preaching* (Leicester, 1996), 112-120; *To Preach*, 103. On the relationship between the sacraments and the word, see G. C. Berkouwer, *The Sacraments, Studies in Dogmatics*, (Grand Rapids, MI, 1969), 43-55

26. Many of these issues are discussed in *To Preach*—see also F. Viola, *Pagan Christianity*; J. G. Davies (ed), *A New Dictionary of Liturgy & Worship* (London, 1986); R. Hanson, *Christian Priesthood Examined* (Guildford, 1979)

27. F. C. Senn, *Christian Liturgy: Catholic and Evangelical* (Minneapolis, MN, 1997), 306

28. One perspective would be represented by Jon Zens in *What's With Paul and Women: Unlocking the Cultural Background of 1 Timothy 2*, Ekklesia Press, 2011; other perspectives can be found in B. B. Warfield, "Paul on Women Speaking in Church," in J. W. Robbins (ed), *The Church Effeminate and Other Essays* (2001), 212-216. A. C. Thiselton, *The First Epistle to the Corinthians* (Grand Rapids, MI/ Carlisle, 2000), 1146-1162; W. D. Mounce, *Pastoral Epistles*, 117-130

29. J. I. Packer, "Authority in Preaching," in M. Eden and D. F. Wells (eds), *The Gospel in the Modern World*, 199-200

30. The priesthood of all believers has been under serious challenge from 200AD onwards. See C. J. Bulley, *The Priesthood of Some Believers: Developments from the General to the Special Priesthood in the Christian Literature of the First Three Centuries* (Carlisle, 2000), 319-326 and cf. *To Preach*, 83

This book was brought to you by Searching Together Magazine and Ekklesia Press. You can get subscriptions to ST.

Annual Subscription:
United States $10
United Kingdom £2 per issue
Australia $10
All other non-US $10 USD
Discounts and free subscriptions are available to those who cannot afford the full subscription price. $35 per year for 5 copies sent to the same address.

Send all correspondence to:
Searching Together/Jon Zens
PO Box 548, St. Croix Falls, WI 54024
Email: jzens@searchingtogether.org
Cell: 715-338-2796
Evenings: 715-755-3048

Website: www.searchingtogether.org

"I read many christian magazines, but only because I have to in order to keep current. I read *Searching Together* because it is always cutting edges and Christ centered.

—Frank Viola

JON ZENS

Jon Zens is a prolific author with more than seven books to his credit. Jon works with Ekklesia Press to publish his books, which challenge the religious status-quo and point people to Christ and one-anothering.

A Church Building (2008) presents four crisp essays in this volume that unravel the reoccurring components of American Christianity and contrasts the reality of the modern religious community with the vision set out in the New Testament. Much of what calls itself church is out of step with the teachings of Christ.

List Price: $10.95

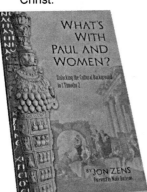

What's With Paul... (2010) takes on one text in the New Testament used as a "clear" mandate to silence women in the church for more than 1500 years. This book exposes that fallacy. This book will help in your quest to discern the mind of the Lord as the gender debate continues.

List Price: $11.95

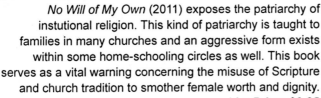

No Will of My Own (2011) exposes the patriarchy of instutional religion. This kind of patriarchy is taught to families in many churches and an aggressive form exists within some home-schooling circles as well. This book serves as a vital warning concerning the misuse of Scripture and church tradition to smother female worth and dignity.

List Price: $8.95

The Pastor Has No Clothes (2011) needs little explanation. The cover says it all... This book demonstrates that putting all the ecclesiastical eggs in the pastor's basket has no precedent in the New Testament.

List Price: $13.95

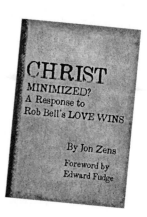

Christ Minimized (2012) is an answer to one of the most controversial books of our generation (*Love Wins*). It examines some traditional views and popular Bible verses about hell, heaven, the afterlife and invites a re-examination.

List Price: $7.95

Ekklesia Press, along with its imprints Trestle Press (for general subjects) and Tamarin Press (for children's books), seeks to help people get published as well as provide the highest quality work in publishing. We do audiobooks, eBooks and both hardbound and trade paperbacks. Our books are printable in three continents and thus they are available around the globe. Here are a few of our titles.

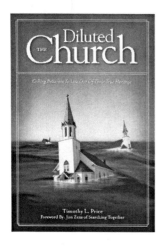

The Diluted Church (2005) is a call to followers of Christ to assume their true heritage and stop being diluted by thinking politics is the only means of influencing people. This book outlines the polluting factors that keep believers from being all God wants them to be. This book is truly unique.

List Price: $16.95

Prepare To Meet Your God (2007) is a book that deals with terminal illness and the preparations one must make on their way to death. This practical and pastoral book is a comfort and challenge to any reader or family facing final events in a loved one's life. It features wide margins and large print.

List Price: $14.95

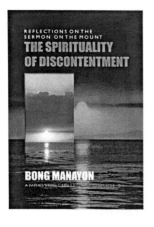

The Spirituality of Discontentment (2011) is about the Sermon on the Mount. Written by a former Filipino pastor to his son. This book is a warm read, but a challenge to see Jesus' sermon in a current applicative sense. Manayon uses Filipino culture and indigenous languages to open up this passage for Western readers. You'll discover this book to be profound.

List Price: $12.95

Shouting At God (2011) relates the personal story of one man's dealing with his father's death. As a pastor he's supposed to have the answers and be comforting everyone else... Yet, when he grapples with the circumstance, faith, belief and an understanding of God takes on a whole new meaning

List Price: $10.95

The First Time... (2012) is a color children's book illustrated and simplified to share the gospel in a way little people can understand. It is told in rhyming verse This book is a wonderful resource.

List Price: $11.95

Happiness... (2010) takes a fresh look at what is required for a person to experience true, lasting happiness. The book helps the reader understand that real inner contentment can be possessed regardless of one's outward circumstances. The key to having this inner joy and happiness is discovering what you are by God's active and personal grace.

List Price: $16.95

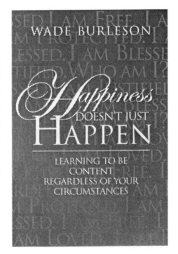